INTRODUCTION TO LOGIC

Introduction

TO

LOGIC

By

ANDREW H. BACHHUBER, S.J.

St. Louis University

APPLETON-CENTURY-CROFTS, INC.

New York

547-1

Library of Congress Card Number: 57-8315

Cum approbatione ecclesiastica

PRINTED IN THE UNITED STATES OF AMERICA

PREFACE

THIS BOOK was written specifically as a textbook for an introductory course in logic. It is hoped, however, that the same qualities intended to make it an effective medium of classroom instruction will likewise appeal to the more serious general reader.

The topics treated are much the same as those discussed in most manuals of Scholastic logic. As far as its contents are concerned, it contains substantially the same definitions, the same rules, the same principles—and even the same classic examples—as countless other books. The special features that justify its publication (in spite of the great number of logic books that have recently come off the press) are not primarily its contents. Rather, they are the new and more effective order and method of presentation, the carefully worked out inductive approach, the inclusion of many thought-provoking exercises, the use of original diagrams, the integration of each section with the rest of the book so that the student will always know where he is headed, and the use of a variety of other pedagogical devices.

In the interests of pedagogical efficiency, Parts I to III are largely functional and, except for the section on the principles of the categorical syllogism, contain a minimum of philosophical considerations. After a streamlined treatment of the term and proposition, the student is immediately introduced to inference. Now, experience has shown that the student grasps the fundamental laws of inference as quickly before he has made a detailed study of the concept and term as after he has made it. Moreover, the student enjoys inference at the beginning of a logic course, but is generally overwhelmed and bewildered by the predominantly metaphysical and epistemological considerations preceding the study of inference in most Scholastic manuals. With the order adopted in this book, the student's initial interest in inference is maintained, and the strictly philosophical considerations come only after he is prepared for them. Another distinct advantage of treating inference early is that the student can then apply the laws of logic to the reading of newspapers, magazines, and so on, throughout the greater part of the course, whereas if the study of inference is delayed, the application of logic to everyday thinking is proportionally curtailed.

Also in the interests of pedagogical efficiency, matter is commonly taken up where it will be used immediately. For instance, in Part I the attributive, or categorical, proposition is explained in detail to supply a background for the study of the categorical syllogism, but the analysis of the conditional syllogism is omitted because, if it were included in this part, several weeks would intervene between its study and its use. Instead, the conditional proposition is discussed in the section on the conditional syllogism where it is used immediately. Similarly, a suggestion is made in a footnote that the conversion of propositions be studied in conjunction with the rules on the quantity of the predicate because the student can grasp both of these together more easily than either of them alone.

The use of examples is a significant feature of the book and is more than a mere pedagogical device. Based on the very nature of our intellect and on the way we acquire knowledge, the use of examples is a necessary means of grasping the rules and principles of logic. We do not first grasp rules and principles in the abstract and then find concrete exemplifications of them. Rather, we *first* grasp individual examples in which the rules and principles are concretized (for instance, simple syllogisms whose validity or invalidity is obvious); and *then,* through insight into these examples, we grasp the rules and principles themselves.

Now, in many logic books the impression is somehow conveyed that we understand definitions, rules, and principles independently of examples and that the sole purpose of examples is to deepen a knowledge that is already possessed in the abstract. In the present book, however, regard has been had in every chapter for the fundamental law of the mind that we do not know the universal except by abstraction and generalization from the particular (that is, from examples). A sustained effort has been made to lead the student by a careful and thorough analysis of examples to an understanding of every definition, rule, and principle.

Special attention is called to the treatment of the principles of the categorical syllogism. Instead of being treated *before* the rules of the syllogism—as is done in most logic books—they are treated *after* the rules and *after* the figures and moods. Only after the student is thoroughly familiar with the mechanics of the syllogism is he able to understand the precise question that the principles answer and the exact function of these principles in a syllogism. When these principles are studied before the rules of the syllogism, experience has shown that they are little more than empty formulae that are memorized blindly; but when they are studied after the rules—and when the question that they answer has been clearly formulated, and their connection with examples clearly analyzed—their study contributes much to the deepening and unifying of the student's understanding of argumentation.

The exercises are an integral part of the book. They have the twofold purpose (*a*) of deepening the student's grasp of definitions, rules, and principles and (*b*) of creating a habit of applying the laws of logic to everyday thinking. It is recommended that a large portion of class time be spent on the exercises as well as on examples that the students themselves have discovered in newspapers, periodicals, textbooks, lectures, conversation, and so on. Every example is a concretization of some principle of logic; and, broadly speaking, the more varied the concretizations, the deeper will be the student's grasp of the principles themselves.

Great pains have been taken to make the explanations at once very thorough and at the same time as simple as the nature of the matter permits. It is hoped, therefore, that many points on which a teacher must ordinarily spend much class time can be mastered through private study with very little help from the teacher, and that the class time thus saved can be devoted to matter whose intrinsic difficulty is such that the student cannot grasp it without the teacher's help.

I have tried to write the book in such a way that the teacher can aim at various levels of understanding by taking or omitting various parts of the book. If the teacher is interested only in the strictly practical aspects of logic, he may well concentrate on Parts I to III, passing lightly over the intricacies of the reduction of propositions to logical form and the more complicated examples of contraposition and inversion, while dwelling at length on the syllogism and fallacies. Perhaps all he will wish to take from Parts IV and V is the treatment of definition and division. As a background for metaphysics, the section on the principles of the syllogism, the many notions explained in Part IV, and the chapter on induction will be of special value. It is suggested that the teacher make a thorough inspection of the Table of Contents to see what parts of the book will serve his purposes best.

In an introductory logic book in the Aristotelian and Thomistic tradition, how much emphasis should be given to symbolic logic? In a decade when symbolic logic is the only logic that many know—when "logic" often means "symbolic logic," and "symbolic logic" means "philosophy"—to ignore it entirely would be a disservice to the student. On the other hand, limitations of space make a thorough treatment impossible. In the appendix on symbolic logic I have restricted myself to a most elementary treatment of the proposition. However, it is precisely at this level that symbolic logic is most vulnerable to attack and most in need of critical appraisal. Hence, although the treatment is extremely brief and extremely elementary, it should nevertheless be of value.

A very special effort has been made to adhere closely to the teachings of St. Thomas Aquinas and to integrate logic with Thomistic metaphysics and epistemology. Yet, in an introductory work of this nature, documentation and lengthy bibliographies seemed out of place. Besides the works of Aristotle and St. Thomas, there are three books to which special attention should be called: Jacques Maritain, *Formal Logic* (Sheed and Ward, New York, 1946); H. W. B. Joseph, *An Introduction to Logic* (Oxford: Clarendon Press, 2nd ed., 1950); and John of St. Thomas, *Outlines of Formal Logic*, translated from the Latin with an introduction by Francis C. Wade, S. J. (Marquette University Press, Milwaukee, 1955). References to the work of Aristotle and St. Thomas can be found in the book by Professor Maritain.

Thanks are due, first of all, to the Reverend William L. Wade, S. J., the head of the Department of Philosophy of Saint Louis University, for many valuable suggestions and for making possible the preliminary editions. Thanks are also due to the teachers who tested the preliminary editions in the classrooms of some twenty colleges and universities and the students in the classes in which the preliminary editions were used, especally those who turned in as homework many of the examples now found in the book. A special debt of gratitude is owed to Messrs. James L. Manning, Lawrence R. Connors, Robert A. Worman, and Elmer H. Luthman, all scholastics of the Society of Jesus and former students of mine, for making the diagrams. Finally, my thanks also go to the Reverend Linus J. Thro, S. J., the Reverend Thomas C. Donohue, S. J., and especially the Reverend Charles W. Mulligan, S. J., for reading the manuscript and for their many kind and helpful criticisms.

A. H. B.

Saint Louis University

CONTENTS

CHAPTER 1

The What and Why of Logic

In Chapter 1 we shall explain briefly what logic is and why we study it.

1. PRELIMINARY DEFINITION OF LOGIC

All of us are familiar with the words "logical" and "illogical." We speak, for instance, of a "logical" candidate, a "logical" procedure, and a "logical" choice. In these contexts the word "logical" means "in accordance with what one would reasonably expect in view of the events or circumstances." Again, using the word "logical" in a slightly different sense, we refer to a man whose thinking is orderly and consistent as a "logical" thinker and to an argument that clearly proves its conclusion as a "logical" argument. On the other hand, we brand as "illogical" an action that is not called for by the circumstances, or a person whose thinking is disorderly and inconsistent, or an argument that does not prove its conclusion but is irrelevant, circular, or self-contradictory. You will notice that in every instance the words "logical" and "illogical" refer to correct thinking—a choice is logical or illogical depending on whether or not it results from correct thinking; a person is logical or illogical depending on whether or not his thinking is correct; and an argument is logical or illogical depending on whether or not it expresses correct thinking.

Now, logic is *the science and art of correct thinking*. Just as chemistry investigates the laws governing the composition, relationships, and affinities of matter, and just as physics studies the laws of matter as endowed with motion and energy, so logic investigates, discovers, and applies the laws we must follow in order to think expeditiously and correctly.[1]

a. Thinking

In the definition of logic as the science and art of correct thinking the word "thinking" does not include absolutely all mental operations but only those mental operations (a) that are directed toward the attainment of truth and (b) by which we elaborate upon knowledge previously possessed. Reverie and day-dreaming, for instance, are not thinking in the sense in which we are using the word here because they are not directed towards the attainment of truth. The operations by which we merely make things present to our minds are not thinking but a prerequisite of thinking, since they involve no elaboration upon knowledge previously possessed. Yet we do think when we analyze what has been made present to our minds—when we compare, classify, define, and divide. Similarly, the operations by which we merely accept a statement as true (like the simple assent to "$2 + 2 = 4$") are not thinking but a possible starting point of thought—logic acknowledges their existence and describes their nature, but cannot lay down laws to govern them.[2] However, we do think when we draw out the implications [3] of statements and "figure out" the connections between them. Thinking, then, includes analysis, comparison, classification, definition, logical division, and so on, and especially the various kinds of inference. *Logic studies these operations insofar as they are instruments of knowledge and means of attaining truth.*

[1] The method of logic, as well as the kind of knowledge it gives us, differs profoundly from that of chemistry and physics. In this paragraph we merely wish to call attention to its general area of investigation.

[2] As an art, logic is concerned only with those mental operations over which it can exercise control; but as a science, it is also concerned with others. For instance, the consideration of induction belongs, at least to some extent, to the science of logic, but not to the art.

[3] An implication is anything that is implied. Now, in logic "to imply" means "to involve the truth or presence of." If two propositions are so related that if the first is true the second must also be true, the first is said to imply the second. The remark "The old skipper is sober today" hints, or suggests, that the skipper is not sober on some other days, but it does not *logically* imply this. It is possible for the skipper to be sober both today and on every other day.

Logic is principally concerned with inference. It studies other operations of the mind chiefly (though not exclusively) because of their relationship to inference. Inference, in its broadest sense, signifies any process by which our minds proceed from one or more propositions (that is, from one or more statements in which anything whatsoever is affirmed or denied) to another proposition so related to the original propositions that if they are true it must also be true. Inference is expressed externally by oral or written argumentation, which is also called inference and of which the following syllogism is a typical example:

> Every dog is an animal;
> but every hound is a dog;
> therefore every hound is an animal.[4]

This example consists of three propositions so related that if the first two (the premises or antecedent) are true, the third proposition (the conclusion or consequent) must also be true. Our mind first accepts the first two propositions as true and then, on seeing the connection between them and the third proposition, asserts it as flowing from them. To establish *general* norms for making this passage from premises (or antecedent) to conclusion (or consequent) legitimately is the main task of logic.

b. Correct Thinking

Our thinking is correct when it conforms to the laws or rules investigated by logic. For instance, definition is correct if it conforms to the rules of definition; logical division is correct if it conforms to its rules; and the various kinds of inference are correct if they conform to their rules. Since very much of logic is a study of the conditions of correctness of thought, we cannot understand the meaning of "correct thinking" unless we first have studied logic.

[4] Examples about dogs, animals, and the like, are chosen because they are perfect illustrations of logical relationships. The fact that they are so commonplace increases their value as illustrations at this stage of our study. Examples with greater intrinsic interest would be likely to draw attention to themselves and distract us from the points they are meant to illustrate.

c. A Science

Logic is a science—at least it is a science in the traditional Aristotelian [5] and Thomistic [6] sense of "science," although not quite in the same sense as physics, chemistry, anatomy, and so on. There is a tendency nowadays to restrict the word "science" to the so-called empirical or inductive sciences, such as physics. Hence, in spite of the fact that logic actually is a science, we do not ordinarily call a logic course a science course.

Science is knowledge, but not all knowledge is science. To rank as science, knowledge must fulfill several special requirements. Science is not mere opinion or hypothesis but certain and demonstrated knowledge; not a mere accumulation or aggregation of data but organized knowledge; not a bare statement of fact or a mere description of events but causal knowledge that tells why things are as they are. Now, logic is a science because it is certain and systematized knowledge of the principles governing correct thinking—it does not give us mere mechanical rules but gives us insight into why its rules must be as they are and cannot be otherwise.

Logic, as a science, investigates, discovers, expresses, systematizes, and demonstrates or explains the laws of correct thinking. But the actual application of these laws—for instance, to the construction and criticism of arguments—takes us out of the sphere of logic as a science and into the sphere of logic as an art.

d. An Art [7]

Art gives facility, first, in reasoning and judging correctly about things to be made—such as statues, paintings, chairs, and syllogisms

[5] Aristotle (384-322 B.C.), a Greek, was one of the world's greatest philosophers and the first man to construct a complete system of logic. He wrote six works on logic, which were later gathered together under the title of *Organon*, or "Instrument" (of knowledge). Their English titles are: (1) *The Categories*, (2) *On Interpretation*, (3) *Prior Analytics*, (4) *Posterior Analytics*, (5) *The Topics*, and (6) *On Sophistical Refutations*. Almost all subsequent writings in logic are based to a considerable extent on the *Organon* of Aristotle.

[6] St. Thomas Aquinas (1225-1274 A.D.) was the greatest of the medieval theologians and philosophers. Among his numerous works are commentaries on many of the writings of Aristotle. These include his commentary on *On Interpretation* and on the *Posterior Analytics*.

[7] It would be a mistake to think that the science and art of logic are completely distinct from one another—that the science excludes the application of

—and, secondly, in actually making them in accordance with the demands of reason.

Logic is an art because it guides man's reason so he can proceed with order and ease and without error in the constructive activity of making definitions, propositions, syllogisms, and so on. Indeed, logic is the "Art of Arts" (*Ars Artium*), or a sort of super-art, for it directs reason itself, which is the director of the other arts. Yet it is an art only in a secondary sense of the word, for its products (unlike those of sculpture, painting, building, and so on) are purely mental and imperceptible to the senses. Since logic perfects the intellect, which is the root of freedom (*libertas*), and since free men (*liberi*) should be pre-eminent in things of the mind, logic has traditionally been called a liberal art.

2. LOGIC AND REASON

a. Insistence on Understanding

The laws and rules of logic are not arbitrary enactments that we submit to out of reverence for authority or because of long-established custom. We submit to these laws and rules only because we clearly see that they must be as they are—that is, the evidence compels us to submit. In a logic course there is to be no blind memorizing and no merely mechanical application of rules that have been learned by rote. The student should not be satisfied with anything short of a thorough understanding of all the fundamentals of logic.

b. Logicians by Nature

All of us are logicians by nature—at least to some extent! [8] We must not suppose that we know nothing at all about logic before

---

the rules of logic or that the art merely accepts the rules ready-made from the science and excludes their understanding.

Strictly speaking, the science of demonstrative logic does not have an art corresponding to it that is distinct from the various sciences that make use of demonstrative logic. In other words, the application of the laws of demonstrative logic to a science (for instance, metaphysics) does not belong to the art of logic but to the science itself. But the science of dialectical logic (or probable and persuasive argumentation) does have a corresponding art.

[8] The student is urged to inspect exercises coming later in the book to see how well he can solve them by natural logic and common sense—for instance, the exercises on pp. 109-110, 150-152, 162-163 and especially 197-201.

we have made a formal study of it. Simply because we are rational beings, we spontaneously know the more general laws of correct thinking and are necessarily subject to them. Just as the law of gravitation was operative before Newton formulated it, so, too, men followed the more general laws of thought before Aristotle and other logicians put them into words. But for a detailed knowledge of these laws and for skill in applying them prolonged study is absolutely necessary.[9]

3. THE LIMITS OF LOGIC

Logic does not give us knowledge of the real world, at least not directly, but only of certain aspects of our thought. It does not consider real things [10] but certain aspects of our knowledge of real things. Hence, (*a*) logic, inasmuch as it is a mere tool of reason, makes no *direct* contribution to the content of our thought and (*b*) logic presupposes means of attaining truth over which it has no control.

a. A Mere Tool of Reason

Students of logic are sometimes disappointed on being told that a *logician as such* does not even know enough to come in out of the rain or that he does not even know that a dog is an animal. As a man, of course, he knows these things, but not as a logician because they lie outside the field of logic. The sole object of logic is certain aspects of our thought—it considers concepts, propositions, arguments; the subject-predicate relationship; the relationship of the minor, middle, and major terms of a syllogism; the logical sequence of propositions; and so on. It does not give us any knowledge at all

[9] It is interesting to note the insistence of St. Thomas not only on the necessity of studying logic but on the necessity of studying it, in spite of its great difficulty, *before* the other sciences. (See *In lib. Boet., 'De Trinit.,'* q. vi, art. 1; also q. v, art. 1, ad 3.)

[10] As opposed to a being of reason, a *real* being, or thing, is one that exists (or at least can exist, or has existed, or will exist) in itself and not just as an object of thought. Socrates, St. Peter, the city of Chicago, and the planet Mars are (or were) real beings or things. A being of reason, on the other hand, has existence only in the mind and as a result of being thought of. Concepts, propositions, arguments, and so on, as listed below, are beings of reason and not real beings.

of real things except insofar as it is a tool of reason and thereby guides us in our thoughts about things and aids the other sciences in attaining truth.

b. Extra-logical Means of Attaining Knowledge

Another limit of logic is suggested by the definition of "thinking." We defined "thinking" as those mental operations (*a*) that are directed toward the attainment of truth and (*b*) by which we elaborate upon knowledge previously possessed. Since we cannot think unless we first have something in our minds to think about, logic presupposes means of attaining truth over which it has no control. It assumes that we accept many truths independently of logic and logical procedures.

1) **EXPERIENCE.** The immediate data of experience are not subject to the control of logic. Many things are immediately evident to us because we experience them—we see, touch, and handle them. The fact that we exist, too, is immediately evident to us because we experience ourselves knowing other things, feeling, willing, and so on.

2) **INSIGHT INTO PRINCIPLES.** Truths like the principle of contradiction ("A thing cannot be and not be in the same respect") and simple relationships of numbers (such as "$2 + 2 = 4$") impose themselves on our minds because by insight into concrete exemplifications of these truths we clearly understand that they must be true. The basic principles of logic and metaphysics are of this sort—we cannot, strictly speaking, *prove* them: we can only *see* them when we inspect examples in which they are illustrated.[11] Now, in the acceptance of truths that are immediately evident (whether they are immediate data of experience or principles grasped by insight into examples), there is no movement of thought from one thing to another, no elaboration of knowledge previously possessed, but only a simple assent to truth. Hence, such acceptance of truth is not "thinking" in the sense in which we understand the word here and therefore lies outside the control of logic.

[11] These principles are grasped by so-called intellective induction. We shall treat of it in Chapter 15.

3) **AUTHORITY.** We accept many statements merely because an authority we consider reliable has proposed them to us as true. Reliance on authority is our reason for accepting much of what we read in the newspapers and hear over the radio and in conversation. Indeed, reliance on authority is often the only possible way of getting information about things that we have not witnessed ourselves. It is also why we accept many of the conclusions of science: no one—not even a great scientist—can examine all the data of science and test the validity of all its conclusions for himself. Reliance on authority is also the reason for accepting the dogmas of revealed religion.

Now, logic has no direct bearing on the acceptance of statements on authority. It can, however, have an indirect bearing. First, it can sometimes help us make a critical examination of the reasons for accepting an authority as worthy of credence. For instance, logic can help us discover inconsistencies of thought; and we will rightly be suspicious of the reliability of an authority (a newspaper columnist, editorialist, historian, and so on) if he makes statements that we find to be either self-contradictory or inconsistent with what we already know to be true. Secondly, logic can guide us when we elaborate on what an authority has proposed to us as true. Thus, authority, just as experience and insight into principles, can supply us with things to think about—that is, with matter that we can subject to logical analysis and use as the starting points of inference.

4. REASONS FOR STUDYING LOGIC

We shall now give a brief answer to the question, Why should we study logic? When you begin a new subject it is helpful to consider the benefits to be gained from its study; and later, as the course progresses, it is often highly advantageous to reflect on whether, and to what extent, these benefits are being attained.

a. The Specific Purpose of Logic

The specific purpose of logic is expressed in its definition by the words "correct thinking." Logic gives us norms for recognizing correct or good thinking, as well as incorrect or bad thinking, and develops in us a habit of analyzing our thought, of distinguishing carefully between our evidence and our conclusions, and of adverting to the structure of our arguments. By familiarizing us with both correct and incorrect procedures, it helps us know for certain whether or not our evidence justifies our conclusions, and teaches us what to look for in order to test the validity of arguments.

How often it happens that we have a vague suspicion that something is wrong with an argument or even know for certain that it is invalid and yet cannot state precisely what is wrong with it! The study of logic will enable us to pinpoint the defects of faulty arguments—to explain exactly what is wrong with them and to give the flaw a name.[12]

Logic, then, has the very practical purpose of helping us think with order and ease and without error. It should enable us to discover defects in the thinking of others and to avoid defects in our own thinking.[13]

The strictly philosophical portions of logic, which show the connection of the laws of logic with the basic principles underlying them, should give us a deep understanding of the conditions of sound argument and therefore a profound trust in the competence of the human mind, as well as great mental satisfaction.

b. An Introduction to Philosophy

Another reason for studying logic is that its study is an apt introduction to philosophy.

1) A BRANCH OF PHILOSOPHY.[14] In the first place, logic is a branch of philosophy at least to the extent that many parts of the science of logic are genuinely philosophical. Hence, logic introduces us to philosophy by inviting (or even compelling) us to philosophize. It introduces us to the abstract thinking of philosophy and familiarizes us with some of its technical terminology. (Now we

[12] The student is urged again to examine exercises occurring later in the book to see how well he can handle them now. The exercises are taken, for the most part, from newspapers, magazines, class lectures, textbooks, and so on, and should show the student the wide range of subject matters to which logic can be applied.

[13] While we extol the benefits of logic, we should not lose sight of its limitations. Logic, if left by itself, is helpless.

[14] Sometimes logic is contrasted with philosophy. But when this is done the word "philosophy" is used in a narrow sense as synonymous with "metaphysics," which is philosophy par excellence.

must not be surprised that philosophy has a technical vocabulary; it is just as impossible to talk about philosophy without at least some knowledge of its technical vocabulary as it is to talk about baseball, football, and tennis without at least a little knowledge of their technical vocabularies.) Indeed, logic is a veritable storehouse of philosophical terms, and by acquainting us with them it prepares us to read philosophical writings intelligently.

2) **A TOOL OF PHILOSOPHY.** Logic is a tool of philosophy just as it is a tool of reason in general. Much of what was said about the specific purpose of logic (under *a*) is applicable in a special way to the use made of logic throughout philosophy.[15]

3) **AN INTRODUCTION TO PROBLEMS OF PHILOSOPHY.** Logic also introduces us to philosophy by introducing us to various philosophical problems that are considered from one point of view in logic and from other points of view in other branches of philosophy. The so-called problem of universals, for instance, has a logical aspect and therefore belongs to logic; but it likewise pervades much of metaphysics, epistemology, and even psychology. The consideration of the principles underlying correct thinking necessarily leads us to principles of metaphysics; and so on. An acquaintance with these problems from the point of view of logic will at once whet our philosophical appetites with a real hunger for their complete solution and fill out our philosophical background so that when the complete solution is given us we will be the better prepared to understand it.

c. *A Historical Reason*

There is also a very cogent historical reason for studying logic. Logic has been an important subject of study for more than 2400 years. From before the time of Aristotle (d. 322 B.C.) down to our own day, the study of logic, and especially of Aristotelian logic, has remained an important part of a liberal education. Even when other branches of philosophy fell into decadence and nearly passed out of existence, as in the so-called Dark Ages, logic continued to be

[15] For St. Thomas's attitude towards logic as an introduction to philosophy see Note 9 on p. 6.

taught. It has had a strong influence on Western thought, and many of its once technical terms have passed into everyday language.

Now, the mere fact that a subject has flourished for over 2400 years and still continues to be taught gives us a very strong presumption in favor of its being worthwhile.

The definition of logic as the science and art of correct thinking defines logic by stating its proximate end or purpose. In our last chapter (Chapter 16), we shall consider logic from another point of view and define it in terms of its formal object. For an adequate understanding of the nature of logic we must consider both its purpose and its formal object. It would be impractical, however, to treat of its formal object at this stage of our study.

PART I

PREREQUISITES OF INFERENCE

GENERAL NOTION OF INFERENCE

LOGIC IS THE SCIENCE and art of correct thinking. We have already seen that the kind of thinking that logic is principally concerned with is inference, which is expressed externally by oral or written argumentation, and that this is likewise called inference. The following syllogism has already been given as a typical example:

> Every dog is an animal;
> but every hound is a dog;
> therefore every hound is an animal.

The main task of logic is to establish norms for determining whether or not an alleged conclusion is actually implied in the premises from which it is said to follow. The main task of logic, in other words, is to formulate general norms, laws, or rules that will help us answer questions like this: *Supposing that* every dog is an animal and that every hound is a dog, does it *follow from this* that every hound is an animal?

In inference the mind proceeds from one or more propositions to another proposition so related to the original propositions that if they are true it must also be true. Consequently argumentation must have two or more propositions as its component parts. Propositions, in turn, are made up of terms (like "dog," "animal," and "hound" in the example given above). Hence, before we can determine the conditions of valid inference, we must know something about propositions; and before we can understand the nature of propositions, we must know at least a little about terms. First of all, therefore, we must treat briefly of the term.

Part I contains three chapters (Chapters 2, 3, and 4). In Chapters 2 and 3 we shall treat of the term and proposition, respectively; in Chapter 4 we shall treat of the general notion of inference.

CHAPTER 2

The Term as a Part of a Proposition

IN THIS CHAPTER we shall say as much about the term as is absolutely necessary for an elementary understanding of the proposition and of the function of the term in inference. First we shall give two preliminary definitions of "term." Next we shall treat of comprehension and extension and their mutual relationship. Finally we shall treat of two divisions of terms—(a) into distributive, or divisive, and collective and (b) into singular, particular, and universal. In Chapter 12 we shall inquire further into the nature of the term.

1. DEFINITION OF "TERM"

The term must be defined from two points of view: from the point of view of its being a sign of a concept and from the point of view of its being the ultimate structural element into which a proposition is resolved. We shall define the *oral term.* ("Term" sometimes signifies the oral term, sometimes the mental term, and sometimes the written term, depending on the context.)

From the point of view of its being a sign of a concept, the oral term is defined as *an articulate sound that serves as a conventional or arbitrary sign of a concept.* We shall explain this definition at length in Chapter 12. We mention it now only to call attention to the fact that logic does not deal with terms insofar as they are mere sounds or mere print on a page but only insofar as they are signs of thought and things—signs, that is, of concepts (or mental terms), mental propositions, and mental argumentation as well as of the things that are set before the mind by thought. This is clear from what we mean when we use words. For instance, when we say "The dog is wagging his tail," we do not mean that the word "dog" is wagging its tail, but that an animal whose nature is signified by "dog" is wagging its tail. Hence, it is clearly not the mere word "dog" but what the word "dog" stands for that is the true subject of this proposition.

From the point of view of the term's being the ultimate structural element into which a proposition and argumentation can be resolved, the term is defined as *a word or group of words that can serve as the subject or predicate of a proposition.* Thus, in the proposition "A dog is an animal," the words "dog" and "animal" are terms—"dog" is the subject and "animal" the predicate.

A term is *simple* if it consists of a single word, as in the examples given above.

A term is *complex* if it consists of a group of words that signify one thing or kind of thing when they are taken together as a unit. For instance, in the proposition "The black little cat-like animal with the white stripe down its back is a skunk," the complete subject ("the black little cat-like animal with the white stripe down its back") consists of a dozen words but still is only one term, because the dozen words constitute a single unit.

Sometimes we use "term" in a broader sense, as signifying any word or group of words that has meaning and that can be a part of a proposition either by itself or in combination with other words. In this sense, "black," "little," "cat-like," "white," and so on, are terms even when they are taken singly.

Most terms signify the quiddity, essence, or nature, of the thing or things they stand for; they express *what a thing is* or, more precisely, *what kind of thing a thing is.* "Quiddity" is derived from the Latin word *quid,* which means "what?"; hence, "quiddity" means "whatness." In this context, "essence" and "nature" are nearly synonymous with "quiddity." Terms that signify quiddities are called *significant terms.*

Significant terms signify concepts directly and immediately. Since concepts are mental representations of things, significant terms also signify things—but only indirectly and through the intermediacy of concepts.

Some terms merely point out things without signifying their quiddities or natures. Such terms are called *nonsignificant terms.*[1] Demonstrative pronouns and adjectives (words, that is, like "this," "that," and "those") are of this sort. When we say "*This* is what I'll buy," we are not expressing the nature of the thing we intend to buy, but are merely pointing it out. ("Demonstrative" is derived from *demonstro,* the Latin word for "I show, indicate, or point out.")

Proper names are likewise nonsignificant terms, since they, too, merely indicate, or point out, an individual person or thing without expressing its nature. When we call a certain man Mr. Smith, for instance, we do not imply that he is a metal worker; and when we call a man Mr. Green, we do not imply that he is green. The proper names "Mr. Smith" and "Mr. Green" do not in any way signify *what kind* of man their bearer is.

2. COMPREHENSION, EXTENSION, AND THEIR INVERSE RELATIONSHIP

On the one hand, we can consider the quiddity (essence, or nature) signified by a term, directing our attention to the *intelligible elements* involved in it—that is, to its definition and properties. If we do this, we are considering the COMPREHENSION of the term (and of the concept signified by the term), as when we think of a triangle as a plane figure bounded by three straight lines. On the other hand, we can consider the *subjects* whose quiddity (essence, or nature) is signified by the term as when we think of a triangle as being either equilateral, isosceles, or scalene. If we do this, we are considering its EXTENSION.

Considerations of comprehension and extension pervade the whole of logic, and a correct understanding of them is absolutely necessary if we are to build our logic on a sound basis.

a. Comprehension

The comprehension of a term (or concept) is the sum total of the intelligible elements of the quiddity signified by the term (or concept). These intelligible elements are referred to as *notes.* This sum

[1] In a certain sense, of course, all terms—including nonsignificant terms—signify something; mere nonsense syllables, which stand for nothing at all, are not terms.

total includes, in the first place, the basic elements that a thing has to have in order to be thought of as the kind of thing signified by the term; it includes, in the second place, whatever is deducible from these basic elements. It includes nothing, however, that a thing does not have to have in order to be the kind of thing signified by the term.

The comprehension of "man," for instance, includes "rational, sentient, animate, corporeal substance" (the notes that are looked upon as basic to the quiddity of man), together with all the notes that are deducible from these, such as "capable of speech," "social being," "risible," and "tool-using." "Man" cannot be thought of, without contradiction, as lacking any of the elements belonging to the comprehension of "man." If a man lacked any element of the comprehension of "man," he would both be a man and not be a man—which is a contradiction and therefore impossible.

Notice how "capable of speech" adds nothing to the comprehension of "man" but merely expresses what is in it implicitly and deducible from it. All a being needs for speech is the ability to think (so he will have something to say) and the ability to make some kind of external movement that can serve as a sign of thought (so he will have something to say it with). As a rational animal, man has each of these abilities. Because he is rational, he has at least the basic ability to think and therefore to have something to say; because he is an animal (that is, a sentient, animate, corporeal substance), he has the ability to make some kind of movement, which is all he needs to express his thought. (These abilities may be undeveloped, as in infants and morons, or accidentally impeded, as in the insane.)

The comprehension of "man" does not include "tall, white, and European," for a man can be thought of without contradiction as neither tall nor white nor European.

Note that the comprehension of a term is not limited to what we explicitly think of when we grasp the meaning of a term; nor does it include only those implications that we actually deduce from a quiddity. Comprehension is not subjective but objective. It includes all the intelligible elements objectively contained in a quiddity, whether we actually think of them or not. The comprehension of a term usually contains many notes of which we have no explicit knowledge at all. For instance, when an eight-year-old child grasps the quiddity of a right triangle, his concept has many implications of which he is completely ignorant. He does not know that the sum of the interior angles is 180°, that the square on the hypotenuse is equal to the sum of the squares on the sides, and so on. Nevertheless, these implications belong to the comprehension of his concept.

Our treatment of the predicables (especially of genus, specific difference, and property) and of definition will throw further light on the nature of comprehension.

b. Extension

The extension of a term includes the subjects signified by the term. Extension is either absolute or functional, depending on whether the term is considered in itself and outside of discourse or as a part of a proposition.

1) **ABSOLUTE EXTENSION.** *The absolute extension of a term and concept is the sum total of the subjects—of the actual subjects as well as the possible subjects—whose quiddity (essence, or nature) is signified by the term and concept.*

This sum total includes everything that has the comprehension of the term—both the kinds of things possessing it, such as genera and species, and the individuals possessing it. Thus, the term "man" includes in its extension all races of men of the past, present, and future; all individual men, both actual and possible; and even, in a way, the men of fiction and fairy tale. "Animal" includes both man and the irrational animals in its extension, for the entire comprehension of "animal" is realized in each of them. A man is an animal; a mouse is an animal; a mosquito is an animal; each of them has all the constitutive notes of "animal" (sentient, animate, corporeal substance) and all their implications.

The subjects whose quiddity (essence, or nature) is signified by a term are called its *inferiors.* In relation to them, the term itself is called a *superior.* "Man," "brute," "winged horse," "dog," "Rover," and so on, are inferiors of the superior "animal."

2) **FUNCTIONAL EXTENSION.** *The functional extension of a term or concept includes only those subjects that it actually sets before the mind when it is used in discourse.* In this sense, the ex-

tension of a term and concept is said to be universal, particular, or singular. It is universal if it sets before the mind each of the subjects whose nature it signifies; for instance, "every dog" and "each man." It is particular if it sets before the mind an indeterminately designated portion of its total possible extension, as do "some men" and "a few animals." It is singular if it sets before the mind one definitely designated individual or group, as do "this man," "that team," and "the tallest man in the room."

This meaning of extension is very important in inference. We shall explain it fully after we have considered the inverse ratio of comprehension and extension and the division of terms into distributive, or divisive, and collective. We shall recur to it a second time when we take up the supposition of terms.

c. *Inverse Ratio of Comprehension and Extension* [2]

In a series in which inferior terms are subordinated to superior terms (as in the series "man, animal, organism, body, substance"), *the greater the comprehension of a term (and concept) the less its absolute extension, and vice versa.* For instance, the comprehension of "man" is greater than that of "animal." Man is a *rational* animal; therefore "man" has all the comprehension of "animal" and, besides that, it also has "rational." But the absolute extension of "animal" is greater than that of "man," for it includes both men and the irrational animals. The diagram on the top of Page 21 displays this inverse ratio graphically. If you start with "substance" at the top of the diagram and go down, you will see how, as the comprehension increases, the extension decreases. "Substance" has the least comprehension, but includes "angel," "mineral," "plant," "brute," and "man" in its extension; "body" includes "corporeal" in its comprehension, but omits "angel" from its extension; and so on. Thus, as the comprehension increases, the extension decreases, all the way to "man," whose comprehension is the greatest of the series, including "rational, sentient, animate, corporeal substance," but whose extension is the smallest, including only "man."

[2] The rule of the inverse ratio of comprehension and extension holds only for universals. It does not hold for the transcendentals (like "being"), which are the greatest not only in extension but also in comprehension (at least implicitly).

	EXTENSION					
SUBSTANCE	Substance	Angel	Mineral	Plant	Brute	Man
BODY	Corporeal substance		Mineral	Plant	Brute	Man
ORGANISM	Animate corporeal substance			Plant	Brute	Man
ANIMAL	Sentient animate corporeal substance				Brute	Man
MAN	Rational sentient animate corporeal substance					Man
	COMPREHENSION					

If asked which of two terms has the greater comprehension, you must ask yourself two questions:

First you must ask yourself whether the terms are related as a superior and an inferior term. For instance, of the two terms "iron" and "silver," you cannot say that either of them has greater comprehension than the other, because they are related as coordinate species rather than as superior and inferior terms—that is, you cannot say "Iron is silver" or "Silver is iron." However, "metal" and "iron" are related as a superior and inferior term because "Iron is metal."

Secondly you must ask yourself which of the two terms gives more information about the subject of which it is predicated—which term gives all the information that the other gives and something else besides. For instance, "iron" has greater comprehension than "metal" because the proposition "This is iron" tells me all that the proposition "This is metal" tells me and something else besides.

Exercise

1. Define comprehension and distinguish between the so-called basic notes and the notes that can be derived from these.
2. Basing your answer on the definition of comprehension, state which term of each of the following pairs has the greater comprehension (unless the comprehension of each is identical), and give the reason for your answer:

   a—"Triangle" and "figure."

   b—"Triangle" and "plane figure bounded by three straight lines."

c—"Triangle" and "plane figure bounded by three straight lines, which enclose three interior angles that are equal to two right angles."
d—"Triangle" and "isosceles triangle."
e—"Right triangle" and "right triangle, on which a square on the hypotenuse is equal to the combined area of the squares on the legs."
f—"Dog" and "animal."

3. Define extension, "absolute extension," "functional extension," inferior, and superior.
4. When we consider the extension of a term, do we prescind entirely from its comprehension? Explain.
5. Which term of each of the pairs given under Question 2 has the greater absolute extension? Explain your answer, basing your explanation on the definition of absolute extension.
6. Compare the members of each of the following groups in both comprehension and extension, and give the reason for your answers—as much as is possible, arrange the terms in the order of increasing comprehension and decreasing extension:

Group 1
a—Rectangle
b—Figure
c—Plane figure
d—Rectilinear plane figure
e—Square
f—Parallelogram

Group 2
a—Dog
b—Organism
c—Cocker spaniel
d—Mammal
e—Vertebrate
f—Material substance
g—Animal

3. DISTRIBUTIVE, OR DIVISIVE, AND COLLECTIVE TERMS

Does a term signify the quiddity (essence, or nature) of individuals taken singly or only of groups of individuals? The answer to this question is the basis for the division of terms into distributive, or divisive, and collective.

a. Distributive or Divisive

A term (and concept) is distributive, or divisive, if it signifies the quiddity (essence, or nature) of individuals taken singly; for instance, "soldier," "player," and "duck."

b. Collective

A term (or concept) is collective if it signifies the quiddity (essence, or nature) of a group of individuals but not of those individuals taken singly. The individuals must have some note in common or must be related to one another in some way, so that the mind can grasp them together as a unit. "Army," "team," and "flock" are collective terms.

Terms like "family," "herd," "bevy," "tribe," "labor union," and so on, are collective by their very nature, since they signify a group by their very definition and independently of the context in which they occur; moreover, the individual member of a family, herd, bevy, tribe, or labor union is not a family, herd, and so on, but only a part of one.

At this point we must call attention to the *collective use* of terms that are not collective by their very nature. For instance, in the proposition "All the ducks covered the entire pond," the subject term "all the ducks" is used collectively. No single duck covered the entire pond but only all of them taken together as a group. Note, however, that the individual ducks of the group covering the entire pond are ducks, whereas the individual birds making up a flock are not a flock.

Note, too, that collective terms can be universal ("every herd"), particular ("some herd"), and singular ("this herd").

4. SINGULAR, PARTICULAR, AND UNIVERSAL TERMS

A thorough understanding of the division of terms into singular, particular, and universal is an absolutely necessary prerequisite to the study of inference.

As we have seen, according to its first meaning, the extension of a term is the sum total of the subjects that the term can be applied to. This is called its absolute extension. According to a second meaning, the extension of a term includes only those subjects to which a term is actually applied in discourse. This is called its functional extension. In this latter sense, the extension of a term is said to be singular if the term is applied to one definitely designated individual or group; particular, if it is applied to an indeterminately designated portion of its absolute extension; and universal, if it is applied to each of the subjects to which it can be applied—that is, if it stands for each one of an unlimited class of subjects, or for its total absolute extension.

This division of terms is so important that we shall explain each of its members in detail.

a. Singular Terms

A term is singular if it stands for one individual or group and designates that individual or group definitely. (Notice that "individual" does not mean "person" only but "person or thing.")

Proper names, such as "Chicago," "France," and "John Jones," are singular. Although many people have the name "John Jones," still, when we use this name, we use it for one definite individual whom we intend to designate definitely.

Superlatives in the strict sense are singular by their very nature. Within any given set of circumstances and from any single point of view, there can be only one best, highest, lowest, tallest, and so on; and the designation of a thing as the best, highest, lowest, tallest, and so on, is a definite designation.

The demonstrative pronouns "this" and "that" are singular inasmuch as they definitely designate a single individual or group.

Common nouns are singular when they are restricted in their application by demonstrative adjectives or other modifiers to a single definitely designated individual or group; for instance, "this man," "that dog," "the tallest man in the room," and "the girl in the front row nearest the window."

Note that collective nouns ("herd," "team," "army," "group") are singular if they stand for a definite group that they designate definitely. Note, too, that nouns that are grammatically plural are singular from the point of view of logic if they definitely designate one group; for instance, "those five men" in the proposition "Those five men make up a basketball team," and "the ducks" in the proposition "The ducks covered the entire pond."

b. *Particular Terms*

A term is particular if it stands for an indeterminately designated portion of its absolute extension.

A term, therefore, is particular, first, if it stands for one individual or group without designating it definitely; and, secondly, if it stands for more than one, but not clearly for all, of the individuals or groups to which it can be applied. "Some man," "some horses," "three boys," "several girls," "a few apples," and "most Americans" are particular.

In the proposition "A horse trampled on the lettuce," the term "a horse" is particular; it stands for a definite horse, but does not designate that horse definitely. On the other hand, in the proposition "This horse trampled on the lettuce," the term "this horse" is singular because it not only stands for a definite individual horse but also designates this horse definitely.

c. *Universal Terms*

A term is universal if it stands for each of the subjects to which it can be applied—that is, if it stands for each one of an unlimited class of subjects. For instance, the terms "every man," "each man," "men without exception," and "whatever is heavier than water" are universal.

Note that a term that is grammatically singular is not necessarily singular from the point of view of logic but might be particular or universal. The definite article "the" is prefixed to both singular and universal terms. "The dog" is singular in "The dog is barking excitedly," but universal (at least virtually) in "The dog is an animal." The indefinite article "a" and "an" is prefixed to both particular and universal terms. "A dog" is particular in "A dog is yelping" but universal (at least virtually) in "A dog is an animal," where "a dog" stands for a dog as such and therefore for every dog.

A term that is used universally (that is, for each individual being as well as for each kind of being to which it can be applied) is said to be *distributed.* A term that is not used for its entire extension is said to be *undistributed.* A singular term actually stands for the only individual or group it can be applied to and is therefore used for its entire extension. Consequently, in a certain limited sense,[3] a singular term is also universal. For this reason universal and singular terms are distributed; particular terms are undistributed.

Exercise

Indicate the quantity, or extension, of the following terms (that is, state whether they are singular, particular, or universal) and give the reason for your answer by quoting pertinent definitions. Ignore the predicate terms except insofar as you must consider them in order to recognize the quantity of the subject.

1. All men (are rational animals).
2. Man (is a rational animal).
3. Captain John Smith.
4. A man (is running down the street).
5. Whoever is in this room (is welcome).
6. Anything that's made of wood (is combustible).
7. A few students (were absent from class).
8. The United States of America.
9. Four herds of buffalo (were in the state).
10. All Americans (are human beings).
11. All Americans (number over 160 millions).
12. This dog (is a collie).
13. Every dog (is an animal).
14. A dog (is barking loudly).
15. Some dogs (are hounds).

[3] We say "in a certain limited sense" because the relationship of a singular term to what it stands for is actually very different from the relationship of a universal term to what it stands for. Still, in the theory of the syllogism and from a purely practical point of view, a singular term is equivalent to a universal term in many respects. For instance, the syllogism "Socrates is a philosopher; but Socrates is a Greek; therefore some Greek is a philosopher" is a valid syllogism although the middle term "Socrates" is singular in each occurrence.

CHAPTER 3

The Attributive Proposition

IN THIS CHAPTER we shall say as much about the proposition as we have to in order to begin our treatment of inference. We shall speak mainly of the attributive proposition.

1. GENERAL NOTION OF THE PROPOSITION

Before treating of the attributive proposition, we shall give a brief explanation of the proposition in general.

A proposition is defined as a statement in which anything whatsoever is affirmed or denied. In some propositions the simple existence of a subject is affirmed or denied, as in "God exists" and "Troy is no longer." In some, an attribute is affirmed or denied of a subject, as in "A dog is an animal" and "A dog is not a cat." In some, again, relationships, or connections, between member propositions are affirmed or denied, as in "If it is raining, the ground is probably wet" and "It is not because he is a Republican that he will not be elected."

A proposition is expressed by what grammarians call a declarative sentence, and must be distinguished from a question, exclamation, wish, command, and entreaty. The following are not propositions: "What is a platyhelminth?," "Ouch!," "May God grant them peace!," "Do it immediately!," and "Please come." These are not propositions because in them nothing whatsoever is either affirmed or denied.

A proposition may also be defined as discourse that expresses either truth or falsity. A proposition is the only kind of discourse that can be true or false in the strict sense, and every proposition is the one or the other. If things actually are as a proposition says they are, it is true; if things are not as it says they are, it is false. Hence, a proposition is the only kind of discourse that you believe, assume, prove, refute, doubt, or deny. "What is a platyhelminth?," "Ouch!," and so on, are neither true nor false; you can neither believe, assume, prove, refute, doubt, nor deny them.

There are many kinds of propositions—existential and nonexistential, simple and compound, categorical and hypothetical, causal, inferential, and so on and so on—but for the present we shall treat only of the ATTRIBUTIVE OR CATEGORICAL PROPOSITION.[1]

2. BASIC ELEMENTS OF THE ATTRIBUTIVE PROPOSITION

An attributive, or categorical, proposition is defined as a proposition in which a predicate (P) is affirmed or denied of a subject (S). It has three basic elements: the subject, the predicate, and the copula.

The SUBJECT is that about which something is affirmed or denied. The logical subject of a proposition is not always the same as its grammatical subject. Take the example, "We should elect Smith." The grammatical subject of this proposition is "we." The logical subject, though (at least in many contexts), is "the one we should elect." In this proposition we are not affirming something about "we." Rather, we are telling who it is that we should elect. "The one we should elect," then, is that about which something is affirmed or denied.

The PREDICATE of an attributive proposition is what is affirmed or denied of the subject.

The COPULA is either "is (am, are)" or "is (am, are) not." If the copula is "is," the proposition is affirmative; if the copula is "is not," the proposition is negative. Affirmative and negative are the two kinds of QUALITY that a proposition can have.

In the affirmative proposition the copula joins, unites, or "copulates," the predicate with the subject; the subject is declared to exist (at least with mental existence) as something identical with the

[1] "Categorical proposition" is generally synonymous with "attributive proposition." Sometimes, however, "categorical proposition" is used in a broader sense and includes not only the subject-predicate type but also propositions that affirm or deny the simple existence of a subject ("God exists" and "Unicorns do not exist").

predicate; and the entire comprehension of the predicate is attributed to, or drawn into, the subject. Thus, when we say "A dog is an animal," we declare that "a dog" and "(some) animal" are identical, that the entire comprehension of "animal" belongs to "dog," and that to exist as a dog is to exist as an animal.

In the negative proposition the copula separates, or divides, the predicate from the subject. The identity of the subject and predicate are denied, and an indeterminate portion of the comprehension of the predicate is excluded from the subject, or vice versa. In other words, the subject and predicate of a negative proposition may have many notes, or intelligible elements, in common; but their comprehension must differ in at least one respect; each must either have an attribute that the other does not have or lack an attribute that the other has. A dog, for instance, is not a cat. Yet both a dog and a cat are substances, bodies, organisms, animals, vertebrates, mammals, and so on; finally, however, you come to differences that make a dog a dog rather than some other animal, and a cat a cat rather than something else; in the notes that are distinctive of each, a dog and a cat must differ.

For a proposition to be negative, the negative particle must modify the copula itself. If the negative particle modifies either the subject or the predicate, but not the copula, the proposition is affirmative. Thus, "Those who have not been vaccinated are likely to get smallpox" and "He who is not with me is against me" are affirmative propositions because the "not" belongs to the subject and does not modify the copula. The following are examples of negative propositions:

1. Socrates is not sick.
2. Some man is not seated.
3. No cat has nine tails.
4. None of the students will go.
5. He will never go.

Notice that in Example 3 we are not affirming something of a being called "no cat," but are denying something of every cat. Similarly in Example 4 we are not affirming something of a being called "none," but are denying something of every student. Hence, since

Numbers 3 and 4 deny something of a subject, they are both negative propositions.

Note that the copula does not always imply the actual real existence of a subject. For instance, the proposition "A chiliagon is a polygon of a thousand angles" does not assert that such a figure actually exists in the real order. All it says is that a chiliagon as conceived in the mind is such a figure. However, *if* a chiliagon exists in the real order, it will exist there as a polygon having a thousand angles.

The mental operation by which we affirm or deny anything whatsoever is called JUDGMENT. The study of judgment belongs to psychology and epistemology rather than to logic. Logic is concerned with the mental proposition, which is the internal product that the act of judgment produces within the mind, and with oral and written propositions insofar as they are signs of mental propositions, but not with judgment itself.

3. QUANTITY, OR EXTENSION, OF PROPOSITION

The quantity, or extension, of a proposition is determined by the quantity, or extension, of the subject term. A proposition is SINGULAR if its subject term is singular, standing for one definitely designated individual or group; it is PARTICULAR if its subject term is particular, standing for an indeterminately designated portion of its absolute extension; and UNIVERSAL if its subject term is universal, standing for each of the subjects that it can be applied to.

If the subject term is INDETERMINATE—that is, if it is not modified by any sign of singularity ("this," "that," and so on), particularity ("some"), or universality ("all," "every," "each")—the proposition too is indeterminate; you must decide by the sense whether it is to be regarded as singular, particular, or universal. For instance, "a man" is universal (at least implicitly) in "A man is a rational animal," but particular in "A man is laughing loudly." In the first example "a man" stands for man as such and therefore includes every man; but in the second example it stands for one individual man designated indeterminately.

Propositions like "Germans are good musicians" and "Mothers love their children" are general propositions. A *general proposition* expresses something that is true in most instances or on the whole. The proposition "Germans are good musicians" means that Germans on the whole, or as a group, are good musicians and is not to be regarded as false because some German here or there is not a good musician. And the proposition "Mothers love their children" is not false because some abnormal mothers do not love their children. Since general propositions admit of exceptions without destroying their truth, they are particular rather than universal.

Usually you can tell for certain whether an indefinite proposition is singular, particular, or universal. In case of doubt, however, you should assume that it is particular and thus avoid attempting to draw more out of your premises than may actually be in them.

We remind you again that many terms, and therefore many propositions, that are singular from the point of view of grammar are particular or universal from the point of view of logic; thus, in the proposition "Man is mortal," "man" is singular grammatically, but universal from the point of view of logic. We also repeat that a proposition is singular if its subject definitely designates one group, even if the subject term is plural grammatically. Thus, the proposition "Those five men make up a basketball team" is a singular proposition even though "five men" is plural grammatically.

The form "No *S* is a *P*" is the ordinary unambiguous way of expressing a universal negative proposition, as in the example "No dog is a cat."

Exercise

Classify the following propositions as singular, particular, or universal; and give the reason for your answer by quoting pertinent definitions.

1. Chicago is a large city.
2. That man is sick.
3. Some man is singing at the top of his voice.
4. All men are mortal.
5. A dog is barking outside my window.
6. Fido is barking outside my window.
7. Our neighbor's dog is barking outside my window.
8. A dog is an animal.
9. Dogs are not cats.

10. Pigeons are eating up the newly planted seed.
11. Pigeons are not mammals.
12. Many men are suffering from arthritis.
13. All the people in the U.S.A. are more than 160,000,000.
14. Whatever is lighter than water floats on water.
15. All the students in this room weigh over two tons.
16. No student in this room weighs over 200 pounds.
17. Woman is fickle.
18. Captain John Smith was a romantic character.
19. Men are selfish creatures.
20. The U.S.A. is a great nation.

4. THE SYMBOLS *A, E, I,* AND *O*

On the basis of both quality and quantity attributive propositions are designated as *A, E, I,* and *O.* These letters are from the Latin words *affirmo,* which means "I affirm," and *nego,* which means "I deny." *A, E, I,* and *O* have the following meanings: *A* and *I* (the first two vowels of *affirmo*) signify affirmative propositions—*A* either a universal or a singular, and *I* a particular; *E* and *O* (the vowels of *nego*) signify negative propositions—*E* either a universal or a singular, and *O* a particular.

	Affirmative	Negative
Universal and Singular	A	*E*
Particular	*I*	*O*

Thus, the following are *A* propositions:

1. All voters are citizens.
2. Every voter is a citizen.
3. A dog is an animal.
4. Without exception, the members of the class passed the examination.

5. John Smith is a doctor.
6. All who have not already been vaccinated must be vaccinated tomorrow.

The following are *E* propositions:

7. No dog is a cat.
8. Dogs are not cats.
9. I am not a colonel.

The following are *I* propositions:

10. Some houses are white.
11. Some cat is black.
12. Dogs sometimes bite strangers.
13. Many men are selfish.
14. Dogs are pests.

The following are *O* propositions:

15. Some cat is not black.
16. Not all cats are black.
17. Not every man is a saint.
18. All that glitters is not gold.
19. All horses can't jump.
20. "Not everyone who says to me: 'Lord, Lord' shall enter into the kingdom of heaven."

Notice that in all of these *O* propositions the predicate is denied of an indeterminately designated portion of the extension of the subject.

Exercise

Classify the following propositions as *A, E, I,* or *O,* and be ready to give the reasons for your answers.

1. All cats are animals.
2. No man is immortal by nature.
3. Some roses are red.
4. Washington is the first president of the United States of America.

5. Some roses are not red.
6. This man is not a sailor.
7. No elephants are native to America.
8. Camels are not native to America.
9. Not all football players are good students.
10. All football players are not good students.
11. No one who does no work will get any pay.
12. Anything as big as an elephant is hard to carry in a wheelbarrow.
13. All the members of that class are philosophy majors.
14. All the members of that class form a philosophical society.
15. Lindbergh was not the first to fly across the Atlantic.

5. THE QUANTITY, OR EXTENSION, OF THE PREDICATE

The rules governing the quantity, or extension, of the predicate are of very great importance both theoretically and practically. A thorough mastery of them is an absolutely necessary prerequisite to an understanding of the conversion of propositions, which we shall treat in Chapter 5, and of the categorical syllogism, which we shall treat in Chapter 7.

We must prefix our treatment of these rules with two very important cautions:

The first caution is a warning never to confuse the quantity of the predicate with the quantity of the proposition itself. The quantity of a proposition, as we saw earlier, is determined solely by the quantity of the subject term; and the quantity of the predicate is irrelevant to the quantity of the proposition. A proposition is singular if the subject term is singular, particular if the subject term is particular, and universal if the subject term is universal. In other words, a proposition is singular, particular, or universal, depending on whether something is affirmed or denied of a definitely designated individual or group, of an indeterminately designated portion of the subject's absolute extension, or of each individual included in the subject's absolute extension.

The second caution is a reminder that the predicate does not have quantity, or extension, in the same way as the subject. The subject term has quantity directly and by its very nature as subject. The subject, according to Aristotelian terminology, indicates "matter," and the predicate expresses a "form" that is received into this subject as into matter (or else denied of it). Now matter, not form, is the basis of quantity; and, until we reflect on the relationship of the subject and predicate, we do not think of the predicate from the point of view of quantity at all, but only from the point of view of comprehension. Suppose, for instance, that you do not know what a platyhelminth is and are then told, "A platyhelminth is a worm." When you grasp the meaning of this proposition, the form "worm" is, as it were, received into the "matter" indicated by "platyhelminth" —the comprehension of "worm" is drawn into the comprehension of "platyhelminth," and the nature of a platyhelminth is revealed to you insofar as a platyhelminth is whatever is signified by the predicate (that is, insofar as it is a worm). Only later, when you have reflected on the subject-predicate relationship, do you see that the extension of the subject is drawn into the extension of the predicate, and so forth. The fact that quantifiers ("every," "some," and so on) are attached to the subject but not to the predicate likewise reveals a difference in the way in which each of them has quantity.

This second caution will save us from the error of thinking that an attributive proposition is nothing more than an assertion of quantitative relationships of terms. This caution will also help us understand both the value and the limitations of diagrams in which, for instance, a circle is enclosed within another circle. These diagrams are visual aids to grasping quantitative relationships of subject and predicate, and only that.

Now that we have given these two cautions, we are ready to treat of the rules governing the quantity, or extension, of the predicate.

Sometimes the predicate of an attributive proposition is singular. *It is singular if it stands for one individual or group and likewise designates this individual or group definitely,* as in the following examples:

1. The first man to make a solo non-stop flight across the Atlantic was Lindbergh.
2. John is not the tallest boy in the room.
3. He is not the first to do that.

Notice that this rule holds for both affirmative and negative propositions. Notice, too, that a singular term is singular independently of its function in a proposition.

If the predicate is not singular, the following rules (which are based on the function of the predicate and on an analysis of the subject-predicate relationship) are applicable:

a. Rule for the Affirmative Proposition

The predicate of an affirmative proposition is particular or undistributed (unless it is singular).

The following diagram displays the most common relationship in extension of the subject and predicate of an affirmative proposition. The large circle represents the extension of "animal." Each of the

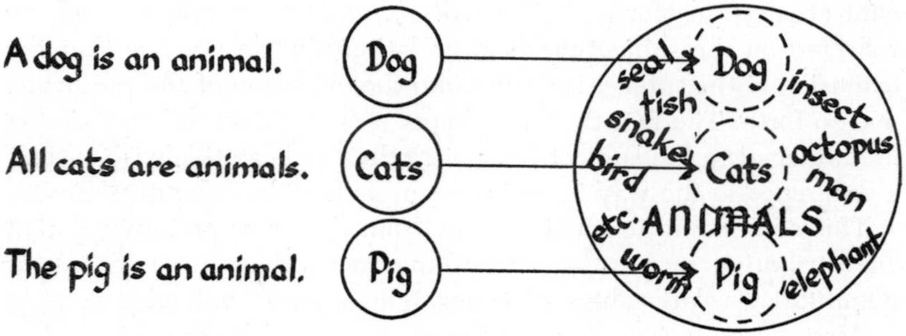

dotted circles represents the indeterminate part of the extension of "animal" embraced by "dog," "cats," and "pig," respectively. The words "bird," "sheep," "elephant," "man," and so on, show that there are, or at least might be, other animals besides "dog," "cats," and "pig." Now, when we say that a dog is an animal, we do not mean that a dog is *every* animal, or *this* or *that* animal, but that a dog is *some* animal: we mean that "dog" is identical with an indeterminately designated portion of the extension of "animal." Thus, we see that the relationship of the subject and predicate in extension is the reverse of their relationship in comprehension: the comprehension of the predicate, as we have seen,[2] is drawn into the subject, with the predicate expressing one of the innumerable attributes of the

[2] See pages 28-29.

subject; but, from the point of view of extension, the subject is drawn into the extension of the predicate and embraces an indeterminately designated part thereof.[3]

b. *Rule for the Negative Proposition*

The predicate of a negative proposition is universal or distributed (unless it is singular).

The subject of a negative proposition is completely excluded from the extension of the predicate, and the predicate is completely excluded from the extension of the subject. Consider the example "No dog is a cat" and the accompanying diagram.

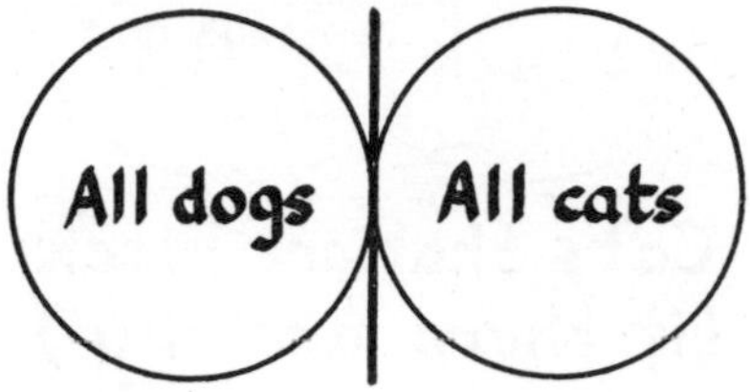

You can go through the entire extension of "cat" without finding a single dog, and through the entire extension of "dog" without finding a single cat. Even the predicate of a singular or particular

[3] The fact that a certain form is in one subject does not exclude its presence in other subjects. For instance, the fact that the form "whiteness" is in this paper does not exclude "whiteness" from a white shirt. Thus, in the proposition "This paper is white," the predicate "white" is particular, since this paper is only one of the innumerable subjects that can have whiteness.

N. B. Predicates expressing the definition or a characteristic property of their subject need a special word of comment. (The terms "definition" and "characteristic property" are defined and explained at length in Chapter 13.) Such predicates have the same comprehension and extension as their subjects and are therefore interchangeable with them. For instance, "rational animal" is the definition of "man"; consequently, just as every man is a rational animal, so every rational animal is a man.

Such predicates are *actually* particular, in accordance with the general rule. This is clear from the fact that, when we say that every man is a rational animal, we do not mean that every man is *every* rational animal, but that every man is *some* rational animal. Still, inasmuch as such predicates can be interchanged with their subjects and made the subjects of universal propositions, they are potentially universal. However, this potential universality does not spring from their function as predicates, but from their matter (that is, from the special character of their thought content).

negative proposition is always universal (unless it is singular), for you can go through the entire extension of the predicate without finding an instance of the subject. For instance, if you are not a Hottentot, we can look at all the Hottentots without finding you; and if some cats are not black, we can look at all black things without finding those cats of which to be black has been denied, as a glance at the diagram below will make clear.

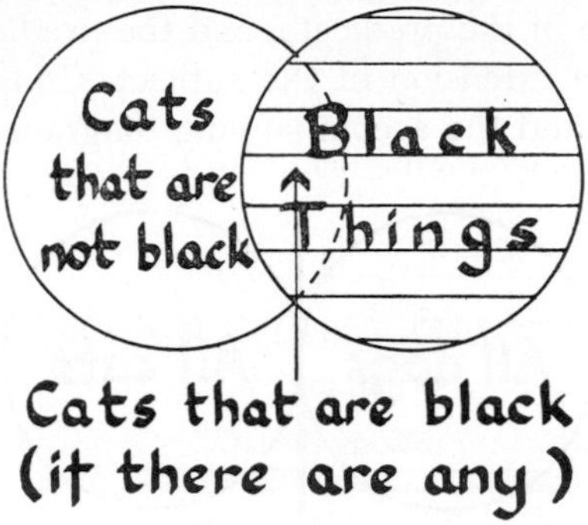

Exercise

I. First state the quantity and quality of the following propositions and then state the quantity of the predicate (that is, whether it is singular, particular, or universal). Notice that in a few instances the predicate is the definition of the subject and therefore "actually particular, but potentially universal by reason of the special character of the thought content or matter." Notice, too, that in No. 1 "rational animal" is not the definition of "John" but of the kind of being he is (that is, of "man"); hence the observation about predicates that are definitions does not apply to this example. The same is true of No. 17.

1. John is a rational animal.
2. John is not a sailor.
3. John is the tallest man in the room.
4. Every man is mortal.
5. Some men are not aviators.
6. The man over there is an American citizen.
7. Rover is a dog.
8. Rover is not a cat.

9. The noisiest dog I ever heard is barking outside my window.
10. The dog that is barking outside my window is the noisiest dog I ever heard.
11. No giraffes are native to America.
12. Some athletes are not good students.
13. A sphere is a solid.
14. A sphere is a solid body bounded by a surface that is equidistant at all its points from a point within that is called its center.
15. A sphere is not a plane figure.
16. A plane triangle is a plane figure bounded by three straight lines.
17. The tiny triangle on the blackboard is a plane figure bounded by three straight lines.
18. New York is a very large city.
19. New York is the most populous city in the United States.
20. The most populous urban area is the world is Greater New York.

II. Do the same with propositions in previous exercises.

6. LOGICAL FORM

First we shall say a few words about logical form in general, and then we shall explain the logical form of the attributive proposition. Finally we shall explain the notion of subject and predicate more fully, and give some practical aids for the reduction of attributive propositions to logical form.

a. General Notion of Logical Form

Logical form in general is defined as *the basic structure, or the basic arrangement of the parts, of a complex logical unit*. Complex logical units include propositions and inferences, or arguments, but not terms.[4] There are as many logical forms as there are distinct structural types of propositions and inferences. The following examples illustrate a few of the innumerable logical forms that we shall study later in the year:

[4] In the present context, where they are opposed to propositions and the various kinds of inference, even so-called complex terms (see p. 16) are simple logical units, which have no logical form.

Propositions—

Every dog is an animal.
John is not a sailor.
If the sun is shining, it is day.
He is either going or not going.
He will be chosen because he is the best man.

Arguments or inferences—

Every dog is an animal;
but every hound is a dog;
therefore every hound is an animal.

No man is twenty feet tall;
but John is a man;
therefore John is not twenty feet tall.

If the sun is shining, it is day;
but the sun is shining;
therefore it is day.

Each of these examples illustrates a different kind of logical unit, with a distinct arrangement of parts, and therefore each illustrates a distinct logical form.

In the present chapter we shall treat only of the logical forms of the attributive, or categorical, proposition; but a glance at the Table of Contents will reveal the many logical forms that we shall treat of later—the forms of the various kinds of propositions (such as conditional, disjunctive, and conjunctive propositions), the forms of eduction (including conversion, obversion, and contraposition), the forms of oppositional inference, the many forms of the categorical and hypothetical syllogism, and so on.

b. Logical Form of the Attributive Proposition

An attributive, or categorical, proposition, as we have already seen, is defined as a proposition in which a predicate (P) is affirmed or denied of a subject (S). This definition indicates the essential parts of the attributive proposition: the subject, the copula, and the predicate. We have already seen that all attributive propositions have the same parts and the same basic structure regardless of their matter or thought content; so far as their structure is concerned, it makes no difference whether they are about men, dogs, swimming pools, peace, walrusses, or Asiatic famines. This basic structure (or *generic logical form*) is: S—copula—P.

This generic basic structure admits of six variations (or *species*) according to differences in the quantity of the subject and the quality of the copula. The subject can be universal, particular, or singular; and the copula can be affirmative or negative. Each of these six varieties of structure is a distinct logical form, or type, of attributive proposition. Thus, we have the following forms of the attributive proposition:

Su is P.	S a P	A
Su is not P.	S e P	E
Sp is P.	S i P	I
Sp is not P.	S o P	O
Ss is P.	S a P	A
Ss is not P.	S e P	E

These six forms, as we have seen, are symbolized by *A, E, I,* and *O:* *A* and *I* signifying affirmative propositions—*A* either a universal or a singular, and *I* a particular; *E* and *O* signifying negative propositions—*E* either a universal or a singular, and *O* a particular.

c. *Reduction to Logical Form*

Reduction to logical form consists in rewording a proposition or argument according to some set plan in order to make its basic structure obvious. The purpose of reduction to logical form is to extricate a part of a complex logical unit (like the subject or predicate of a categorical proposition, or the minor, middle, or major terms of a categorical syllogism) to make it an object of special consideration or to facilitate various logical processes (for instance, conversion).

The logical form of most of the sample propositions we have had up to the present is very obvious, for most of them have been arranged in the order *S*—copula—*P*, and there has been no difficulty in recognizing the quantity of the subject term. It is easy to see, for instance, that the proposition "Every dog is an animal" has the logical form "Su is *P*," which is also expressed "*S* a *P*," or simply *A*.

Many propositions, however, do not display their logical form so clearly as these. Consider, for instance, the proposition "He writes editorials." In this proposition the word "writes" expresses both the copula and a part of the predicate, and (at least in most contexts) the words "writes editorials" are equivalent to "is a writer of editorials." Hence, if we wish to express this proposition in the order "S—copula—*P*," we must change the wording to "He—is—a writer of editorials." Thus, the reduction to logical form of an attributive proposition consists in rewording it so as to state, first, its logical subject together with an appropriate sign of quantity, such as "all," "every," "some," and so on; next, its copula; and then its predicate. For instance, reduced to logical form, the proposition "Violinists play the violin" becomes "All violinists—are—ones who play the violin."

We shall now make some observations that should help us to discover the logical subject, copula, and predicate of an attributive proposition and at the same time throw greater light on their nature.

The logical subject, as we have seen, expresses that about which anything whatsoever is affirmed or denied. To find the logical subject of a proposition, ask yourself, About whom or what is the statement made? About whom or what is new information given? Often you will be helped by also asking yourself, To what question does the proposition give an answer? With these suggestions in mind, let us re-examine the proposition "We should elect Smith" in order to determine what its logical subject is in various contexts.

If the proposition "We should elect Smith" is an answer to the question "Whom should we elect?," a statement is made, and information is given us, about the one we should elect; hence, "the one we should elect" is the subject, and "Smith" is the predicate. If the proposition is an answer to the question "Who should elect Smith?," information is given about the ones who should elect Smith; and so the logical subject is "the ones who should elect Smith," and "we" is the predicate. On the other hand, if the proposition is an answer to the question "What should we do?," "what we should do" is the logical subject and "to elect Smith" is the predicate.

To determine the quantity, ask yourself, Is the statement made about the whole extension of the subject, about an indeterminately designated portion of its extension, or about one definitely designated individual or group? We have already mentioned some of the usual signs of universality, particularity, and singularity when we treated of the division of terms into universal, particular, and singular. We might add that words such as "never," "nowhere," "at no time," "always," "without exception," and so on, are often signs of universality. Words such as "a few," "many," "hardly any," "generally," "often," "sometimes," "most," and so on, are usually signs of particularity.

The copula is always "is (am, are)" or "is (am, are) not"; that is, it is always the present indicative of the verb "to be" either with or without a negative particle. Indications of time expressed by the past and future tenses of verbs do not belong to the copula but to the predicate.

The predicate is whatever is affirmed or denied of the subject. Whatever new information is given belongs to the predicate. Often a predicate term can be discovered by asking the question to which a proposition gives the answer and by then giving the answer to this question in a minimum number of words and in an incomplete sentence. For instance, suppose that the proposition "We should elect Smith" is an answer to the question, Whom should we elect? The answer is "Smith." Hence, "Smith" is the predicate; and, reduced to logical form, the proposition is: "The one we should elect —is—Smith." Or suppose that the proposition "Tex put the saddle on the horse" is an answer to the question, Where did Tex put the saddle? The answer, expressed in a minimum number of words, is: "on the horse." Hence, this is the predicate. Expressed in logical form the sentence becomes: "(The place) where Tex put the saddle —is—on the horse."

Often you will have to supply words such as "one," "thing," and so on, with the predicate—for instance, when reduced to logical form, the proposition "All men have free will" becomes "All men—are—ones having free will." Sometimes you will have to use nouns, adjectives, participles, or relative clauses to express a predicate contained in a verb. For instance, "He runs" becomes "He—is—running" if "runs" signifies a present action, or "He—is—a runner" if "runs" signifies a habitual action.

Many propositions are of mixed type. "All but a few will go," for instance, is at once *I* and *O*. Reduced to logical form, it becomes "Most (some) are ones who will go; the rest (some) are not ones who will go."

We shall now give a few examples of the reduction of propositions to logical form.

1. "When under pressure, he does his best work" becomes "He is one who does his best work when under pressure." This is an *A* proposition. "When under pressure" belongs to the predicate.

2. "Not all who are here will go to the concert" becomes "Some who are here are not ones who will go to the concert." This is an *O* proposition.

3. "Few men get all they want" can be reduced to either of two logical forms. It can be looked upon as an *A* proposition and reduced as follows: "The number of men who get all they want is small." It can also be looked upon as a combination of *I* and *O* and reduced as follows: "Some men are ones who get all they want; many men (some) are not ones who get all they want." "Few" frequently means "some, but not many."

4. "Dogs are a nuisance" becomes "Some dogs are a nuisance." All lovers of dogs, at least, will insist that this is an *I* proposition and not an *A*.

5. "Canaries sing" becomes "Canaries are singers." In this context "sing" does not signify a present action but a habitual or frequently repeated action; it means that canaries can sing and do it often, but not that they are actually singing here and now.

Exercise

Reduce the propositions given below to logical form. When the logical form depends on the context, construct a context by asking the question that you want the proposition to answer. Next, state whether the propositions are *A, E, I,* or *O;* and, lastly, indicate the quantity of the predicates.

1. An attributive proposition consists of a subject, copula, and predicate.
2. Time marches on.
3. "Blessed are the poor in spirit."
4. Cats have whiskers.

5. Fortune favors the brave.
6. A distinguished man called on me this afternoon.
7. "This is my commandment, that you love one another."
8. Men seek wealth.
9. Hardly anyone will go.
10. All horses can't jump.
11. Mothers generally love their children.
12. Nearly all voted against the bill.
13. All's well that ends well.
14. Few manage to get all they want.
15. A few will be unable to go.

CHAPTER 4

General Notion of Inference

1. SOME DEFINITIONS

INFERENCE, *according to its broadest meaning,* signifies any process by which the mind proceeds from one or more propositions to other propositions seen to be implied in the former. However, *in its strict and proper sense,* inference signifies the operation by which the mind gets new knowledge by drawing out the implications of what it already knows. The distinction between inference in the broad sense and inference in the strict and proper sense will be clearer after we have contrasted immediate and mediate inference.

The word "inference" is also applied to any series of propositions so arranged that one, called the CONSEQUENT, flows with logical necessity from one or more others, called the ANTECEDENT. Sometimes the name is given to the consequent alone, viewed in relation to the antecedent from which it flows.

Etymologically, "antecedent" (derived from the Latin *antecedo*) means "that which goes before"; it is defined as "that from which something is inferred." "Consequent" (derived from the Latin *consequor*) means "that which follows after"; it is defined as "that which is inferred from the antecedent."

The antecedent and consequent of a valid inference are so related that the truth of the antecedent involves the truth of the consequent (but not vice versa); and the falsity of the consequent involves the falsity of the antecedent (but not vice versa). In other words, if the antecedent is true, the consequent (if it really is a consequent) is also true; and if the consequent is false, the antecedent is false. However, if the antecedent is false, the consequent is indifferently false or true (and therefore doubtful); and if the consequent is true, the antecedent is indifferently true or false (and therefore doubtful).

The connection by virtue of which the consequent flows with logical necessity from the antecedent is known as consequence or simply SEQUENCE. The sequence (which is signified by "therefore," "consequently," "accordingly," "hence," "thus," "and so," "for this reason," and so on) is the very heart of inference; and when we make an inference, our assent bears on it directly.

A genuine sequence is called *valid;* a pseudo sequence is called *invalid.* Notice that an invalid sequence is really not a sequence at all but is merely called a sequence because it mimics one (just as counterfeit money is called money, although it really is not money but only make-believe money).

SYNOPTIC SCHEMA

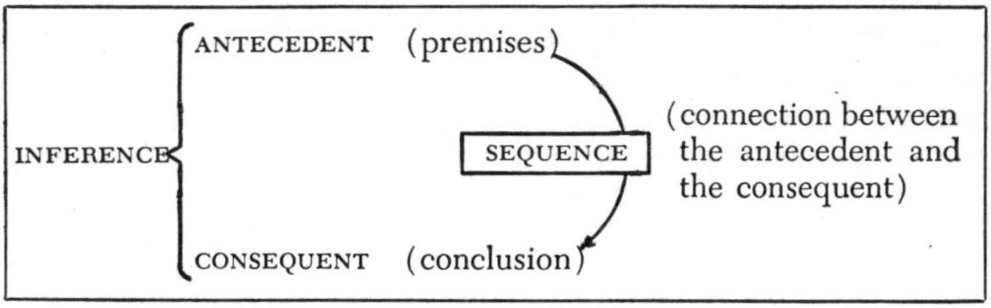

Exercise

Which of the following illustrate inference? Explain and defend your answer. Notice that the adverbs "therefore," and so on, do not always signify logical sequence; sometimes they express mere factual dependence of what is stated in the "therefore" clause on what is stated in the preceding clause or clauses (as in Nos. 2 and 7). Sometimes the antecedent is not intended to prove the consequent, but merely to explain it (as in No. 11). Notice, too, that sometimes no special word is used to signify sequence.

1. All men are mortal; but you are a man; therefore you are mortal.
2. He broke his leg and is therefore using crutches.
3. He's a man and therefore mortal.
4. The barometer is very low and the humidity is very high; consequently, it's likely to rain within a few hours.

5. I wonder how far it is from Calcutta to Bombay.
6. Carrots are vegetables, dogs bark, and cows give milk.
7. His mother is sick; that's why he did not come to school today.
8. He blushes; therefore he is guilty.
9. Smoke is pouring out of the windows; the house must be on fire.
10. Since the consequent of that syllogism is false, its antecedent must also be false.
11. It rains so much in Darjeeling because humid winds are chilled as they hit the mountainside and thereupon precipitate their moisture.
12. He studies logic because it's a required course.

2. FORMAL AND MATERIAL SEQUENCE

Valid sequence springs either from the form of inference or from the special character of the matter or thought content. If the sequence springs from the form of inference, the sequence is FORMAL and the argument is said to be formally valid or formally correct; if the sequence springs from the special character of the thought content, the sequence is MATERIAL and the argument is said to be materially valid.

The LOGICAL FORM of inference is the order that the parts of an inference have towards one another. We refer primarily to the order of concepts and propositions *in the mind.* The connection, however, between our thoughts and their written expression is so close that we can represent the logical form of inference by the arrangement of terms and propositions on a printed page. For instance, the following example illustrates one kind of inference that is formally valid:

Every S is a *P;*
therefore some *P* is an S.

We can substitute anything we want to tor S and *P,* and the consequent will always be true if the antecedent is true. If we substitute "dog" for S and "animal" for *P,* we get:

Every dog is an animal;
therefore some animal is a dog.

If we substitute "voter" for *S* and "citizen" for *P*, we get:

> Every voter is a citizen;
> therefore some citizen is a voter.[1]

We shall now examine an inference that is *formally invalid but materially valid:*

> Every triangle is a plane figure bounded by three straight lines;
> therefore every plane figure bounded by three straight lines is a triangle.

In this example the consequent does not flow from the antecedent because of the form; but it does flow because of the special character of the thought content. "Plane figure bounded by three straight lines" is a definition of "triangle" and is therefore interchangeable with it. Suppose, however, that we retain the same form but substitute "dog" for "triangle" and "animal" for "plane figure bounded by three straight lines." Suppose we argue:

> Every dog is an animal;
> therefore every animal is a dog.

This inference is obviously invalid; yet it has exactly the same form as the materially valid inference given above. The form is:

> Every *S* is a *P;*
> therefore every *P* is an *S.*

As we shall see when we study the conversion of propositions, an inference with this arrangement is always formally invalid.

Whenever we use the terms "sequence," "inference," "validity," "correctness of argumentation," and so on, without qualification, we shall understand them in their formal sense unless it is clear from the context that we are speaking of material sequence.

3. TRUTH AND FORMAL VALIDITY

Logical truth consists in the conformity of our minds with reality. A proposition, as we explained above, is true if things are as the proposition says they are. Logic studies reason as an instrument for

[1] We may not proceed from an antecedent that does not assert the actual real existence of a subject to a consequent that does assert its actual real existence.

acquiring truth, and the attainment of truth must ever remain the ultimate aim of the logician. Still, in the chapters on formal inference, we shall study only one part of the process of attaining truth. We shall not be directly concerned with acquiring true data but rather with conserving the truth of our data as we draw inferences from them. In other words, we shall aim at making such a transition from data to conclusion that if the data (antecedent, premises) are true, the conclusion (consequent) will necessarily be true. *Formal validity, correctness, rectitude,* or *consistency* will be our immediate aim. We shall not ask ourselves, Are the premises true?, but, Does the conclusion flow from the premises so that *IF* the premises are true, the conclusion is necessarily true?

The following syllogism is correct in this technical sense although the premises and the conclusion are false:

> No plant is a living being;
> but every man is a plant;
> therefore no man is a living being.

This syllogism is correct *formally* because the conclusion really flows from the premises by virtue of the form, or structure, of the argument. *IF* the premises were true, the conclusion would also be true.

The following syllogism is not correct formally although the premises and the conclusion are true:

> Every dog is an animal;
> but no dog is a *plant;*
> therefore no *plant* is an animal.

This syllogism is not correct because the conclusion does not really flow from the premises. Its invalidity will be obvious if we retain the same form but change the matter by substituting "cow" for "plant."

> Every dog is an animal;
> but no dog is a *cow;*
> therefore no *cow* is an animal.

In this syllogism (it is really only a make-believe or apparent syllogism), an obviously false conclusion comes after obviously true premises; so the syllogism must be incorrect, for in a correct or valid syllogism only truth can follow from truth.

4. IMMEDIATE AND MEDIATE INFERENCE

Inference is either immediate or mediate. Immediate inference consists in passing directly (that is, without the intermediacy of a middle term or a second proposition) from one proposition to a new proposition that is a partial or complete reformulation of the very same truth expressed in the original proposition. Except for terms prefixed by "non-" and their equivalents, immediate inference has only two terms, a subject term and predicate term (at least in most of its forms), and, strictly speaking, involves no advance in knowledge. Since immediate inference involves no advance in knowledge, it is inference only in the broad, or improper, sense.[2]

Mediate inference, on the other hand, draws a conclusion from two propositions (instead of one) and does involve an advance in knowledge. Consequently, mediate inference is inference in the strict, or proper, sense. It is mediate in either of two ways. In the categorical syllogism it unites, or separates, the subject and predicate of the conclusion through the intermediacy of a middle term; in the hypothetical syllogism the major premise "causes" the conclusion through the intermediacy of a second proposition.

The goal of mediate inference is not only a new proposition but also a new truth, for in mediate inference, as we have seen, there is an advance in knowledge. This advance is either in the order of discovery or in the order of demonstration or explanation.

The advance in knowledge is in the order of discovery when we proceed from a known truth to a new truth that we did not hitherto know to be true. The new truth, of course, must be contained somehow or other in the premises; for if it were not in the premises, it could not be gotten out of them. Still, it was in the premises only virtually and implicitly, whereas in the conclusion it is stated actually and explicitly.

The advance in knowledge is in the order of demonstration when we already knew the truth of what is stated in the conclusion but now either accept it for a new reason or have come to understand why it is true. Previously we may have accepted it on authority or as an object of opinion or natural certitude. But now we see its

[2] Some logicians object to calling it inference at all.

connection with more basic principles, and thus we possess it in a more perfect manner.

First we shall treat of immediate inference, and then of mediate inference.

SYNOPSIS

Immediate inference	Mediate inference
a) passes from one proposition	a) passes from two propositions
b) without a medium	b) through a medium
c) to a new proposition but not to a new truth.	c) not only to a new proposition but also to a new truth.

5. DEDUCTION AND INDUCTION

Deduction is the process by which our minds proceed from a more universal truth to a less universal truth, as in the syllogism "All men are mortal; but Peter is a man; therefore Peter is mortal." Induction, on the other hand, is the process by which our minds proceed from sufficiently enumerated instances to a universal truth, as in the example "This ruminant (a cow) is cloven-hoofed; this one (a deer) is cloven-hoofed; and this one (a goat) and this (an antelope) and this (an elk); therefore all ruminants are cloven-hoofed."

Induction precedes deduction. It is principally by induction that we get the universal principles that constitute the premises of deductive arguments; it is by induction, too, that we grasp the rules governing deduction as well as the principles underlying them. Nevertheless, it is customary in logic courses to treat of deduction before induction.

All formal inference and many instances of material inference are deductive. All induction, however, is material inference. At present we shall content ourselves with merely mentioning the division of inference into deduction and induction; in later chapters we shall treat of each of them in detail.

PART II

KINDS OF IMMEDIATE INFERENCE

In Part II we shall consider certain types of so-called immediate inference, treating of eduction in Chapter 5 and of oppositional inference in Chapter 6.

Note again that, since immediate inference terminates only in a new proposition and not in a new truth, it is inference in the broad or improper sense, and that only mediate inference is inference in the strict and proper sense.

The study of immediate inference will be helpful for the following reasons. First of all, it will give us facility in recognizing the quantity of terms and the quantitative relationships of subject and predicate. Secondly, it will help us to recognize equivalent propositional forms—often the same truth can be expressed in various forms, and it is important that we know which forms are equivalent and which are not. Thirdly, the study of immediate inference will help us understand the relationship of propositions to one another as to truth and falsity—how, if one proposition is true, certain other propositions must be false, and vice versa. Besides, it will give us practice in disengaging the form of propositions from their matter. For all these reasons, a study of immediate inference will provide a useful background for the study of inference in the strict and proper sense.

CHAPTER 5

Eduction

EDUCTION IS the formulation of a new proposition by the interchange of the subject and predicate of an original proposition and/or by the use or removal of negatives. We shall consider four kinds of formal eduction: conversion, obversion, contraposition, and inversion. Then we shall append a note on certain types of so-called material eduction.

1. CONVERSION

Conversion is the formulation of a new proposition by interchanging the subject and predicate of an original proposition but leaving its quality unchanged. "No cat is a dog," for instance, is converted to "No dog is a cat." The original proposition is called the *convertend,* the new proposition the *converse,* and the process itself *conversion.* Conversion is either simple or partial.

a. Simple Conversion

Conversion is simple if the quantity of the converse is the same as the quantity of the convertend. Hence, in simple conversion, if the convertend is universal, the converse is also universal; if the convertend is particular, the converse is particular; and if the convertend is singular, the converse is singular.

By simple conversion we can convert *E* propositions, *I* propositions, and singular propositions whose predicates are singular terms. Thus, "No cat is a dog" is converted by simple conversion to "No dog is a cat"; "Some houses are white" to "Some white things are houses"; and "The man near the door is John" to "John is the man near the door."

A consideration of the following diagrams will help us understand why *E* and *I* can be converted by simple conversion. "No cat is a dog" can be diagrammed as follows:

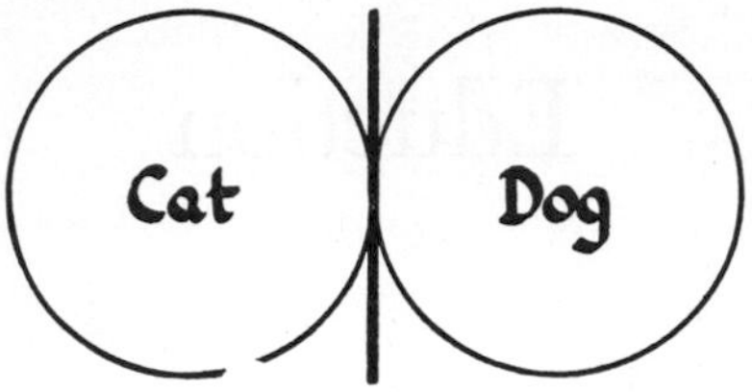

Neither of the two is the other; each is completely excluded from the extension of the other; hence, each can be denied of the other. Just as no cat is a dog, so too no dog is a cat.

"Some houses are white" can be diagrammed as follows:

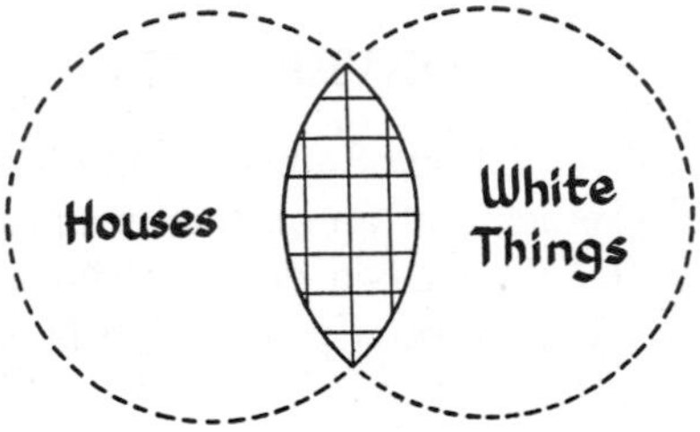

The space enclosed by both circles represents houses that are white and, as well, white things that are houses. Hence, just as some houses are white, so too some white things are houses.

A propositions cannot be converted by simple conversion. The original predicate, on being made the subject of a universal proposition, would be changed from a particular term to a universal term. For instance, you cannot argue "All dogs are animals; therefore all animals are dogs."

O propositions cannot be converted at all. The original subject, on being made the predicate of a negative proposition, would be changed from a particular term to a universal term. Thus, you cannot convert "Some dogs are not hounds" to "Some hounds are not dogs."

b. Partial Conversion

Conversion is partial if the quantity of the proposition is reduced from universal to particular. Partial conversion is also called accidental conversion, conversion by limitation, and reduced conversion. *A* is converted by partial conversion to *I*, and *E* is converted to *O*.

A propositions, if we regard their form alone, can be converted only by partial conversion. For instance, "All men are mortal beings" is converted by partial conversion to "Some mortal beings are men." Note again how the subject of an affirmative proposition is drawn into the extension of the predicate and embraces an indeterminately designated portion of it.

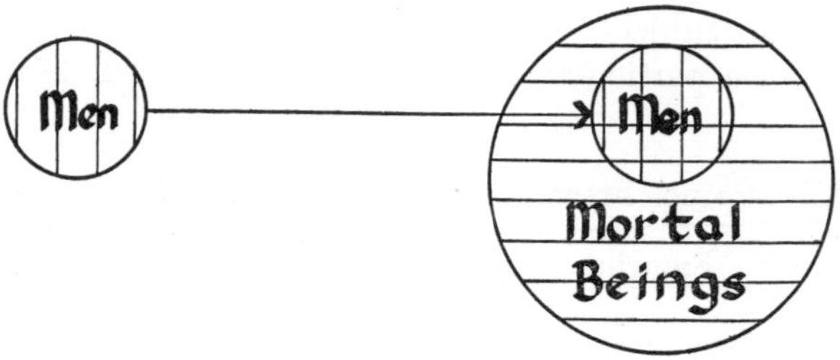

Men do not include all the mortal beings—plants and the other animals can die too—hence, we may not argue: "All men are mortal beings; therefore all mortal beings are men." In doing this, we would extend the term "mortal being" from particular to universal. We would assert something about all mortal beings in the converse after having given information about only some mortal beings in the convertend.

An *A* proposition whose predicate is the definition or a characteristic property of the subject may be converted by simple conversion because of the special character of the matter or thought content. Such a predicate, as we saw above,[1] is interchangeable with its subject. Thus, "Every man is a rational animal" may be converted by simple conversion to "Every rational animal is a man." This conversion is *materially* valid but *formally* invalid.

Since *E* propositions can be converted by simple conversion, they

[1] See the footnote on p. 37.

can obviously also be converted by partial conversion. If no cat is a dog, it is obvious that some dog is not a cat.

c. Four Notanda

1–Often it is advisable to reduce propositions to logical form before attempting conversion. This will save you from mistakes as illogical as the attempted conversion of "The dog bit the man" to "The man bit the dog."

2–Beware of converting *A* propositions by simple conversion. This is a common fallacy and is intimately related to the fallacies of the undistributed middle and the illicit process of a term, which we shall study when we take up the categorical syllogism.

3–*O* propositions, as we explained above, cannot be converted. Their original subject, on becoming the predicate, would be changed from a particular term to a universal term. You may not argue:

Some *MEN* are not Frenchmen;	*Sp* are not *Pu*
therefore some Frenchmen are not *MEN*	*Pp* are not *Su*

You must be especially careful when the apparent converse of an *O* proposition is, or at least seems to be, true. Take the example "Some cats are not black; therefore some black things are not cats." It is most assuredly true that some black things are not cats; but this cannot be inferred from the mere fact that some cats are not black. The formal invalidity of this inference is made obvious by a comparison with the following example, which has identical form, "Some dogs are not hounds; therefore some hounds are not dogs."

4–The actual real existence of a subject may not be asserted in the converse if it has not been asserted in the convertend. There is special danger of doing this in converting *A* to *I* or *E* to *O*.

Synopsis

1. Brief rules for conversion:

    (1). Interchange *S* and *P*.
    (2). Retain quality.
    (3). Do not extend any term.

2. Kinds of conversion:

   (1). Simple (*E* to *E*, *I* to *I*).
   (2). Partial (*A* to *I*, *E* to *O*).

3. Examples of conversion:

   A to *I:* "Every cat is an animal" to "Some animal is a cat."
   E to *E:* "No cat is a dog" to "No dog is a cat."
   I to *I:* "Some house is white" to "Some white thing is a house."
   O cannot be converted.

Exercise

I. Give the converse of the following (if they have one):
   1. Every *A* is a *B*.
   2. No *A* is a *B*.
   3. Some *A* is a *B*.
   4. Some *A* is not a *B*.
   5. Some dogs are very fierce animals.
   6. Giraffes are animals with long necks.
   7. Some men are not very good orators.
   8. Some of the most cheerful people I know are continually sick.
   9. Good example is the most effective way of influencing another to good.
   10. What is sauce for the goose is sauce for the gander.

II. Reduce to logical form, and then convert:
   1. Tex put the saddle on the horse.
   2. Jack ate Jill's candy.
   3. The policeman caught the thief.
   4. Some philosophers base their arguments on false principles.
   5. No sane man would do that.
   6. A lion bit his keeper.
   7. Many men followed his example.
   8. Lindbergh was the first to make a solo, non-stop flight across the Atlantic.
   9. We'll all be there.
   10. Pupils teach their professors many things.

III. Convert the propositions given in previous exercises.

IV. Criticize the following examples. First, note whether the propositions are *A, E, I,* or *O*. Then, applying the rules for conversion, state whether the inference is valid or invalid and give the reason for your answer.

1. All men have free will; therefore all having free will are men.
2. All truly democratic governments respect human rights; therefore all governments that respect human rights are truly democratic.
3. If all whales are mammals, there can be no doubt that some mammals are whales.
4. If true democracies are free countries, all free countries must be true democracies.
5. Some football players are good students; therefore some good students are football players.
6. Some football players are not good students; therefore some good students are not football players.
7. Some animals are not dogs; therefore some dogs are not animals. (This has the same form as No. 6.)
8. No mere man is entirely without sin; therefore none who is entirely without sin is a mere man.

2. OBVERSION

Obversion is the formulation of a new proposition by retaining the subject and quantity of an original proposition, changing its quality, and using as predicate the contradictory of the original predicate. "Every dog is an animal," for instance, is obverted to "No dog is a non-animal." Notice that obversion involves either the use or removal of two negatives: the use or omission of the one negative changes the quality, the use or omission of the other negative changes the predicate to its contradictory. The original proposition is called the *obvertend,* the new proposition the *obverse,* and the process itself *obversion.*

The RULES OF OBVERSION may be briefly expressed as follows:

Rule 1. Retain the subject and the quantity of the obvertend.

Rule 2. Change the quality. If the obvertend is affirmative, the obverse must be negative; and if the obvertend is negative, the obverse must be affirmative.

From Rules 1 and 2 we see that *A* propositions are obverted to *E*, *E* to *A*, *I* to *O*, and *O* to *I*.

Rule 3. As predicate, use the contradictory of the predicate of the original proposition. Under certain conditions you can make a *materially* valid obversion by using as predicate the immediately opposed contrary of the predicate of the original proposition.[2]

First we shall explain and exemplify obversion in which the predicate of the obverse is the contradictory of the predicate of the obvertend.

A to *E*. "Every dog is an animal" is obverted to "Every dog is *NOT* a *NON*-animal," which is normally expressed, "No dog is a non-animal." Note that both the obvertend and the obverse are universal propositions and that the one negative particle negates the copula and the other negates the predicate.

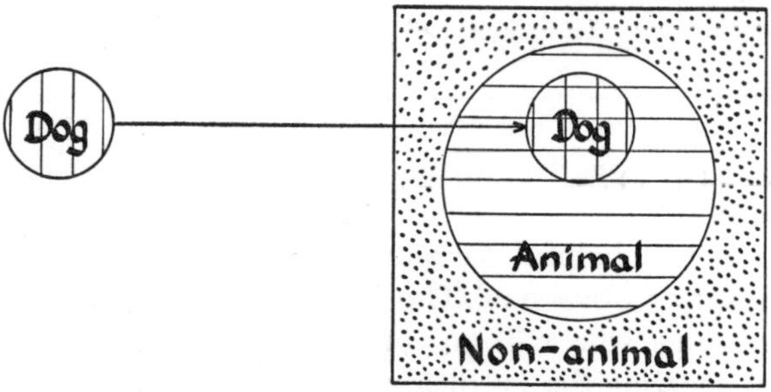

Obviously, if every dog is within the big circle, no dog is outside of it.

[2] Contradictory terms are terms that are so related that the one is the simple negation of the other; for instance, "man" and "non-man," and "being" and "non-being."

Contrary terms signify concepts that belong to the same genus but differ from one another as much as possible within that genus; for instance, "hot" and "cold," and "first" and "last." Contrary terms are immediately opposed if there is no middle ground between them; for instance, "mortal" and "immortal." Contrary terms are mediately opposed if there is a middle ground between them; for instance, "hot" and "cold," "expensive" and "cheap," "high" and "low," and so on.

Contradictory and contrary terms are explained at length on p. 217.

E to *A*. "No dog is a cat" is obverted to "Every dog is a *NON*-cat." The subject "dog" is universal in the obvertend; so it stays universal in the obverse. The quality is changed from affirmative to negative. The negative particle is transferred from the copula to the predicate.

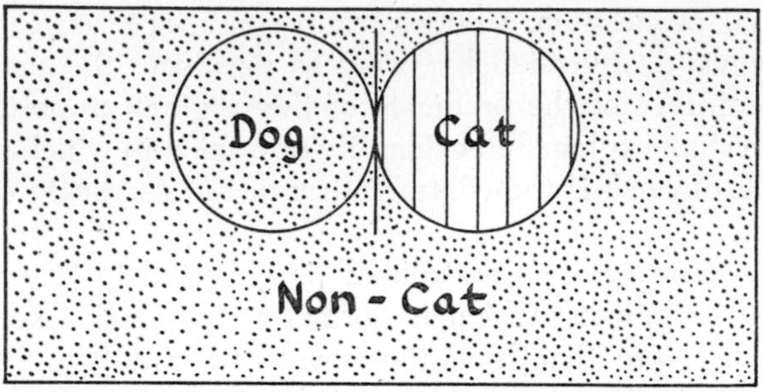

A glance at the diagram makes it obvious that, if no dog is a cat, every dog is a non-cat.

I to *O*. "Some man is a voter" is obverted to "Some man is *NOT* a *NON*-voter."

O to *I*. "Some man is not a voter" is obverted to "Some man is a *NON*-voter." The negative, again, is transferred from the copula to the predicate.

Sometimes it is helpful to reduce propositions to logical form before attempting obversion. The logical form of "He will not go" is "He is not one who will go" or "*Ss* is not *P*." By changing the quality and negating the predicate, you get the obverse, "He is one who will not go" or "*Ss* is *non-P*."

We shall now explain and exemplify *materially valid* obversion in which the immediately opposed contrary of the predicate of the obvertend becomes the predicate of the obverse. Such obversion may be made when the subject of the propositions belongs to the same genus that the two immediately opposed contraries belong to. For instance, "living being" is the genus (or quasi genus) of both "mortal" and "immortal," and within this genus whatever is not mortal is immortal and vice versa. Hence, when the subject of the proposition is a living being, if what is signified by the subject is not mortal, it is immortal; if it is mortal, it it not immortal; and so on. Thus, you can legitimately obvert "Angels are not mortal" to "Angels are immortal." But you cannot legitimately obvert "A stone is not mortal" to "A stone is immortal," because a stone—a non-living being—does not belong to the genus of beings that must be either mortal or immortal. It is legitimate, though, to obvert "A stone is not mortal" to "A stone is non-mortal."

Mediately opposed contraries are of no use in obversion, because there is a middle ground between them. You can obvert "The house is not white" to "The house is non-white," but not to "The house is black." The reason for this is that there are many other colors besides white and black; hence, a house that is not white is not necessarily black.

You can easily be deceived in the use of terms prefixed by "in-," "im-," "un-," and so on. Often a term and the corresponding term having one of these prefixes are contraries, but often they are not. For instance, "flammable" and "inflammable," "habitable" and "inhabitable," "vest" and "invest," and so on, are not contraries.

Synopsis

1. Brief rules for obversion:

   (1). Retain subject and quantity.

   (2). Change quality.

   (3). As predicate, use contradictory of original predicate.

2. Examples of obversion:

   A to *E*: "Every cat is an animal" to "No cat is a non-animal."

   E to *A*: "No cat is a dog" to "Every cat is a non-dog."

   I to *O*: "Some house is white" to "Some house is not non-white."

   O to *I*: "Some house is not white" to "Some house is non-white."

Exercise

I. Give the obverse of the following:

1. Every *A* is a *B*.
2. No *A* is a *B*.

3. Some *A* is a *B*.
4. Some *A* is not a *B*.
5. Wood is inflammable.
6. Wood is not magnetic.
7. All men are mortal.
8. He is ineligible.
9. Parts of Asia are not habitable.
10. Asbestos is noninflammable.

II. Criticize the following; state whether they are valid or invalid and, if they are valid, whether they are valid formally or only materially. Explain.

1. All men are mortal; therefore no men are immortal.
2. No stone is immortal; therefore every stone is mortal.
3. No murderer will enter the kingdom of heaven; therefore all murderers are ones who will not enter the kingdom of heaven.
4. His lecture was not without humor; hence, it must have had some humor.
5. His rendition was not particularly inspiring; hence, it must have been somewhat uninspiring.
6. If the officer was not tactful, he must have been tactless.
7. No mere man is entirely free from sin; therefore every mere man is somewhat blemished by sin.
8. If all soldiers are combatants, no soldiers are noncombatants.
9. What is not visible is invisible.
10. Some judges are unjust; therefore some judges are not just.

3. CONTRAPOSITION

Contraposition is the formulation of a new proposition whose subject is the contradictory of the original predicate. It is a combination of obversion and conversion. Like conversion, it involves the interchange of the subject and predicate; and like obversion, it involves either the use or the removal of negatives affecting the copula and terms. The original proposition is called the *contraponend,* the new proposition the *contraposit* or *contrapositive,* and the process itself *contraposition.* There are two types.

a. Type 1

The first type of contraposition (which is sometimes called partial, or simple, contraposition) consists in the formulation of a new proposition (1) whose *subject* is the contradictory (or, in certain circumstances, the immediately opposed contrary) of the original predicate, (2) whose *quality* is changed, and (3) whose *predicate* is the original subject. Thus, "Every dog is an animal" becomes "Every *NON*-animal is *NOT* a dog," which is normally expressed as "No non-animal is a dog."

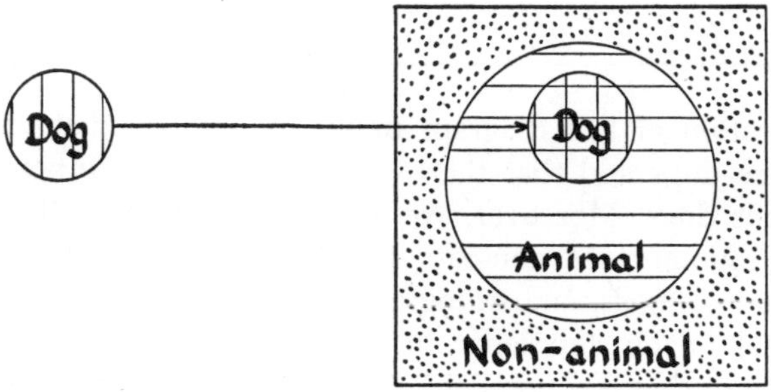

A glance at this diagram makes it obvious that if every dog is an animal, no dog is a non-animal and no non-animal is a dog.

To get Type 1:

(1). Obvert

(2). Then convert the obverse

Thus, beginning with "Every dog is an animal," first obvert this to "No dog is a non-animal," and then convert this to "No non-animal is a dog."

By contraposition of the first type—that is, by partial, or simple, contraposition—*A* is changed to *E*, *E* to *I*, and *O* to *I*. Just as *O* has no converse, so *I* has no contraposit. Note that the use of immediately opposed contraries is the same in contraposition as it is in obversion.

A to *E*. We have already illustrated and diagrammed the contraposition of *A* to *E*. As we have seen, we may argue, "Every dog is an animal; therefore no non-animal is a dog."

E to *I*. "No dog is a cat" becomes "Some non-cat is a dog." You may not argue, "No dog is a cat; therefore every non-cat is a dog."

This involves a violation of the rule for conversion that you should not extend a term.

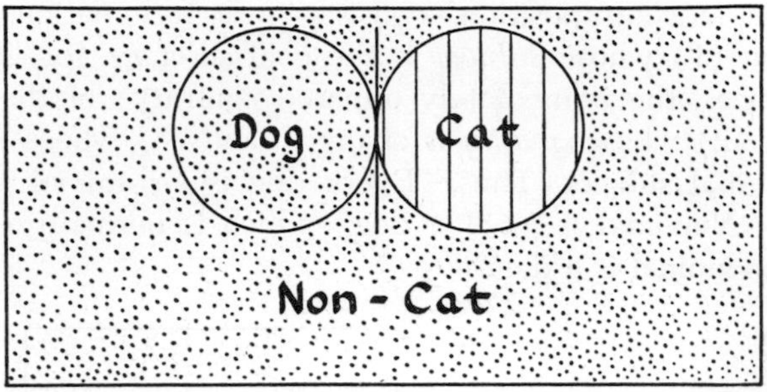

A consideration of this diagram makes it obvious that only some non-cats are dogs and that there at least might be other non-cats that are not dogs. Moreover, we know that, as a matter of fact, there are innumerable non-cats that are not dogs; for instance, horses, stones, angels, and triangles.

Let us take each step separately. First, we obvert "No dog is a cat" to "Every dog is a non-cat." As the predicate of an affirmative proposition, "non-cat" is particular. Then we convert this either to "Some non-cat is a dog" or to "Some non-cats are dogs."

O to *I*. "Some man is not a voter" may be changed by simple contraposition to "Some non-voter is a man." First we obvert "Some man is not a voter" to "Some man is a *NON*-voter." Then we convert this by simple conversion of "Some non-voter is a man."

I propositions have no contraposit. The first step in contraposition is obversion. If we obvert *I*, we get *O*. The second step is conversion, and we have seen that *O* cannot be converted. Hence, since *O* cannot be converted, *I* cannot be contraposed.

b. Type 2

The second type of contraposition (which is sometimes called complete contraposition) is the formulation of a new proposition (1) whose *subject*, just as with Type 1, is the contradictory (or, in certain circumstances, the immediately opposed contrary) of the original predicate, (2) whose *quality* is unchanged, and (3) whose *predicate* is the contradictory of the original subject. This is the sense in which the older Scholastic logicians used the term "contraposition." Frequently they called it "conversion by contraposition."

To get Type 2:

(1). Obvert
(2). Then convert the obverse
(3). Then obvert the converse of the obverse

In other words, the contraposit of the second type is the obverse of the contraposit of the first type. (Hence, the contraposit of the second type is sometimes called "the obverted contraposit," as opposed to the first type, which is called the "simple contraposit.")

By contraposition of the second type, *A* is changed to *A*, *E* to *O*, and *O* to *O:*

A to *A:* "Every man is mortal" to: "Every non-mortal is a non-man."
E to *O:* "No dog is a cat" to: "Some non-cat is not a non-dog."
O to *O:* "Some man is not a voter" to: "Some non-voter is not a non-man."

With Type 2, just as with Type 1, *I* has no contraposit, because one of the steps would involve the conversion of an *O* proposition.

Synopsis

1. Brief rules for contraposition:

Type 1. Simple	Type 2. Complete
(1). The *subject* is the contradictory of the original predicate.	(1). The *subject* is the contradictory of the original predicate.
(2). The *quality* is changed.	(2). The *quality* is not changed.
(3). The *predicate* is the original subject.	(3). The *predicate* is the contradictory of the original subject.
To get Type 1:	To get Type 2:
(1). Obvert	(1). Obvert

(2). Then convert the obverse	(2). Then convert the obverse (3). Then obvert the converse of the obverse

2. Examples of contraposition (note that Type 2 is the obverse of Type 1):

Type 1. Simple		Type 2. Complete	
A to *E*.	"Every *S* is a *P*" to "No *non-P* is an *S*."	*A* to *A*.	"Every *S* is a *P*" to "Every *non-P* is a *non-S*."
E to *I*.	"No *S* is a *P*" to "Some *non-P* is an *S*."	*E* to *O*.	"No *S* is a *P*" to "Some *non-P* is not a *non-S*."
O to *I*.	"Some *S* is not a *P*" to "Some *non-P* is an *S*."	*O* to *O*.	"Some *S* is not a *P*" to "Some *non-P* is not a *non-S*."
I cannot be contraposed.		*I* cannot be contraposed.	

Exercise

I. Give the contraposit (both types) of the following (if they have a contraposit). To get Type 1, obvert, then convert; to get Type 2, obvert the converse of the obverse.

1. Every *A* is a *B*.
2. No *A* is a *B*.
3. Some *A* is a *B*.
4. Some *A* is not a *B*.
5. All voters are citizens.
6. No aliens are voters.
7. Some Asiatics are not favorably disposed towards Americans.
8. Some blackboards are green.
9. No atheist is a Christian.
10. All belonging to the class will go to the museum.

II. Criticize the following:

1. If dogs are animals, no non-animals are dogs and all non-animals are non-dogs.
2. Some animals are dogs; therefore some non-dogs are not animals; hence, too, some non-dogs are non-animals.

3. Whatever is a fungus is a plant; hence whatever is not a plant is not a fungus. In other words, non-plants are non-fungi; that is, nothing but plants are fungi.
4. Whatever is inseparable from a thing is found wherever the thing is found; hence, what is not found wherever a thing is found is not inseparable from the thing.
5. Since all ruminants are cloven-hoofed, as soon as we see that an animal is not cloven-hoofed, we see that it is not a ruminant.
6. A good definition is convertible with the term defined; hence, what is not convertible with the term defined cannot be a good definition.
7. No animals that do not suckle their young are mammals; therefore some non-mammals are animals that do not suckle their young.
8. Since all reptiles are vertebrates, we can be sure that all non-vertebrates are not reptiles.
9. If no non-vertebrates are reptiles, it follows that all non-reptiles are non-vertebrates.
10. Since no atheists are Christians, only non-Christians are atheists.

4. INVERSION [3]

Just as there are two types of contraposition, so too there are two types of inversion. Both types consist in the formulation of a new proposition whose subject is the contradictory of the original subject. In the first type (called partial or simple inversion), the quality is changed, but the predicate is the same as in the original proposition. In the second type (called complete inversion), the quality is unchanged, but the predicate is the contradictory of the original predicate. Immediately opposed contrary terms may be used just as in obversion and contraposition. The original proposition is called the *invertend,* the new proposition the *inverse,* and the process itself *inversion.*

Inversion is effected by a series of obversions and conversions. Experiment will show that only *A* and *E* can be inverted. By Type 1, *A* is inverted to *O,* and *E* to *I;* by Type 2, *A* is inverted to *I,* and *E* to *O.*

[3] The value of studying inversion lies principally in the facility it gives us in recognizing quantitative relationships of the subject and predicate. This section may be omitted without serious loss.

The second type of inverse is the obverse of Type 1, and is therefore sometimes called the "obverted inverse," as opposed to Type 1 which is called the "simple inverse."

If you subject an *A* proposition to the following processes, you finally get its inverse:

INVERTEND: *A*. Every *S* is a *P*. ("Every cat is an animal.")
Obvert to: *E*. No *S* is a *non-P*. ("No cat is a non-animal.")
Convert to: *E*. No *non-P* is an *S*. ("No non-animal is a cat.")
Obvert to: *A*. Every *non-P* is a *non-S*. ("Every non-animal is a non-cat.")
Convert to: *I*. Some *non-S* is a *non-P*. ("Some non-cat is a non-animal.") (This is inverse, Type 2.)
Obvert to: *O*. Some *non-S* is not a *P*. ("Some non-cat is not an animal.") (This is inverse, Type 1.)

If you subject an *E* proposition to the following processes, you finally get its inverse. Note that you must convert first and then obvert.

INVERTEND: *E*. No *S* is a *P*. ("No cat is a dog.")
Convert to: *E*. No *P* is an *S*. ("No dog is a cat.")
Obvert to: *A*. Every *P* is a *non-S*. ("Every dog is a non-cat.")
Convert to: *I*. Some *non-S* is a *P*. ("Some non-cat is a dog.") (This is inverse, Type 1.)
Obvert to: *O*. Some *non-S* is not a *non-P*. ("Some non-cat is not a non-dog.") (This is inverse, Type 2.)

TABLE OF EDUCTIONS

<table>
<tr><th></th><th>A</th><th>E</th><th>I</th><th>O</th></tr>
<tr><td>ORIGINAL PROPOSITIONS</td><td>S a P</td><td>S e P</td><td>S i P</td><td>S o P</td></tr>
<tr><td>1. Obverse</td><td>S e -P</td><td>S a -P</td><td>S o -P</td><td>S i -P</td></tr>
<tr><td>2. Converse</td><td>P i S</td><td>P e S</td><td>P i S</td><td rowspan="2">O has no converse</td></tr>
<tr><td>3. Obverted converse</td><td>P o -S</td><td>P a -S</td><td>P o -S</td></tr>
<tr><td>4. Contraposit, Type 1</td><td>-P e S</td><td>-P i S</td><td rowspan="2">I has no contraposit.</td><td>-P i S</td></tr>
<tr><td>5. Contraposit, Type 2</td><td>-P a -S</td><td>-P o -S</td><td>-P o -S</td></tr>
<tr><td>6. Inverse, Type 1</td><td>-S o P</td><td>-S i P</td><td rowspan="2" colspan="2">I and O have no inverse.</td></tr>
<tr><td>7. Inverse, Type 2</td><td>-S i -P</td><td>-S o -P</td></tr>
</table>

The table on the bottom of Page 70 summarizes the results of eduction. The quality and quantity of each proposition is indicated by inserting *a, e, i,* or *o* between S and *P*. Contradictory terms are indicated by a minus sign (—). Needless to say, the student is not expected to memorize this table; however, he will find that going through the table step by step will be a very profitable exercise on the quantitative relationships of terms.

5. A NOTE ON MATERIAL EDUCTIONS

Up to the present we have been treating, for the most part, of formal inferences; that is, of inferences that depend for their validity on the quality of propositions and the quantity of their terms without any regard for the special character of their matter or thought content. There is another kind of inference, of much less importance, known as material eduction, which is based on the meanings of terms.

a. Eduction by Added Determinant

Eduction by an added determinant is the formulation of a new proposition in which both the subject and the predicate of the original proposition are limited by the addition of some modifier which has exactly the same meaning in relation to both of them. For instance, "Citizens are men; therefore *honest* citizens are *honest* men" is valid; "honest" has exactly the same meaning with both "citizens" and "men." But we may not argue: "A mouse is an animal; therefore a *big* mouse is a *big* animal," because "big" does not have exactly the same meaning with "mouse" as it has with "animal" in general.[4] A thief is a man, but a *good* thief is not therefore a *good* man. A soprano is a woman, and a *shrieking* soprano is a *shrieking* woman; but a *flat* soprano is not necessarily a *flat* woman, nor is a *bad* soprano necessarily a *bad* woman.[5]

[4] See "Relative Concepts" in the second meaning, p. 216. Nothing is big or small absolutely but only relatively, that is, with reference to a standard.

[5] See the division of terms into univocal, equivocal, and analogous on pp. 224-229.

b. Eduction by Complex Conception

Eduction by complex conception is the formulation of a new proposition whose subject consists of a term modified by the subject of the original proposition and whose predicate consists of the very same term modified by the predicate of the original proposition. In eduction by added determinants, a new term modifies the original subject and predicate; in eduction by complex conception, a new term is modified by them.

"If a horse is an animal, *the head of* a horse is *the head of* an animal, and *the tail of* a horse is *the tail of* an animal." You must be especially careful in the use of words expressing quantitative proportions; for instance, "Dogs are animals, and *ten* dogs are *ten* animals." Yet it is false that *half of* the dogs in the world are *half of* the animals in the world. In "Dogs are animals," "animals" is particular; that is, "dogs" embraces an indeterminately designated portion of the extension of "animals." Since the portion is indeterminate to begin with, half of it is also indeterminate.

Ordinarily nothing can be educed by complex conception from a negative proposition. For instance, you may not argue: "A dog is not a cat; therefore the owner of a dog is not the owner of a cat."

c. Eduction by Omitted Determinant

Eduction by omitted determinant is the formulation of a new proposition in which a modifier of the original predicate is omitted. Care must be had that the meaning of what is left of the original predicate is not altered, as in: "This locket is false gold, therefore it is gold." Consider also: "It is a *pretended* fact; therefore it is a fact;" "It is *stage* money; therefore it is money;" and "It is *nothing;* therefore it is."

Nothing can be educed in this way from negative propositions. You may not argue: "A dog is not a *rational* animal; therefore a dog is not an animal." The reason for this is clear from what we know of the relationship in comprehension of the subject and predicate of negative propositions.[6]

[6] For an explanation of the relationship in comprehension of the subject and predicate of a negative proposition see Chapter 3, p. 29.

d. Eduction by Converse Relation

Eduction by converse relation is the formulation of a new proposition in which a relationship is expressed that is the reverse of the relationship expressed in the original proposition. For instance, "A mouse is smaller than an elephant; therefore an elephant is larger than a mouse"; "Johnny is Mary's nephew; therefore Mary is Johnny's aunt"; "Since he is my father, I must be his son (or daughter)"; and "Chicago is northeast of St. Louis; therefore St. Louis is southwest of Chicago."

CHAPTER 6

Oppositional Inference

Opposite, or opposed, propositions are propositions that cannot be simultaneously true or that cannot be simultaneously false, or that cannot be either simultaneously true or simultaneously false. In other words, they are so related to one another that if one is true, the other is false; or if one is false, the other is true; or if one is true the other is false, *and vice versa.* Such propositions are said to be opposed, opposite, or repugnant, to one another because either the truth of one excludes the truth of the other or the falsity of one excludes the falsity of the other, or both. *This impossibility of being simultaneously true, or false, or either true or false is the essential note of logical opposition.*

The abstract term "OPPOSITION" signifies the relationship that opposite propositions have towards one another. OPPOSITIONAL INFERENCE consists in proceeding from the known (or assumed) truth or falsity of a proposition to the truth or falsity of any of its opposites. The meaning of these definitions will be clearer after we have made a detailed examination of the various kinds of opposition.

In the present section we shall emphasize the opposition of *quantified* attributive, or categorical, propositions (that is, of *A, E, I,* and *O* propositions). These are opposed if they have THE SAME SUBJECT AND PREDICATE but differ from one another in QUALITY, or QUANTITY, or BOTH QUALITY AND QUANTITY. Each of the opposed attributive propositions is to have exactly the same subject and predicate. The subject and predicate are to have exactly the same meaning in both propositions and, except for the differences in quality and quantity, must be used in exactly the same way (that is, must have the same supposition).

Besides, unless the real existence of a subject is asserted in an original proposition, it may not be asserted in an inferred proposition.

The SQUARE OF OPPOSITION is a visual aid to understanding and remembering the various kinds of opposition and their laws. Below is the square of opposition for quantified attributive, or categorical, propositions.

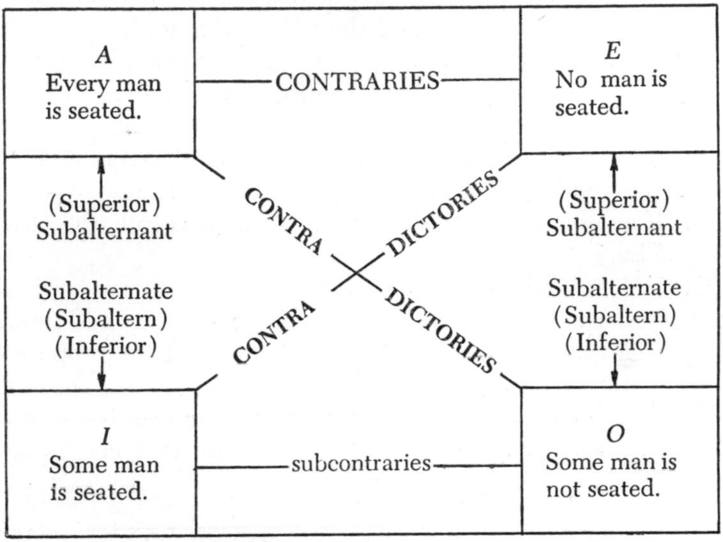

1. CONTRADICTORY OPPOSITION

Contradictory opposition is the opposition of a pair of propositions so related to one another that they cannot be either simultaneously true or simultaneously false. The truth of one excludes the truth of the other, and the falsity of one excludes the falsity of the other. In other words, contradictory propositions are so related to one another that if one is true, the other is false, and vice versa. This exclusion of both simultaneous truth and simultaneous falsity is the essential note of contradictory opposition.

Because contradictory opposition excludes both simultaneous truth and simultaneous falsity, it is the most perfect kind of opposition and is of great importance in controversy and debate. To refute a thesis or destroy the truth of a proposition, it is sufficient and necessary to prove its contradictory: to prove more is superfluous, to prove less is inadequate.

Quantified attributive propositions having the same subject and predicate but differing in BOTH QUALITY AND QUANTITY (that is, *A* and *O*, and *E* and *I*) are contradictories. For instance, the universal affirmative proposition "Every man is seated" is the contradictory of the particular negative proposition "Some man is not seated," and vice versa; and the universal negative proposition "No man is seated" is the contradictory of the particular affirmative proposition "Some man is seated," and vice versa. (See the square above.)

The Rules of Contradictories are based on the very notion of contradiction and may be briefly stated as follows:

(1). If one of two contradictory propositions is true, the other is false.

(2). If one is false, the other is true.

In case these rules are not already perfectly clear, they will be clarified by an inspection of the following diagrams of the propositions "Every man is seated" and "No man is seated."

If *every man is seated,* then it is false that *some man is not seated;* and if *some man is not seated,* then it is false that *every man is seated.*

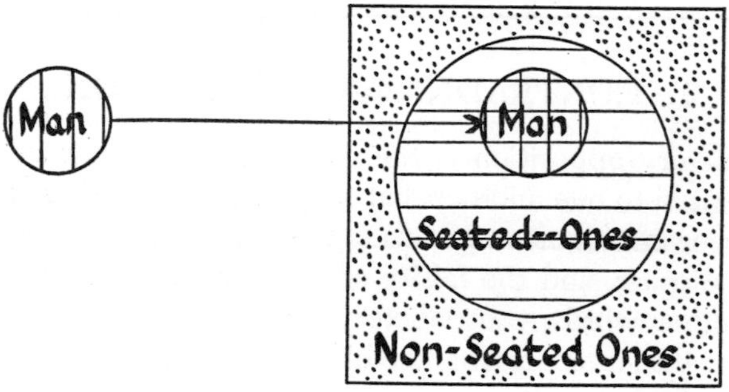

If every man is inside the big circle, it is false that some man is outside it; and if some man is outside it, it is false that every man is inside it; and so on.[1]

[1] Diagrams such as these can help us understand the quantitative relationships of terms and propositions. They are visual aids to recognizing the validity,

Similarly, if *no man is seated,* it is false that *some man is seated;* and if *some man is seated,* it is false that *no man is seated.* Consider the following diagram, in which the quantitative relationship of "man" and "seated ones" is displayed:

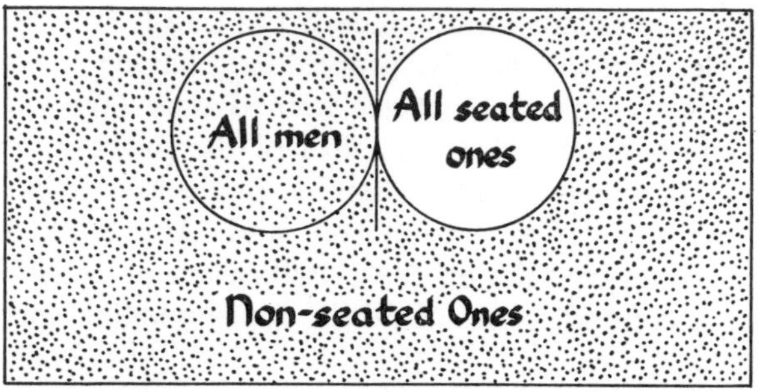

If no man is among the seated ones, it is false that some man is among them, and vice versa.

We shall now give some examples of contradictory propositions that are not quantified attributive propositions. Notice that the members of each pair are so related to one another that if one is true the other is false, and vice versa, and that this incompatibility in both truth and falsity is the essential note of contradictory opposition.

1. "Socrates *is* sick" and "Socrates *is not* sick."
2. "Bobby is *always* eating" and "Bobby is *sometimes not* eating."
3. "Johnny is *never* sick" and "Johnny is *sometimes* sick."
4. "If it is raining, the ground is wet" and "It is false that if it is raining, the ground is wet"—which can also be expressed as "If it is raining, it does not follow that the ground is wet," for the "if . . . then" type of proposition asserts a sequence, while "it does not follow" denies a sequence.
5. "Both John and Mary will go" and "Either John or Mary

---

or invalidity, of inferences, but are not intended to serve as a basis for a theory of inference. We must not think that inference consists of enclosing the things we think about in circles, as we drive sheep into a pen, or of excluding the things we think about from circles, as we drive sheep out of a pen. Definitely, by our use of such diagrams, we run a calculated risk that at least some students will formulate for themselves a false theory of predication.

or both will not go"—which can also be expressed as "Either John will not go, or Mary will not go, or neither of them will go."

Propositions having the same subject but having contradictory terms as predicates are also contradictory propositions. Thus, the propositions "This is a man" and "This is a non-man" are related to one another as contradictories, since if the one is true the other is false, and vice versa. Similarly, propositions having the same subject but having predicates that are immediately opposed contrary terms are contradictories if the subject of the propositions belongs to the genus to which the immediately opposed contrary terms belong—for instance, "Angels are mortal" and "Angels are immortal."

Later on, when we take up the classification of propositions, we shall give the contradictories of all the types needing special attention.

2. CONTRARY OPPOSITION

Contrary opposition is the opposition of a pair of propositions so related to one another that they cannot be simultaneously true but can be simultaneously false (at least as far as their form is concerned). The truth of one excludes the truth of the other, but the falsity of one does not exclude the falsity of the other. In other words, contrary propositions are so related that if one is true the other is false, but if one is false the other is doubtful. This exclusion of simultaneous truth but not of simultaneous falsity is the essential note of contrary opposition.

Universal attributive, or categorical, propositions having the same subject and predicate but differing in quality (that is, *A* and *E*) are contraries. For instance, the universal affirmative proposition "Every man is seated" is the contrary of the universal negative proposition "No man is seated," and vice versa. (See the square above.)

The Rules of Contraries are based on the very notion of contrary opposition and may be stated briefly as follows:

(1). If one of two contrary propositions is true, the other is false.

(2). If one is false, the other is doubtful.

A consideration of the diagram given to illustrate contradictory opposition will also confirm the rules of contrary opposition.

We shall now give examples of contrary propositions that are not quantified attributive propositions. Notice that the members of each pair are so related to one another that only one of them can be true but both of them can be false (at least as far as their form or structure is concerned).

The propositions "Both men and women are admitted" and "Neither men nor women are admitted" are contraries, as they cannot be simultaneously true but can be simultaneously false—for instance, if men are admitted but not women or if women are admitted but not men.

"This house is entirely white" and "This house is entirely black" illustrate contrary opposition, as both propositions cannot be true but both can be false—as would be the case if the house were partly white and partly black, or of some altogether different color such as red, brown, or green. The following pairs of propositions likewise illustrate contrary opposition:

1. "Johnny is *never* sick" and "Johnny is *always* sick."
2. "Socrates is seated" and "Socrates is standing."
3. "All his answers are right" and "All his answers are wrong."
4. "He got 100% in his examination" and "He got 50% in his examination."
5. "He should go" and "He should not go."

If you study these pairs of propositions, you will see that the members of each pair are so related to one another that if one is true the other is false, but both of them can be false.

3. SUBCONTRARY OPPOSITION

Subcontrary opposition is the opposition of two propositions that cannot be simultaneously false but can be simultaneously true: if one is false, the other must be true; but both of them can be true (at least as far as their form is concerned).

Subcontraries get their name from their position on the square of opposition "under" (*sub*) the contraries. Usually the name is limited to *I* and *O*, that is, to particular propositions having the same subject and predicate but differing in quality; thus, "Some man is seated" and "Some man is not seated" are subcontraries.

The Rules of Subcontraries may be stated briefly as follows:

(1). If one is false, the other is true.

(2). If one is true, the other is doubtful.

Thus, if "Some man is seated" is false, "Some man is not seated" is obviously true. On the other hand, if "Some man is seated" is true, it is impossible to tell whether or not some man is not seated; maybe some are seated and some are not, and maybe all are seated.

4. SUBALTERNS

Subalterns are not, strictly speaking, opposites at all because (as far as their form is concerned) neither the truth nor falsity of either of them excludes the truth or falsity of the other. In other words, both of them can be true and both of them can be false. Nevertheless, subalterns (or, more accurately, a subalternant and its subaltern) are frequently called opposites because of their connection with the strict mutually repugnant opposites that we have already studied.

Subaltern opposition is the relationship of attributive, or categorical, propositions having the same subject, predicate, and quality, but differing in quantity. Usually the universal proposition (*A* or *E*) is called the *subalternant* or *superior,* and the particular proposition (*I* or *O*) is called the *subalternate* or *subaltern,* but sometimes both are called subalterns.

Rule of Subaltern Opposition. The rules of subaltern opposition may be stated briefly as follows:

(1). If the universal is true, the particular is true; but if the universal is false, the particular is doubtful.

(2). If the particular is true, the universal is doubtful; but if the particular is false, the universal is false.

A consideration of the examples given on the square will make these rules clear.

Note that induction, which we shall study later, proceeds from *I* to *A;* that is, from a limited number of instances to a universal law. Induction, however, is not formal inference but *material* inference; hence, the rules given here do not govern induction.

Synopsis of Rules

1. CONTRADICTORIES (*A–O, E–I*):
   (1). If the one is true, the other is false.
   (2). If the one is false, the other is true.
2. CONTRARIES (*A–E*):
   (1). If the one is true, the other is false.
   (2). If the one is false, the other is doubtful.
3. SUBCONTRARIES (*I–O*):
   (1). If the one is true, the other is doubtful.
   (2). If the one is false, the other is true.
4. SUBALTERNS (*A–I, E–O*):
   (1). If the universal is true, the particular is true; but if the universal is false, the particular is doubtful.
   (2). If the particular is true, the universal is doubtful; but if the particular is false, the universal is false.

SYNOPTIC SCHEME

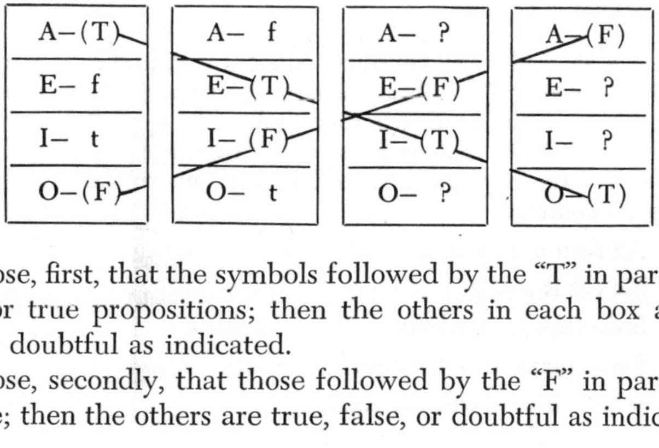

Suppose, first, that the symbols followed by the "T" in parentheses stand for true propositions; then the others in each box are true, false, or doubtful as indicated.

Suppose, secondly, that those followed by the "F" in parentheses are false; then the others are true, false, or doubtful as indicated.

Exercise

I. In the first row of squares, supposing in turn that *A, E, I,* and *O* are true, mark the remainder as true, false, or doubtful by writing "t," "f," or "?" in the appropriate parentheses. Do the same in the second set of squares, beginning with *O, I, E,* and *A,* respectively, as false.

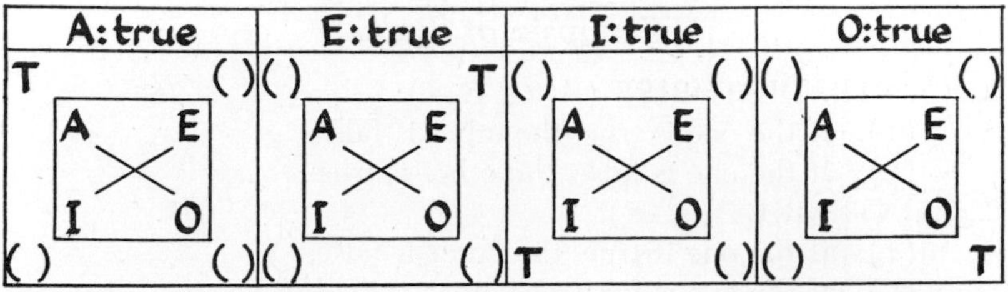

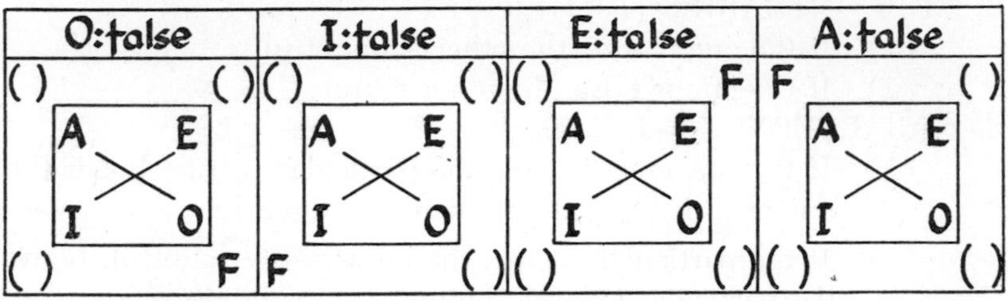

Note that the two sets of squares are exactly the same. You get the same results if you start with a proposition as true or with its contradictory as false.

II. Give the contradictory, contrary, subcontrary, and subaltern of each of the following (if it has one); and, supposing that the original proposition is true, state whether each of its opposites is true, false, or doubtful. Note that each type of proposition (*A*, *E*, *I*, and *O*) has only three opposites: *A* and *E* have no subcontrary; *I* and *O* have no contrary.

1. All men are mortal.
2. No cat is a dog.
3. Some house is white.
4. Some house is not white.
5. John is a very wealthy man.
6. If the sun is shining, it is day.
7. John says he is not going.
8. He went to the hospital because he was sick.
9. Every A is a B.
10. Some A is a B.

III. Supposing that the propositions after each of the numbers are true or false as indicated, state whether the propositions following them are true, false, or doubtful, and tell what kind of opposition is illustrated by each example.

1. If it is true that *every A is a B,*
   a—that no A is a B is . . . .
   b—that some A is a B is . . . .
   c—that some A is not a B is . . . .
2. If it is false that *every A is a B,*
   a—that no A is a B is . . . .
   b—that some A is a B is . . . .
   c—that some A is not a B is . . . .
3. If it is true that *some A is a B,*
   a—that every A is a B is . . . .
   b—that no A is a B is . . . .
   c—that some A is not a B is . . . .
4. If it is false that *some A is a B,*
   a—that every A is a B is . . . .
   b—that no A is a B is . . . .
   c—that some A is not a B is . . . .
5. If it were false that *all women are human beings,*
   a—that no women are human beings would be . . . .
   b—that some women are human beings would be . . . .
   c—that some women are not human beings would be . . . .
6. If it were true that *every cat is a dog,*
   a—that no cat is a dog would be . . . .
   b—that some cat is a dog would be . . . .
   c—that some cat is not a dog would be . . . .
7. If "some aliens are seditious" is true,
   a—that all aliens are seditious is . . . .
   b—that no aliens are seditious is . . . .
   c—that some aliens are not seditious is . . . .
8. If it is true that *all horses can't jump,*
   a—that all horses can jump is . . . .
   b—that no horse can jump is . . . .
   c—that some horse can jump is . . . .

IV. State the kind of opposition illustrated in each example; and, wherever an inference has been made, state whether it is valid or invalid.

1. All hounds are dogs; therefore some hounds are dogs.
2. Some dogs are hounds; therefore some dogs are not hounds.
3. Some dogs are not hounds; therefore some dogs are hounds.
4. It is false that all men are angels; therefore it is true that no men are angels.

5. If it is true that all jewelers have jewels to sell, it is false that no jeweler has jewels to sell.
6. If it were true that no jewelers sold jewels, it would be false that some jeweler did not sell them.
7. It is false that no jeweler sells jewels; therefore it is true that some jeweler does sell jewels.
8. "I always tell my salesmen not to be discouraged if the first couple customers on a block give them trouble. They know then that there'll be at least a few soft touches near the end."
9. "I told the workers that since some labor unions are not honestly managed, it follows that some are honestly managed, and that ours was one of these."
10. "Every single American is desirous to improve the living conditions of the lower classes. America, they say, will then be a true democracy, with all the citizens living, if not on similar levels of luxury, wealth, and importance, at least on an equal basis of freedom. But unfortunately several big businessmen, controlling monopolies, and thus able to ruin thousands of other business men, do not desire to help the poor. Therefore, probably little improvement will be carried out until the power of this minority is overcome."
11. If it is false that he plays neither the saxophone nor the clarinet, it must be true that he plays either a saxophone, or a clarinet, or both a saxophone and a clarinet.
12. If it is false that beggars should be choosers, it follows that beggars should not be choosers.
13. Suppose it's false that John should drink milk; it follows that John should not drink it.
14. If the speaker is not telling the truth, he must be lying.
15. "It is a fallacy to argue from the variety of systems and the extravagant character of certain philosophies to the impotence of all metaphysics. If the system of one philosopher is to a great extent the expression of his personal temperament, it does not necessarily follow that a like judgment can be passed on the system of another philosopher: if some of the arguments of a given philosopher are sophistical, it does not follow that all his arguments are sophistical." (From a book review)

V. This is an exercise in both eduction and opposition. Assuming that the marked propositions are true or false as indicated, mark the remaining propositions as "t," "f," or "?." Notice that Nos. 1, 5, 9, and 13 are *A, E, I,* and *O,* and that the propositions directly under each of these are equivalent to *A, E, I,* and *O,* respectively. Notice the relationship of Nos. 16 and 17 to No. 4.

	a	*b*	*c*	*d*	*e*	*f*	*g*	*h*
1. Every A is a B.	T	F	( )	( )	( )	( )	( )	( )
2. No A is a non-B.	( )	( )	( )	( )	( )	( )	( )	( )
3. No non-B is an A.	( )	( )	( )	( )	( )	( )	( )	( )
4. Every non-B is a non-A.	( )	( )	( )	( )	( )	( )	( )	( )
5. No A is a B.	( )	( )	T	F	( )	( )	( )	( )
6. Every A is a non-B.	( )	( )	( )	( )	( )	( )	( )	( )
7. No B is an A.	( )	( )	( )	( )	( )	( )	( )	( )
8. Every B is a non-A.	( )	( )	( )	( )	( )	( )	( )	( )
9. Some A is a B.	( )	( )	( )	( )	T	F	( )	( )
10. Some B is an A.	( )	( )	( )	( )	( )	( )	( )	( )
11. Some A is not a non-B.	( )	( )	( )	( )	( )	( )	( )	( )
12. Some B is not a non-A.	( )	( )	( )	( )	( )	( )	( )	( )
13. Some A is not a B.	( )	( )	( )	( )	( )	( )	( )	( )
14. Some A is a non-B.	( )	( )	( )	( )	( )	( )	( )	( )
15. Some non-B is an A.	( )	( )	( )	( )	( )	( )	( )	( )
16. Some non-A is a non-B.	( )	( )	( )	( )	( )	( )	( )	( )
17. Some non-B is a non-A.	( )	( )	( )	( )	( )	( )	( )	( )
18. Every B is an A.	( )	( )	( )	( )	( )	( )	T	F
19. No B is a non-A.	( )	( )	( )	( )	( )	( )	( )	( )
20. No non-A is a B.	( )	( )	( )	( )	( )	( )	( )	( )
21. Every non-A is a non-B.	( )	( )	( )	( )	( )	( )	( )	( )
22. Some B is not an A.	( )	( )	( )	( )	( )	( )	( )	( )
23. Some B is a non-A.	( )	( )	( )	( )	( )	( )	( )	( )
24. Some non-A is a B.	( )	( )	( )	( )	( )	( )	( )	( )

PART **III**

MEDIATE DEDUCTIVE INFERENCE

IN CHAPTER 4 we gave a brief, preliminary explanation of inference. We defined some important terms—such as "inference," "antecedent," "consequent," "sequence," "form," "validity," "truth," and so on—and called attention to the difference between formal and material validity, between truth and validity, between so-called immediate and mediate inference, and, finally, between deduction and induction. In Part II we treated of two general types of immediate inference—eduction and oppositional inference—and of various subdivisions of each. In Part III we shall treat of mediate deductive inference, which is expressed by the syllogism.

A syllogism, in its broadest sense, is any argumentation in which from two propositions, called the premises, we infer a third proposition, called the conclusion, which is so related to the premises taken jointly that if they are true, it must also be true. This definition is broad enough to include both the categorical syllogism and the hypothetical syllogism. Frequently, however, the term "syllogism" is defined in so narrow a sense as to include only the categorical syllogism.

We shall treat of the syllogism in Chapters 7, 8, and 9 according to the following outline.

CHAPTER 7. *The Simple Categorical Syllogism*

1. Basic Structure
2. The General Rules of the Categorical Syllogism
3. The Logical Forms of the Categorical Syllogism: Figures and Moods
4. Principles of the Categorical Syllogism
5. Reduction of the Imperfect Figures to the First Figure

CHAPTER 7

The Simple Categorical Syllogism

1. BASIC STRUCTURE

THE SIMPLE CATEGORICAL syllogism is the most important elementary type of syllogism. It consists of three categorical, or attributive, propositions so put together that the subject (t) and predicate (T) of the conclusion are united or separated through the intermediacy of a middle term (M). For instance, in the following example "dog" and "mortal" are united through the union of each of them with "animal."

> Every animal is mortal;
> but every dog is an animal;
> therefore every dog is mortal.

The first proposition of this example is the major premise; the second proposition is the minor premise; and the third is the conclusion. "Mortal," the predicate of the conclusion, is the major term; "dog," the subject of the conclusion, is the minor term; and "animal," which occurs in both the premises but not in the conclusion, is the middle term.

a. Major Term

The major term is the predicate of the conclusion. The major term must occur in the conclusion and in one of the premises, generally the first, which is therefore called the MAJOR PREMISE. We shall designate the major term by *T*, or, to display the structure of a syllogism more graphically, by a rectangle (▭).

b. Minor Term

The minor term is the subject of the conclusion. The minor term must occur in the conclusion and in the premise in which the major term does not occur. This MINOR PREMISE is often introduced by the adversative conjunction "but" (because in controversy it introduces a turn of thought contrary to the expectations of an opponent). We shall designate the minor term by *t,* or, to display the structure of a syllogism more graphically, by an ellipse ( ).

c. Middle Term

The middle term occurs in each of the premises but not in the conclusion. In the major premise it occurs in conjunction with the major term; and in the minor premise, in conjunction with the minor term. It is the medium through which the major and minor terms are united in the affirmative syllogism and separated in the negative syllogism. As opposed to the middle term, the minor and major terms are called the EXTREMES.[1]

The structure, or form, of the syllogism given above can be displayed in any of the following ways:

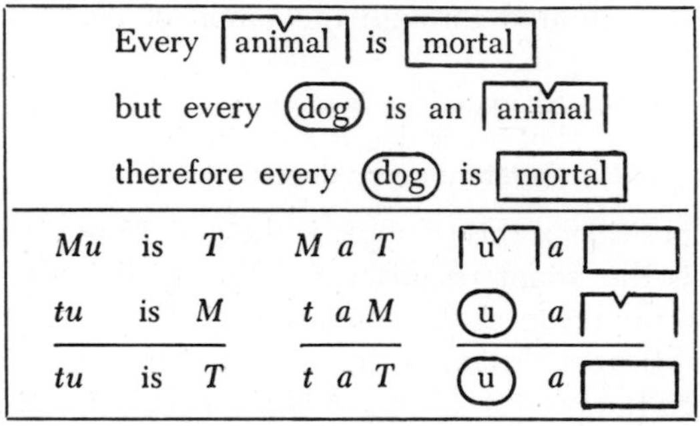

The relationship of the terms of a syllogism towards one another —and consequently the validity of a syllogism—can often be made

[1] These preliminary definitions of major, minor, and middle term are practical working definitions that are suitable for our present purposes but need some qualification. Strictly speaking, in an affirmative syllogism, the major term is the term with the greater extension and the minor term with less extension (*major* and *minor* are the Latin words for "greater" and "lesser," respectively). In the so-called fourth figure the major term is the subject and the minor term the predicate of the conclusion. However, in the practical working out of syllogisms we can pass over these subtle distinctions and call the predicate of the conclusion the major term and its subject the minor.

In an affirmative syllogism of the first figure (which is the "perfect" figure), the middle term gets its name not only because it is a medium for uniting the major and minor terms but also because it is midway between them in extension.

evident through the use of diagrams. We shall now examine two syllogisms and their accompanying diagrams, first an affirmative syllogism and then a negative syllogism.

Consider the following affirmative syllogism and the accompanying diagram:

Every animal is mortal;
but every dog is an animal;
therefore every dog is mortal.

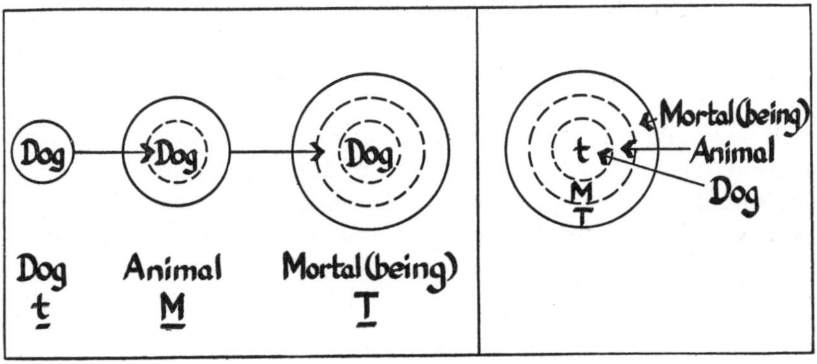

"Dog" (t) is drawn into the extension of "animal" (M), and "animal" (M) is drawn into the extension of "mortal (being)" (T). Since every dog *is* an animal, what is true of every animal must also be true of every dog. Hence, since every animal is mortal, every dog must be mortal too.

Now consider the following negative syllogism and the accompanying diagram:

No animal is an angel;
but every dog is an animal;
therefore no dog is an angel.

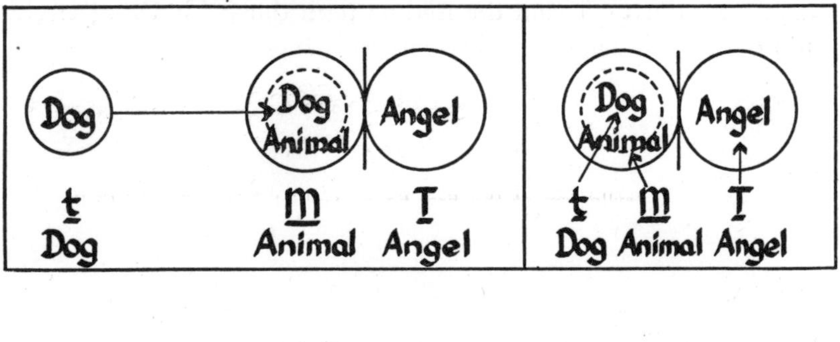

"Dog" (t) is drawn into the extension of "animal" (M); "animal" (M) is completely excluded from the extension of "angel" (T). Since every dog *is* an animal, what is denied of every animal must also be denied of every dog. Hence, just as no animal is an angel, so too no dog is an angel.

In analyzing a syllogism, first pick out the conclusion, noting its subject (t) and predicate (T). Then, if you are analyzing a categorical syllogism, look for the premise in which the minor term (t) occurs; this is the minor premise and should contain the minor (t) and middle (M) terms. Then look for the premise in which the major term (T) occurs; this is the major premise and should contain the major (T) and middle (M) terms. At first, most of our examples will be arranged in the order of major premise, minor premise, conclusion, which is the order required by the *logical form* of the syllogism. But very few syllogisms in newspapers, magazines, and books—with the exception of logic books—are arranged in this order. Sometimes the minor premise comes first; perhaps even oftener the conclusion is placed first. Indeed, the latter is a very natural order, for it first centers our attention on what is to be proved and then on the proof itself.

Exercise

First pick out the conclusion of each of the following syllogisms. Then pick out the minor and major terms, then the minor and major premises, and, finally, the middle term. If the three propositions are not already arranged in the order required by the logical form of the syllogism, rewrite the example as in the model given below. Wherever necessary, reduce the propositions to the logical form of the attributive proposition. Then mark the minor term thus ◯, the major term thus □, and the middle term thus ⌈M⌉. Using circles as in the model, diagram at least some of the syllogisms.

An Example

Whales are not fish. The reason for this is that whales are mammals, whereas fish are not mammals.

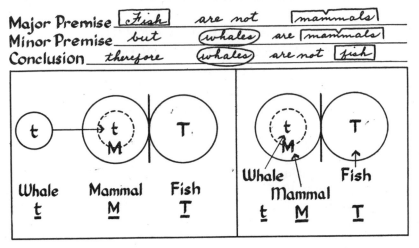

Major Premise: Fish are not mammals
Minor Premise: but whales are mammals
Conclusion: therefore whales are not fish

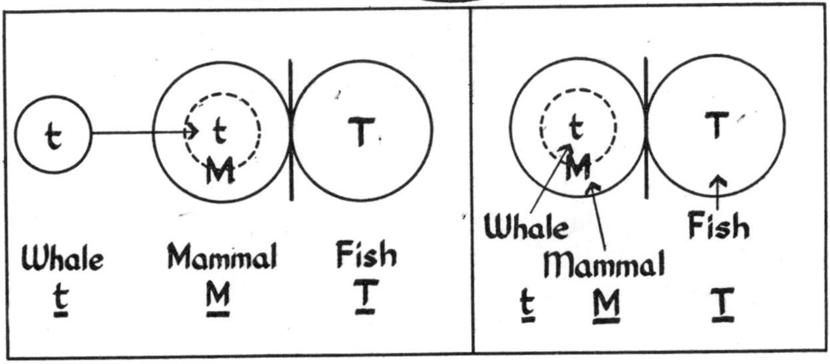

1. All metals are conductors of electricity;
   but copper is a metal;
   therefore copper is a conductor of electricity.
2. No insulator is a good conductor of electricity;
   but copper is a good conductor of electricity;
   therefore copper is not an insulator.
3. George W. Carver was a Negro;
   but George W. Carver was an eminent scientist;
   therefore some eminent scientist was a Negro.
4. The building on the corner of Grand and Lindell must be a church. Why? Because it is a building having a steeple with a cross on it, and all such buildings are churches.
5. Every *X* is a *Y;* therefore, since every *Y* is a *Z,* every *X* must also be a *Z.*
6. A good leader has the confidence of his followers; Joe Doe, though, does not have the confidence of his followers, and is therefore not a good leader.
7. Since winesaps are apples and apples are fruit, winesaps, too, must be fruit.
8. Some metals are precious; this follows from the fact that gold and silver, which are metals, are precious.

9. Diamonds are precious; and, since diamonds are stones, it follows that some stones are precious.
10. Some mortals are rather stupid. You can infer this from the fact that all men are mortals, and some men are rather stupid.

2. GENERAL RULES OF THE CATEGORICAL SYLLOGISM

We shall now state and explain the general rules of the categorical syllogism. Pay special attention to the headings that are supplied to help you see the order of the rules. Note that the first four rules are rules of the terms—Rules 1 and 2 treating of their number and arrangement, Rules 3 and 4 treating of their quantity; and that the remaining rules are rules of the propositions—Rules 5, 6, and 7 treating of the quality of the propositions, Rules 8 and 9 of their quantity, and Rule 10 of their existential import.

The following outline will be of great help both in remembering the rules and in seeing their relationship to one another:

a. The Rules of the Terms

1. Their Number and Arrangement
   (1). Their Number: ...
   (2). Their Arrangement: ...
2. Their Quantity, or Extension
   (3). The Quantity of the Minor and Major Terms: ...
   (4). The Quantity of the Middle Term: ...

b. The Rules of the Propositions

1. Their Quality
   (5). If both premises are affirmative, ...
   (6). If one premise is affirmative and the other negative, ...
   (7). If both premises are negative, ...
2. Their Quantity (Corollaries of Rules 3 and 4)
   (8). At least one premise must be ...
   (9). If a premise is particular, the conclusion must be ...

3. Their Existential Import
   (10). If the actual real existence of a subject has not been asserted in the premises, . . .

a. The Rules of the Terms

1) THEIR NUMBER AND ARRANGEMENT

Rule 1. *There must be three terms and only three—the major term, the minor term, and the middle term.*

The necessity of having only three terms follows from the very nature of a categorical syllogism, in which a minor (t) and a major (T) term are united or separated through the intermediacy of a third term, the middle term (M).

The terms must have exactly the *same meaning* and (except for certain legitimate changes in supposition)[2] must be used in exactly the same way in each occurrence. A term that has a different meaning in each occurrence is equivalently two terms. We must be especially on our guard against ambiguous middle terms.

This rule is violated in each of the following examples.

> 1. Men must eat;
> but the picture on the wall is a man;
> therefore the picture on the wall must eat.

In Example 1 the pseudo middle term ("men" and "man") has two meanings and is therefore really two terms. In its first occurrence it signifies men of flesh and blood; however, the picture on the wall is not a man of flesh and blood but is merely called a man by extrinsic denomination because of its resemblance to a real man.

> 2. "Man" rimes with "ban";
> but you are a man;
> therefore you rime with "ban."

In Example 2 "man" likewise stands for something different in each occurrence. The *word* "man" rimes with "ban"; however, you are not the word "man" but a being having a human nature.

[2] Supposition of terms is a property that terms acquire in propositions and by which they stand for a definite one of the various things they can stand for. Notice that in Examples 1 and 2 the supposition of "man" changes; the word stands for one thing in the major premise and for a different thing in the minor premise. We shall treat of supposition of terms at length in Chapter 12.

3. Wisconsin is next to Illinois;
but Illinois is next to Missouri;
therefore Missouri is next to Wisconsin.

Example 3 has six terms: "Wisconsin," "next to Illinois," "Illinois," "next to Missouri," "Missouri," and "next to Wisconsin."

4. A short and thin man cannot weigh 250 pounds;
but John is short;
therefore John cannot weigh 250 pounds.

In the major premise the term "a short and thin man" means "a man who is both short and thin." But the argument proceeds as though the term meant "a man who is either short or thin." On account of this ambiguity, the term "a short and thin man" is equivalent to two terms, and the syllogism incurs the fallacy of four terms.

Rule 2. *Each term must occur in two propositions. The major term must occur in the conclusion, as predicate, and in one of the premises, which is therefore called the major premise. The minor term must occur in the conclusion, as subject, and in the other premise, which is therefore called the minor premise. The middle term must occur in both premises but not in the conclusion.* Hence, there must be three propositions.

The necessity of having three terms arranged in this way in three propositions also follows from the very nature of a categorical syllogism. Two propositions (the premises) are required for the middle term to fulfill its function of uniting or separating the minor and major terms, and a third proposition (the conclusion) is required to express the union or separation of the minor and major terms.

2) THE QUANTITY, OR EXTENSION, OF THE TERMS

Rule 3. *The major and minor terms may not be universal (or distributed) in the conclusion unless they are universal (or distributed) in the premises.*

The reason for this rule is that we may not conclude about *all* the inferiors of a term if the premises have given us information about only *some* of them. The conclusion is an effect of the premises and must therefore be contained in them implicitly; but *all* are not necessarily contained in *some*—at least not by virtue of the form of argumentation alone.

Violation of this rule is called either *extending a term* or an *illicit process* of a term. There is an *illicit process of the major term* if the major term is particular in the premise but universal in the conclusion; and an *illicit process of the minor term,* if the minor term is particular in the premise but universal in the conclusion.

Note that there is no illicit process if the major or minor term is universal in the premises and particular in the conclusion. To go from a particular to a universal is forbidden—just as on the square of opposition; but to go from a universal to a particular is permissible.

We shall now examine five examples of syllogisms in which this rule is violated. The conclusions of some of them are true *by accident;* that is, the conclusions do not actually flow from the premises but are true for some other reason. It will be helpful to display the logical form of these syllogisms and to mark the quantity of each proposition and of the predicate terms as well. An arrow is used to indicate an illicit process of a term.

1. All dogs are mammals;

   but no men are dogs;

   therefore no men are mammals.

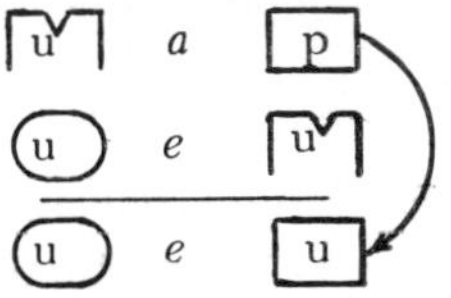

A consideration of the following diagram will help us see why this syllogism is invalid and how the rules of the categorical syllogism are intimately related to the rules governing eduction and oppositional inference.

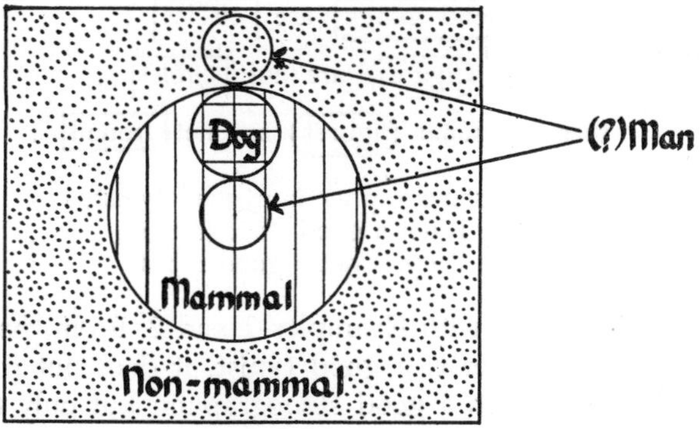

All dogs are mammals; therefore *some* mammals are dogs. If *I* is true, *O* is doubtful; hence, there might be some mammals that are not dogs, and men might be among them. In other words, it might be possible not to be a dog and still be a mammal. From the mere fact, then, that man is not a dog, you cannot tell whether or not he is a mammal.

The conclusion of Example 1 ("therefore no men are mammals") is false. Example 2 has exactly the same form as Example 1; the conclusion, however, is true by accident.

2. Horses are irrational animals;
   but men are not horses,
   therefore men are not irrational animals.

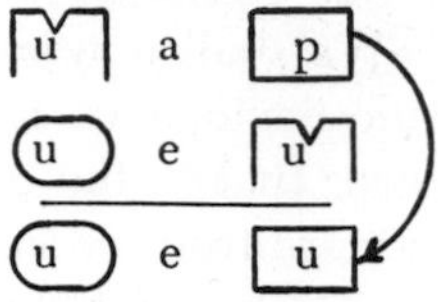

3. Every circle is round;
   but every circle is a figure;
   therefore every figure is round.

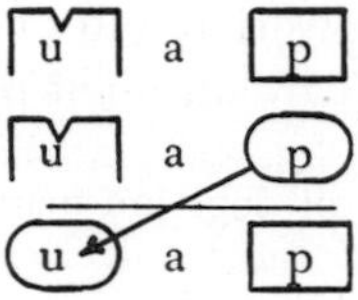

Example 3 has an illicit process of the minor term. The minor term "figure" is particular, or undistributed, in the minor premise where it is the predicate of an affirmative proposition, but universal, or distributed, in the conclusion where it is universalized by the quantifier "every."

What is wrong with Examples 4 and 5?

4. Some round things are circles ;
   but some figures are not circles ;
   therefore some figures are not round .

5. A good stenographer is a good typist;
   but Mary is not a good stenographer;
   therefore Mary is not a good typist.

Compare Example 5 with Examples 1 and 2. From the fact that every good stenographer is a good typist, it does not follow that every good typist is also a good stenographer, but only that some good typist is a good stenographer. Hence, from the mere fact that Mary is not a good stenographer, you cannot tell whether or not she is a good typist. She may be one of the good typists—if there are any—who are not good stenographers.

Note that an illicit process of the minor term is never incurred if the conclusion is particular and that an illicit process of the major term is never incurred if the conclusion is affirmative.

Rule 4. *The middle term must be universal, or distributed, at least once.*[3]

The reason for this rule is that when the middle term is particular in both premises it might stand for a different portion of its extension in each occurrence and thus be equivalent to two terms, and therefore fail to fulfill its function of uniting or separating the minor and major terms.

We shall now examine five examples of syllogisms in which this rule is violated.

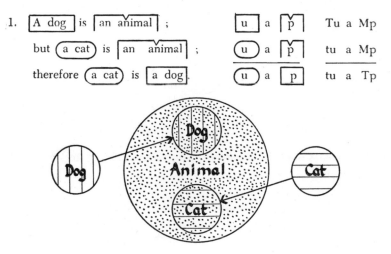

1.	A dog is an animal;	u a p	Tu a Mp
	but a cat is an animal;	u a p	tu a Mp
	therefore a cat is a dog.	u a p	tu a Tp

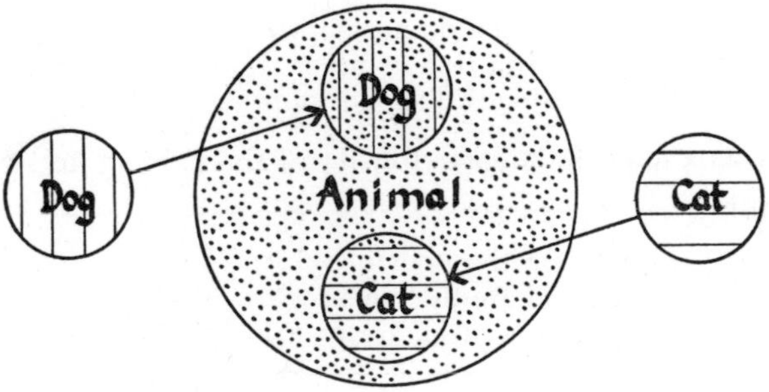

A consideration of the diagram shows us that "animal" stands for a different portion of its extension in each of the premises and thus does not unite "cat" and "dog." Both of them are animals but not the same animals.

[3] A syllogism is valid if the middle term is singular in both occurrences. See "The Expository Syllogism," p. 108.

2.	Many rich men oppress the poor;	Mp i Tp
	but Jones is a rich man;	ts a Mp
	therefore Jones oppresses the poor.	ts a Tp

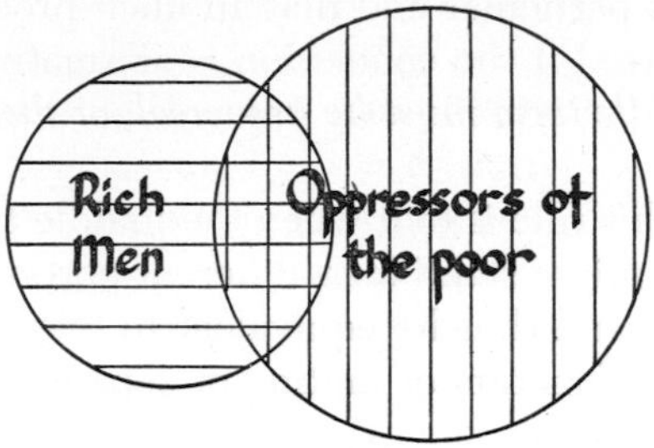

In the major premise "rich men" stands only for the rich men enclosed within the big circle representing all those who oppress the poor; but for all we know, "rich man" in the minor premise stands for a rich man outside the big circle. Hence, we cannot tell whether Jones is one of the rich men who oppress the poor or one of those (if there are any) [4] who do not oppress the poor.

The same diagram will throw light on Example 3.

3. Many rich men do not oppress the poor;
but Jones is a rich man;
therefore Jones does not oppress the poor.

In Example 4 note the inverted order of the subject and predicate in the premises.

4. Blessed are the poor in spirit;
but blessed are the meek;
therefore the meek are poor in spirit.

5. A sick man needs medicine;
but castor oil is medicine;
therefore a sick man needs castor oil.

Notice that the middle term *may* be universal in both occurrences, but *has to be* universal only once.

[4] Of course, there are rich men who do not oppress the poor, but you cannot infer this from the fact that some rich men oppress the poor—if *I* is true, *O* is doubtful.

Violation of this rule is often called the fallacy of the *undistributed middle.*

b. The Rules of the Propositions

1) THE QUALITY OF THE PROPOSITIONS

Rule 5. *If both premises are affirmative, the conclusion must be affirmative.*

The reason for this rule is that affirmative premises either unite the minor and major terms, or else do not bring them into relationship with one another at all—as when there is an undistributed middle. In neither case may the major term be denied of the minor term. Hence, to get a negative conclusion you must have one—and only one—negative premise.

The following four examples illustrate either real or *apparent* violations of this rule.

1. All sin is detestable;
   but some pretense is sin;
   therefore some pretense is not detestable.

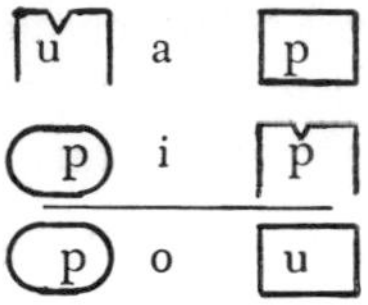

"Some pretense is detestable" is a valid conclusion of the premises; note how we tend to proceed invalidly from an implicit *I* to an *O.* This example, besides violating Rule 5, also illustrates an illicit process of the major term.

As soon as you see that both premises are affirmative but the conclusion negative, you can be sure that your syllogism is invalid. Be on your guard, however, against *apparent* affirmative or negative propositions. The following syllogism is valid although it *seems* to violate this rule.

2. Animals differ from angels;
   but man is an animal;
   therefore man is not an angel.

Example 2 is valid because "differ from" is equivalent to "are not."

3. Man is two-legged;
   but a horse is four-legged;
   therefore a man is not a horse.

Example 3 is also valid—at least materially. When we say that man is two-legged, we do not mean that he has at least two legs (and maybe more) but that he has two and only two. Hence we imply that he is not four-legged.

4. A lion is an animal;
but a fox is an animal;
therefore—since the middle term "animal" is undistributed—a fox is not a lion.

Rule 6. *If one premise is affirmative and the other negative, the conclusion must be negative.*

The reason for this rule is that the affirmative premise unites the middle term with one of the extremes (that is, with either the minor or the major term) and the negative premise separates the middle term from the other extreme. Two things, of which the one is identical with a third thing and the other is different from that same third thing, cannot be identical with one another. Hence, if a syllogism with a negative premise concludes at all, it must conclude negatively. Thus, Example 1 is invalid.

1. Every *B* is a *C;*	Mu a T
but some *A* is not a *B*.	tp o M
therefore some *A* is a *C*.	tp i T

From the fact that some *A* is not a *B* you cannot tell whether or not some *A* is a *C*. It is possible that no *A* is either a *B* or a *C*.

There are *apparent* exceptions to this rule, but they will cause no difficulty if we keep in mind that many negative propositions are equivalent to affirmative propositions and can be changed into them by one or the other kinds of immediate inference. Number 2, for instance, is a valid syllogism.

2. Dogs are not centipedes;
but hounds are dogs;
therefore hounds differ from centipedes.

The conclusion is equivalently negative, since "differ from" is here equivalent to "are not."

Rule 7. *If both premises are negative—and not equivalently affirmative—there is no conclusion at all.*

To fulfill its function of uniting or separating the minor and the major term, the middle term must itself be united with at least one of them. But if both premises are negative, the middle term is denied of each of the extremes and we learn nothing about the relationship of the extremes towards one another. Some examples and a diagram will make this clear.

1. A stone is not an animal;	Mu e T
but a dog is not a stone;	tu e M
therefore a dog is not an animal.	tu e T

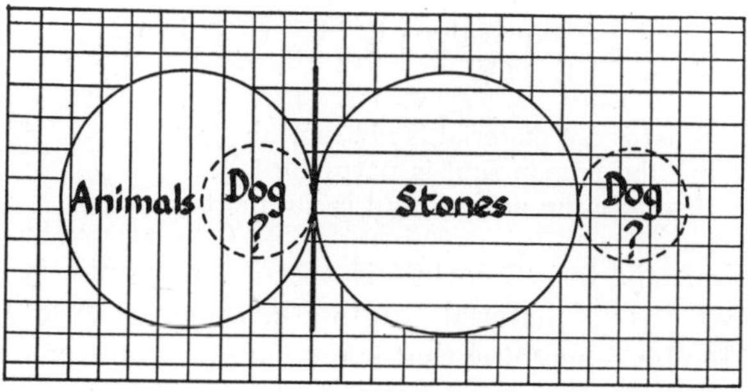

The non-animals, represented by the horizontal lines, and the non-stones, represented by the vertical lines, overlap; hence, from the fact that a dog is not a stone, you cannot tell whether or not a dog is an animal. Some non-stones are animals, and others are not.

Example 2 has the same form as Example 1; but the conclusion is true by accident.

2. A dog is not a cat;
but a rat is not a dog;
therefore a rat is not a cat.

3. The poor do not have security;
but these men are not poor;
therefore these men have security.

4. No murderer shall enter into the kingdom of heaven;
but John is not a murderer;
therefore John shall enter into the kingdom of heaven.

5. Insulators are not conductors of electricity;
but glass is not a conductor of electricity;
therefore glass is an insulator.

The following examples illustrate *apparent* but not real violations of this rule. Note how the mind sometimes spontaneously substitutes for a proposition its obverse or some other kind of immediate inference.

1. No *B* is not a *C;*
   but no *A* is not a *B;*
   therefore no *A* is not a *C*
   (or: therefore every *A* is a *C*).

The major premise of Example 1 is equivalent to "Every *B* is a *C*"*;* the minor premise is equivalent to "Every *A* is a *B*"*;* and the conclusion, to "Every *A* is a *C*."

2. What is not material is not mortal;
   but the human soul is not material;
   therefore the human soul is not mortal.

In Example 2, the term "mortal" in the major premise is denied of the term "what is not material," and in the minor premise the human soul is said to be "something that is not material" (obversion). Thus, if what is not material is not mortal and if the human soul is something that is not material, it must also be something that is not mortal.

3. Non-voters are not eligible;
   but John is not a voter;
   therefore John is ineligible.
4. No man is not mortal;
   but no American citizen is not a man;
   therefore no American citizen is immortal.
5. What is not metallic is not magnetic;
   but carbon is not metallic;
   therefore carbon is not magnetic.

2) THE QUANTITY OF THE PROPOSITIONS

The rules on the quantity of the propositions are corollaries of the rules on the quantity of the terms.

Rule 8. *At least one premise must be universal.*[5]

[5] An expository syllogism (that is, a syllogism whose middle term is singular) may have two particular premises if the middle term is the predicate of each of them. See "Expository Syllogism," p. 108.

We shall consider every possible arrangement of the terms in categorical syllogisms in which both the premises are particular propositions and see how in every arrangement either Rule 3 or Rule 4 is violated.

1–If both premises are affirmative, the middle term is particular in each occurrence, and Rule 4 is violated. Let *a, e, i,* and *o* indicate the quality and quantity of the propositions and *t, M,* and *T* the minor, middle, and major terms, respectively. We shall now diagram the four possible arrangements.

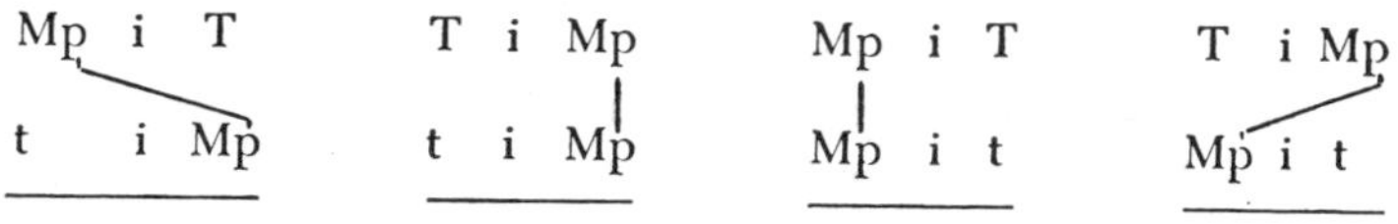

If the middle term (*M*) is subject, it is particular, because we are here dealing with particular propositions. If the middle term is predicate, it is also particular, because the predicate of an affirmative proposition is particular.

2–If one premise is affirmative and the other negative, either Rule 3 or Rule 4 is violated. If the middle term is the predicate of the negative premise, there will always be an illicit process of the major term and thus Rule 3 will always be violated, as illustrated in the first and second diagrams. Rule 4, which requires that the middle term be universal at least once, is violated in two cases: first, if the middle term is the subject of both premises and, second, if the middle term is the subject of the negative premise and the predicate of the affirmative premise, as is illustrated in the third and fourth diagrams.

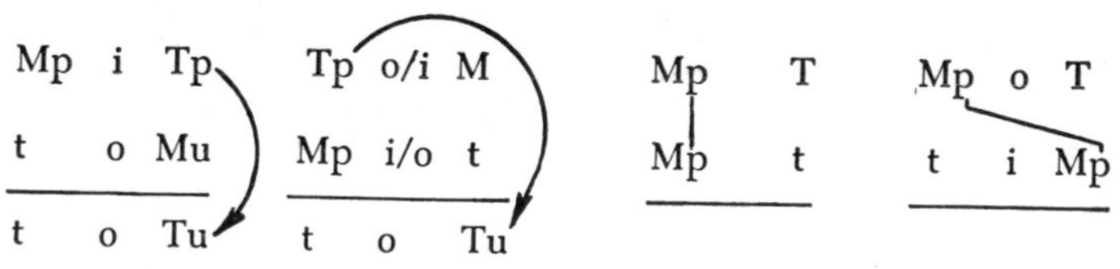

3–If both premises are negative, Rule 7, of course, is violated.

Exercise

Both premises of the following syllogisms are particular propositions. State which of the rules of the terms is violated in each example.

1. Some Russians are Communists;
   but some atheists are Russians;
   therefore some atheists are Communists.
2. Some Russians are Communists;
   but some atheists are not Russians;
   therefore some atheists are not Communists.
3. Some Russians are not Communists;
   but some atheists are Russians;
   therefore some atheists are not Communists.
4. Some wealthy men are not happy;
   but many virtuous men are happy;
   therefore some wealthy men are not virtuous.
5. Some misers sit in their apartments all day counting their gold pieces;
   but many people don't do that;
   therefore many people are not misers.

Rule 9. *If a premise is particular, the conclusion must be particular.*

According to Rule 3, the minor term may not be universal in the conclusion unless it is universal in the minor premise. But an examination of cases reveals that in a valid syllogism having a particular premise the minor term can never be universal in the minor premise. Let us consider syllogisms whose major and minor premises, respectively, are *I-E, A-O,* and *I-A.*

The combination, *I-E,* is always invalid because, as the following diagram shows, it always contains an illicit process of the major term.

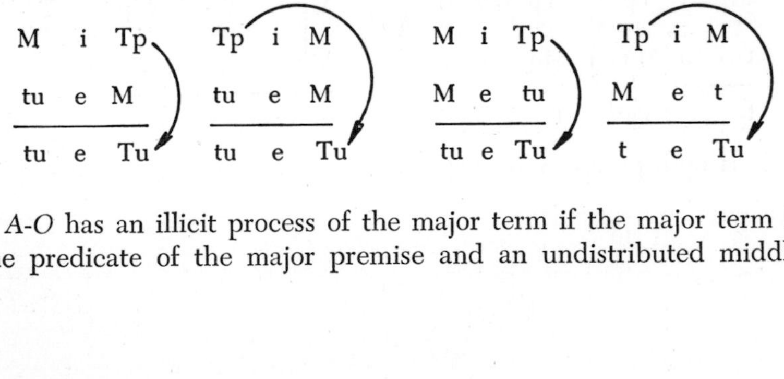

A-O has an illicit process of the major term if the major term is the predicate of the major premise and an undistributed middle whenever the middle term is predicate of the major premise and subject of the minor premise.

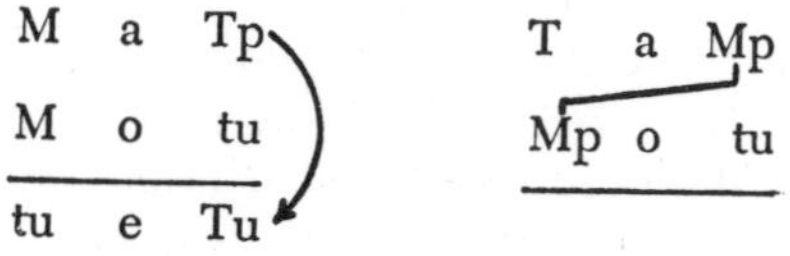

I-A has an undistributed middle if the middle term is the predicate of the minor premise.

We have examined the arrangements which give us a minor term that is universal in the minor premise, and have discovered that all of them contain an illicit process of the major term or an undistributed middle.

Hence, in syllogisms having a particular premise, we can conclude validly only when the minor term is particular in the premises; and, according to Rule 3, when it is particular in the premises, it must also be particular in the conclusion. If the minor premise is *I*, the minor term may be either the subject or the predicate; if the minor premise is *A*, the minor term must be the predicate; if it is *O*, the minor term must be the subject. As we have already seen, the minor premise may never be *E*. The following schema gives us a synopsis of all the valid forms of syllogisms having a particular premise. We can see at a glance that in all of them the conclusion must be particular.

M a T	T a M	M e T	T E M	M e T	M a T	M i T	T i M	M o T
tp i M	tp o M	tp i M	tp i M	M i tp	M i tp	M a tp	M a tp	M a tp
tp i T	tp o T	tp o T	tp o T	tp o T	tp i T	tp i T	tp i T	tp o T

3) THE EXISTENTIAL IMPORT OF THE PROPOSITIONS

Rule 10. *The actual real existence of a subject may not be asserted in the conclusion unless it has been asserted in the premises.*

The reason for this rule is the general principle that nothing may ever be asserted in the conclusion that has not been asserted implicitly in the premises. This rule takes us out of the domain of formal logic, which does not consider existence except incidentally. We mention it only as a practical aid to argumentation.

A Note on the Expository Syllogism. An expository syllogism differs from an ordinary syllogism in that its middle term is singular in both premises. It is not an inference at all in the strictest sense of the word but rather an appeal to experience. As its name suggests, it "exposes" a truth to the senses by setting an example before the mind.

An expository syllogism is useful for refuting *A* and *E* propositions by establishing their contradictories. For instance, the statement "All wood floats" can be refuted as follows:

> This does not float;
> but this is wood;
> therefore not all wood floats.

Or if someone were to assert "No Greek was a philosopher," he could be refuted as follows:

> Socrates was a philosopher;
> but Socrates was a Greek;
> therefore some Greek was a philosopher.

The expository syllogism follows the general rules of the categorical syllogism except on two counts: the first is that the middle term is singular and not universal; the second is that both premises may be particular if the middle term is the predicate of each of them. For instance, in the following example, both premises are particular but the syllogism is nevertheless valid:

> One of the largest cities in the world is Bombay;
> but one of the largest port cities is Bombay;
> therefore one of the largest port cities is one of the largest cities in the world.

Obviously, if the middle term were not singular in this example, it would have to be particular since it is the predicate of an affirmative proposition, and the syllogism would be invalid. But this fallacy is avoided because it is singular.

Exercise

I. State the general rules of the categorical syllogism, following the outline prefixed to the explanation of the rules.

II. Apply the general rules of the categorical syllogism to the following examples.

1. All animals are substances;
 but all frogs are animals;
 therefore all frogs are substances.
2. All cows are animals;
 but no horses are cows;
 therefore no horses are animals.
3. Murder is sinful;
 but abortion is murder;
 therefore abortion is sinful.
4. Contradictories are opposites;
 but black and white are opposites;
 therefore black and white are contradictories.
5. All mammals have lungs;
 but most fish do not have lungs;
 therefore most fish are not mammals.
6. No dog is a man;
 but Fido is not a man;
 therefore Fido is a dog.
7. Democracies are free;
 but some of the governments of the Middle Ages were not democracies;
 therefore some of the governments of the Middle Ages were not free.
8. All mammals are viviparous;
 but whales are viviparous;
 therefore whales are mammals.
9. Those who are not sick may go;
 but Johnny is not sick;
 therefore Johnny may go.
10. No dog is not an animal;
 but no hound is not a dog;
 therefore all hounds are animals.

III. Which of the ten rules are violated in syllogisms whose major premise, minor premise, and conclusion, respectively, are the following types of propositions?

1. A I A.	6. I O I.
2. A E A.	7. E I E.
3. E E E.	8. E I I.
4. A A E.	9. E O O.
5. I I I.	10. I E O.

IV. Pick out the conclusion of each of the following syllogisms. Then pick out the minor and major terms, then the minor and major premises, and then the middle term. Next apply the general rules of the categorical syllogism. In some instances it may be necessary to reduce a syllogism to logical form. Be careful, however, not to do violence to the sense.

1. He is obviously a Communist, since he's always screaming about the evils of capitalism, and that's exactly what the Communists are always screaming about.
2. Willingness to admit a wrong is the mark of a big man. John . . . , Conclave President, proved himself big Monday night when he told the Conclave he had made a mistake in the attempted firing of Thomas . . . , Arts representative to the student government.
3. All true democracies have respect for the dignity of the human person; hence, since Vatican City has respect for the dignity of the human person, it must be a true democracy.
4. Americans will never tolerate tyranny. From their earliest days they have been accustomed to freedom of opportunity and to freedom of thought and expression. No nation with such a background will ever submit to an arbitrary and self-seeking despot.
5. All true democracies have respect for the dignity of the human person; hence, since Vatican City is not a true democracy, it does not have respect for the dignity of the human person.
6. He thinks that labor unions should be abolished. The reason he gives is that they cause strikes and, according to his way of thinking, whatever causes strikes should be done away with.
7. No cats are dogs, because no cats are spaniels, and all spaniels are dogs.
8. "Whoever is not just is not of God. Nor is he just who does not love his brother." You see, then, that he who does not love his brother is not of God. (1 *Jn.* 3/11)
9. "Everyone who hates his brother is a murderer. And you know that no murderer has eternal life abiding in him." Hence, you

see that none who hates his brother has eternal life abiding in him. (1 *Jn.* 3/15)

10. Whatever encourages tenants already in possession to use space wastefully at low rents brings about the appearance of a housing shortage. Many tenants would move if it were legal to demand of them the amount of rent that their apartments are worth. Hence, rent control has itself brought about an appearance of a housing shortage.

V. Study the exclusive proposition and the exceptive proposition on pp. 289-290, and then evaluate the following syllogisms:

1. Only citizens over twenty-one are voters;
but John is a citizen over twenty-one;
therefore John is a voter.
2. None but registered students are members of this class;
but John is a member of this class;
therefore John is a registered student.
3. Only the brave deserve the fair;
but he is brave;
therefore he deserves the fair.
4. None but the clean of heart shall see God;
but he is not clean of heart;
therefore he shall not see God.
5. None but the clean of heart shall see God;
but he is clean of heart;
therefore he shall see God.
6. All members of the class who did the special exercises passed the examination;
but all but four did the special exercises;
therefore all but four passed the examination.

3. LOGICAL FORMS OF THE CATEGORICAL SYLLOGISM: FIGURES AND MOODS

Logical form, as we have seen, is the basic structure, or the basic arrangement of the parts, of a complex logical unit. Now the categorical syllogism is a complex logical unit having as its parts (a) terms and (b) propositions in which these terms are affirmed or denied of one another. The logical form, then, of the categorical syllogism includes (a) the arrangement of the terms—which is called figure—and (b) the arrangement of the propositions according to quality and quantity—which is called mood.

A study of the logical forms of the categorical syllogism will serve several purposes. At present its chief fruit will be to deepen our understanding of the general rules of the syllogism and to give us practice in applying them. Later on it will serve as a background for the consideration of the principles underlying the syllogism and for the reduction of syllogisms of the second, third, and fourth figures to syllogisms of the first figure.

First we shall explain the general nature of the figures and moods; then we shall derive the valid moods of each of the figures; finally we shall show why the first figure is the perfect figure.

a. General Nature of the Figures and Moods

1) **FIGURE.** The figure of a categorical syllogism consists of the arrangement of the *terms* in the premises. There are four figures and each is defined by the position of the middle term. In the first figure, the middle term is the subject of the major premise and the predicate of the minor premise (*sub-pre*). In the second figure, the middle term is the predicate of both premises (*pre-pre*). In the third figure, the middle term is the subject of both premises (*sub-sub*). In the fourth figure, the middle term is the predicate of the major premise and the subject of the minor premise (*pre-sub*). The so-called fourth figure differs only accidentally from the first—it is an inverted first figure—but for practical purposes we shall treat of it separately.

First Figure (sub-pre)	Second Figure (pre-pre)	Third Figure (sub-sub)	Fourth Figure (pre-sub)
M T	T M	M T	T M
t M	t M	M t	M t

2) **MOOD.** The mood of a categorical syllogism consists of the disposition of the premises according to quality and quantity. There are sixteen possible arrangements of the premises according to quality and quantity. The possible arrangements are:

Major premise:	A A A A	E e E e	I i i i	O o o o
Minor premise:	A E I O	A e I o	A e i o	A e i o[6]

By applying the general rules we shall see that only eight of these arrangements are ever valid. Rule 7 ("If both premises are negative, there is no conclusion") excludes *e-e, e-o, o-e,* and *o-o.* Rule 8 ("at least one of the premises must be universal") excludes *i-i, i-o, o-i,* and *o-o*—the last of which was already excluded by Rule 7. Rule 3 ("The major and minor terms may not be universal in the conclusion unless they are universal in the premises") excludes *i-e,* for the major term would be universal in the conclusion but particular in the premise. The moods indicated by the capital letters remain:

A A A A	E E	I	O
A E I O	A I	A	A

But not all of these are valid in every figure.

b. The Valid Moods of Each Figure

We shall now apply the general rules of the categorical syllogism to determine the valid moods of each figure.

1) THE FIRST FIGURE. In the first figure the middle term is the subject of the major premise and the predicate of the minor premise (*sub-pre*).

M	T
t	**M**

As we saw above, the eight possible moods are:

A a A a	E E	i	o
A e I o	A I	a	a

By experiment we shall find that of these eight moods only the four indicated by the capital letters are valid.

[6] The valid moods are indicated by capital letters, the invalid moods by small letters. The same procedure is followed when we indicate the moods of each of the four figures.

M a T	M a Tp	M a T	M a Tp
t a M	t e M	t i M	t o M
t a T	t e Tu	t i T	t o Tu

M e T	M e T	Mp i T	Mp o T
t a M	t i M	t a Mp	t a Mp
t e T	t o T		

Rule 3 ("The major and minor terms may not be universal in the conclusion unless they are universal in the premises") excludes *a-e* and *a-o.* In the premise, the major term is the predicate of an affirmative proposition and therefore particular; but in the conclusion it is the predicate of a negative proposition and therefore universal.

Rule 4 ("The middle term must be universal at least once") excludes *i-a* and *o-a.* As subject of an *I* or *O* proposition, the middle term is particular; and as predicate of an *A* proposition, it is also particular in its second occurrence.

Only four moods remain:	A	A	E	E
	A	I	A	I
They conclude in:——	A	I	E	O

An inspection of these moods enables us to draw up the following RULES OF THE FIRST FIGURE:

1. *The major premise must be universal* (*A* or *E*).
2. *The minor premise must be affirmative* (*A* or *I*).

Exercise

I. In syllogisms of the first figure, why must the major premise be universal, and the minor premise affirmative?

II. Apply both the general rules and the special rules of the first figure to the following syllogisms.

1. Every *B* is a *C;*
   but no *A* is a *B;*
   therefore no *A* is a *C.*

2. No *Z* is an *X;*
   but every *Y* is a *Z;*
   therefore no *Y* is an *X*.
3. Every cat is an animal;
   but no dog is a cat;
   therefore no dog is an animal.
4. Some people are difficult to get along with;
   but all Americans are people;
   therefore some Americans are difficult to get along with.
5. Some men are walking;
   but Peter is a man;
   therefore Peter is walking.

2) THE SECOND FIGURE. In the second figure, the middle term is the predicate of both premises (*pre-pre*).

T	**M**
t	**M**

Beginning with the eight possible moods, we shall proceed, just as with the first figure, by applying the general rules to each of them. The eight possible moods are:

a	A	a	A	E	E	i	o
a	E	i	O	A	I	a	a

Whenever both premises are affirmative, the middle term will be particular in each occurrence; hence, Rule 4 ("The middle term must be universal at least once") excludes *a-a, a-i,* and *i-a.* Rule 3 ("The major and minor terms may not be universal in the conclusion unless they are universal in the premises") excludes *o-a;* as the subject of *O,* the major term is particular in the premise but, as the predicate of a negative proposition, is universal in the conclusion.

Only *four moods* remain:	A	A	E	E
	E	O	A	I
They conclude in:——	E	O	E	O

An inspection of these moods enables us to draw up the following RULES OF THE SECOND FIGURE:

1. *The major premise must be universal* (*A* or *E*).
2. *One premise must be negative.*

Exercise

I. In syllogisms of the second figure, why must the major premise be universal and why must one premise be negative?

II. Apply both the general rules and the special rules of the second figure to the following:

1. Some metal floats on water;
   but potassium floats on water;
   therefore potassium is a metal.

2. Democratic governments protect freedom;
   but this government protects freedom;
   therefore this government is democratic.

3. Americans are generous;
   but Silas is not generous;
   therefore Silas is not an American.

4. All mammals are viviparous;
   but some fish are viviparous;
   therefore some fish are mammals.

5. *C* is not *B;*
   but *A* is *B;*
   therefore *A* is not *C*.

3) **THE THIRD FIGURE.** In the third figure the middle term is the subject of both premises (*sub-sub*).

M T
M t
———

We shall proceed just as with the first and second figures. The eight possible moods are:

A	a	A	a	E	E	I	O
A	e	I	o	A	I	A	A

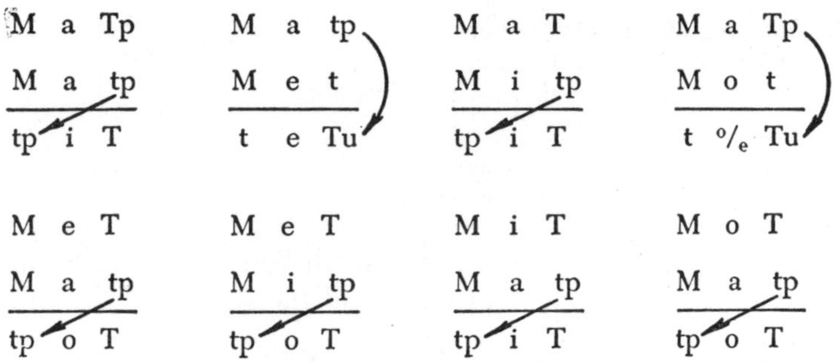

An inspection of the forms given above reveals that Rule 3 ("The major and minor term may not be universal in the conclusion unless they are universal in the premises") excludes *a-e* and *a-o*. Note that every conclusion is particular.

There remain *six moods:*	A	A	E	E	I	O
	A	I	A	I	A	A
They conclude in:——	I	I	O	O	I	O

An inspection of these moods and conclusions enables us to draw up the following RULES OF THE THIRD FIGURE:

1. *The minor premise must be affirmative.*
2. *The conclusion must be particular.*

Exercise

I. In syllogisms of the third figure, why must the minor premise be affirmative and why must the conclusion be particular?

II. Apply both the general rules and the special rules of the third figure to the following.

1. Potassium floats on water;
   but potassium is a metal;
   therefore some metal floats on water.
2. Some Inquisitors were cruel;
   but some Inquisitors were good men;
   therefore some good men were cruel.
3. Ebony does not float on water;
   but ebony is wood;
   therefore some wood does not float on water.

4. Socrates was a philosopher;
   but Socrates was a Greek;
   therefore some Greek was a philosopher.
5. Some men are silly;
   but every man is an animal;
   therefore some animals are silly.

4) THE FOURTH FIGURE. In the fourth figure, the middle term is the predicate of the major premise and the subject of the minor premise.

T	**M**
M	t

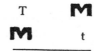

The eight possible moods are:

A	A	a	a	E	E	I	o
A	E	i	o	A	I	A	a

T a M	T a M	T a Mp	T a Mp
M a tp	M e tu	Mp i t	Mp o t
tp i T	tu e T		
T e M	T e M	T i M	Tp o M
M a tp	M i tp	M a tp	M a tp
tp o T	tp o T	tp i T	t o Tu

Rule 4 ("The middle term must be universal at least once") excludes *a-i* and *a-o*. Rule 3 ("The major and minor terms may not be universal in the conclusion unless they are universal in the premises") excludes *o-a*.

There remain five moods:	A A	E	E	I	
	A E	A	I	A	
They conclude in:——————	I E	O	O	I	

An inspection of these moods and conclusions enables us to draw up the following RULES OF THE FOURTH FIGURE (inverted first figure):

1. *If the major premise is affirmative, the minor premise must be universal.*
2. *If the minor premise is affirmative, the conclusion must be particular.*
3. *If a premise (and the conclusion) is negative, the major premise must be universal.*

Violation of the first rule involves an undistributed middle; of the second, an illicit process of the minor term; and of the third, an illicit process of the major term.[7]

Exercise

I. State the three rules of the fourth figure and give the reason for each of them.

II. Apply both the general rules of the categorical syllogism and the special rules of the fourth figure to the following:

1. Every hound is a dog;
   but every dog is an animal;
   therefore some animal is a hound. (Notice that this concludes more naturally in *A:* "therefore every hound is an animal.")
2. All men have free will;
   but some beings having free will are potential doers of evil;
   therefore some potential doers of evil are men.
3. No person under twenty-one years of age is a voter;
   but some voters are university students;
   therefore some university students are not under twenty-one years of age.
4. All voters are over twenty-one years of age;
   but some who are over twenty-one years of age are university students;
   therefore some university students are voters.

[7] The problem as to whether the so-called fourth figure is an independent figure or merely an inverted first figure whose major and minor premises are interchanged is too complicated to be treated in an elementary manual. For a discussion of this problem see Maritain, *Logic,* pp. 186-92, especially the footnote on p. 187, and Joseph, *Introduction to Logic,* pp. 280-86.

5. All voters are over twenty-one years of age;
but some over twenty-one years of age are not university students;
therefore some university students are not voters.

c. *The Perfect Figure*

The first figure is considered the perfect figure. In the first place, as we shall see later,[8] the principles underlying the categorical syllogism regulate syllogisms of the first figure most directly and most obviously. Secondly, only the first figure can have a universal affirmative conclusion, which is the kind of conclusion with which science is principally concerned. Thirdly, the first figure is the only figure in which the middle term gives, or at least can give, the reason why what is signified by the major term belongs to what is signified by the minor term.[9] Examine, for instance, the following syllogism:

A spiritual substance is immortal;
but the human soul is a spiritual substance;
therefore the human soul is immortal.

In this syllogism, the middle term "spiritual substance" contains the reason why immortality belongs to the human soul—it is that the human soul is a spiritual substance, and a spiritual substance, *as such,* must be immortal. For these reasons the first figure is the figure of scientific and philosophical demonstration.

4. PRINCIPLES OF THE CATEGORICAL SYLLOGISM

a. *The Problem and a Brief Answer*

Now that we are familiar with the mechanics of the categorical syllogism and have made a study of the various figures, we are ready to take up the principles underlying the logical movement of the categorical syllogism. We shall endeavor to penetrate more deeply into the nature of the syllogism by trying to grasp the principles

[8] Pp. 131-132. Also see Joseph, *Introduction to Logic,* pp. 305-7.

[9] In the first figure the middle term can give not only the *ratio cognoscendi* (the reason for knowing) of the conclusion but also the *ratio essendi* (the reason for being). It can give not only the reason why we *know* that the conclusion is true but also the reason why it actually *is* true—that is, the reason why what is signified by the minor term has the attribute signified by the major term.

that are operative every time a minor and major term are united (or separated) through the intermediacy of a middle term. Previously we grasped the validity of individual syllogisms and of various types of syllogisms but without adverting to the most general principles illustrated in each; in the present section we shall try to disengage these principles from the examples in which they are illustrated and to enunciate them explicitly.[10] For instance, from our previous study we know that the following syllogism is valid:

> A dog is an animal;
> but a hound is a dog;
> therefore a hound is an animal.

We can tell that this syllogism is valid because, aided by the rules of the syllogism, we clearly grasp the relationship of the terms "hound," "dog," and "animal"—we clearly see that if a dog is an animal and a hound is a dog, a hound must also be an animal. We see this directly and need not appeal to any principle at all. Yet, on reflection, we see that this argument fulfills certain basic conditions —that certain basic principles underlie its logical movement—and that the fulfillment of these conditions is the reason for its validity. To discover what these conditions and principles are is the aim of our present inquiry.

A PRINCIPLE is something that is first and from which something else either is or becomes or is known. A PRINCIPLE OF KNOWLEDGE is knowledge from which other knowledge flows or on which other knowledge somehow depends. The premises of a syllogism, for instance, are a principle of the conclusion because the conclusion flows from them and because (at least in some cases) our knowledge of the conclusion is dependent on our knowledge of the premises.

Notice that a principle of knowledge is not necessarily known first chronologically. Chronologically, we may first know particular exemplifications of the principle; then, by generalization, we work

[10] These principles are grasped by so-called intellective induction, which is explained in Chapter 16.

Some authors give the false impression that we first grasp the principles underlying the logical movement of the syllogism and that we then derive the rules from them by deduction.

back to the principle itself (as is the case with the principles of the syllogism).

Some principles are first, or ultimate, principles; others are derived principles. A FIRST PRINCIPLE is first absolutely and is not dependent on any broader principle. A DERIVED PRINCIPLE is first in its own order but not absolutely. It is either a particularization of some broader principle (as are the principles of the identifying and separating third), or a conclusion deduced from premises (as a conclusion of mathematics may be a principle in physics).

In the present section we are concerned with the *principles of knowledge* of the categorical syllogism. We are concerned not with the principles serving as premises from which the conclusion is deduced but with the principles underlying the logical movement itself.

The first question that we shall endeavor to answer is this: What are the *special* principles on which the validity of the categorical syllogism (but of no other type of syllogism) ultimately depends? The answer (as we shall soon see) is the PRINCIPLE OF THE IDENTIFYING THIRD in an affirmative syllogism and the PRINCIPLE OF THE SEPARATING THIRD in a negative syllogism. If one of these principles underlies the logical movement of a categorical syllogism, the conclusion must be true if the premises are true.

But we must also answer a second question: How are we to know whether or not the principles of the identifying or separating third underlie a syllogism? Two other principles give the answer. They are the DICTUM DE OMNI ("law of all") for the affirmative syllogism and the DICTUM DE NULLO ("law of none") for the negative syllogism. The various rules governing the syllogism are nothing but practical aids for telling whether or not these principles are operative in a syllogism.

The principles of the identifying and separating third are particularized formulae of the more general principles of identity and contradiction (which are the basic principles of absolutely all judgment and inference), phrased in such a way as to be more immediately applicable to the syllogism. Hence, first of all (under *b*), we shall treat of the principles of identity and contradiction. Next (under *c*), we shall treat of the principles of the identifying and separating third. Finally (under *d*), we shall treat of the *dictum de omni* and the *dictum de nullo*.[11]

b. The Principles of Identity and Contradiction

We shall now state the principles of identity and contradiction, which are the absolutely first principles of all judgment and inference, in their most general formulae.

1) **THE PRINCIPLE OF IDENTITY** has several formulae. The two that seem most correct philosophically are: "What is, is" and "Everything is what it is." Notice that this principle is true of things as they are in themselves and independently of their being thought of. For this reason it is not only a logical principle but also a metaphysical principle.

2) **THE PRINCIPLE OF CONTRADICTION** also has several formulae. Sometimes it is enunciated as a metaphysical principle in a formula that is true of things as they are in themselves; sometimes, again, it is enunciated as a purely logical principle in a formula that is not applicable to things as they are in themselves but only to things as they exist in the mind as a result of being known.

Insofar as the principle of contradiction is a metaphysical principle, it has two common formulae. The first and broadest is: "A thing cannot be and not be in the same respect." The second formula, which is narrower inasmuch as it does not extend to all existence but only to the presence or absence of attributes, is as follows: "A thing cannot both have and not have the same attribute in the same respect." Notice that the principle does not assert that a thing cannot be at one time and not be at another, or have an attribute in one respect and not have it in another. For instance, there is no contradiction in John's being good at basketball but not good at dominoes, in his being heavy in comparison with George but not heavy in comparison with Jim, or in his having a puppy as a pet one day but not having it the next. Inasmuch as this principle, as stated in both of these formulae, is true of things as they are in

[11] In a certain sense, sense experience is the principle of all human knowledge, since, as will be explained in the philosophy of human nature, there is nothing in the intellect that was not somehow or other in the senses first. In the order of apprehension (but not in the orders of judgment and inference), being is the principle of all knowledge.

themselves and independently of our thought of them, it is a metaphysical principle.

As a purely logical principle, the principle of contradiction is also expressed in two formulae corresponding to the formulae given above. The first and broadest formula is: "The same thing cannot be both affirmed and denied in the same respect." The second is: "The same attribute cannot be both affirmed and denied of the same subject in the same respect." Thus expressed, the principle is a purely logical principle because it is not applicable to things as they are in themselves but only to things insofar as they are known, or mentally reproduced.

The purely logical principle of contradiction is *grounded* on the metaphysical principle enunciated above—contradictory propositions, in other words, cannot both be true because things cannot be and not be in the same respect. Yet the logical principle is not deducible from the metaphysical principle since it brings in a new element, the impossibility of *knowingly* asserting each of two contradictories at the same time.

A little reflection will show that, although we have not stated the principle of contradiction explicitly, we have nevertheless made constant use of it throughout our study of inference.

Why, for instance, is the partial conversion of an *A* proposition (*A* to *I*) a formally valid inference, whereas the simple conversion of *A* (*A* to *A*) is invalid? Let us examine an example of the conversion of *A* to *I:*

> Every dog is an animal;
> therefore some animal is a dog.

Now, to affirm the antecedent ("every dog is an animal") and to deny the consequent ("some animal is a dog") is to affirm and deny the same thing in the same respect and thus to run counter to the principle of contradiction. Let us now examine an example of the conversion of *A* to *A:*

> Every dog is an animal;
> therefore every animal is a dog.

This example is obviously invalid; but why? Because to affirm the antecedent and to deny the consequent (or pseudo consequent) does not involve affirming and denying the same thing in the same respect and does not run counter to the principle of contradiction: The fact that every dog is an animal does not exclude the possibility of animals that are not dogs.

An examination of any example of valid inference will show that it is valid precisely because the admission of the antecedent and the denial of the consequent involve a contradiction. Our use of the principle of contradiction is perhaps most obvious in contradictory opposition. The principle of contradiction also governs the categorical syllogism, the conditional syllogism, and so on.

c. *The Principles of the Identifying and Separating Third*

We shall now treat of the principles of the identifying and separating third, which are specialized, or particularized, statements of the principles of identity and contradiction phrased in a way that is directly applicable to the categorical syllogism and only to it.

1) THE PRINCIPLE OF THE IDENTIFYING THIRD. The principle of the identifying third is stated as follows: "Two things that are identical with the same third thing are identical with one another."

Notice that in this formula the words "two things" and "third thing" do not refer to three really distinct existing things, but to one thing (or one kind of thing) that is grasped in three distinct concepts. The "three things," therefore, are three only in the mind, as will be explained below. In the real order, for instance, the very same being is at once a hound, a dog, and an animal.

The following example and diagram are not presented as a proof of the principle but merely as an illustration. If we examine the example and consider the relationship of the terms as displayed in the diagrams, we shall, by insight into this example, clearly understand the principle itself.

Moreover, the explanation given here presupposes the *dictum de omni* ("law of all"), which will be explained in the next section.

Let us now examine the following syllogism and the accompanying diagrams and explanations:

Every dog is an animal;
but every hound is a dog;
therefore every hound is an animal.

For convenience in diagramming, we shall invert the order of the premises, giving the minor premise first and the major premise second.

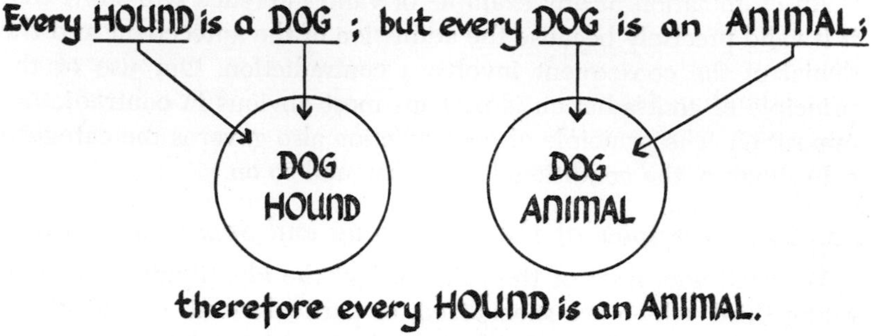
Every HOUND is a DOG ; but every DOG is an ANIMAL;
DOG
HOUND
DOG
ANIMAL
therefore every HOUND is an ANIMAL.

What is presented to the mind under the formality of "hound" is the very same thing that is presented under the formality of "dog"; and what is presented under the formality of "dog" is the same as that presented under the formality of "animal." Let us unite the two parts of our diagram.

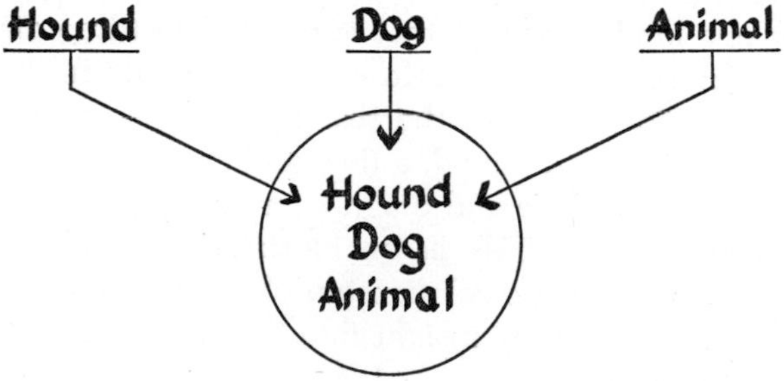
Hound
Dog
Animal
Hound
Dog
Animal

What is signified by "hound" has been shown to be identical with what is signified by "animal" because what is signified by each of them is identical with what is signified by "dog." The very same reality is at once hound, dog, and animal. The middle term "dog" is the identifying third because, through it, the minor term "hound"

and the major term "animal" have been identified in the sense explained above.

The principle of the identifying third can be grasped directly through insight into an example and without any appeal to the broader principles of identity or contradiction. However, we can easily show how a denial of the principle of the identifying third implies a denial of the principle of contradiction. If, for instance, after admitting that every dog is an animal and that a hound is a dog, you nevertheless deny that a hound is an animal, you implicitly deny what you have explicitly affirmed, simultaneously asserting both an *A* and an *O* proposition. By denying that every hound is an animal you are implicitly asserting that some dog (namely a hound) is not an animal (*O*), thus denying the universal proposition "every dog is an animal" (*A*), which you already admitted as a premise.

Notice that we did not say that a "hound" is *equal* to a "dog" and an "animal," nor that "hound" is *similar* to "dog" and "animal"; but that a hound *is* a dog and therefore *is* an animal.[12]

2) THE PRINCIPLE OF THE SEPARATING THIRD. The principle of the separating third is stated thus: "Two things of which the one is identical with the same third thing but the other is not are not identical with one another."

Notice that one of the two things must be identical with the same third thing and the other not. It is not enough if neither of the two is identical with the same third thing. From the fact, for instance, that neither a cow nor a horse is a man, it is impossible to tell whether or not a cow is a horse. (Recall the rule that a syllogism cannot conclude if both of its premises are negative.)

Let us examine the following syllogism together with the diagrams given below.

Every dog is an animal;
but no animal is an angel;
therefore no dog is an angel.

[12] The principle of the identifying third should not be confused with the mathematical principle "Two things *equal* to the same third thing are *equal* to one another."

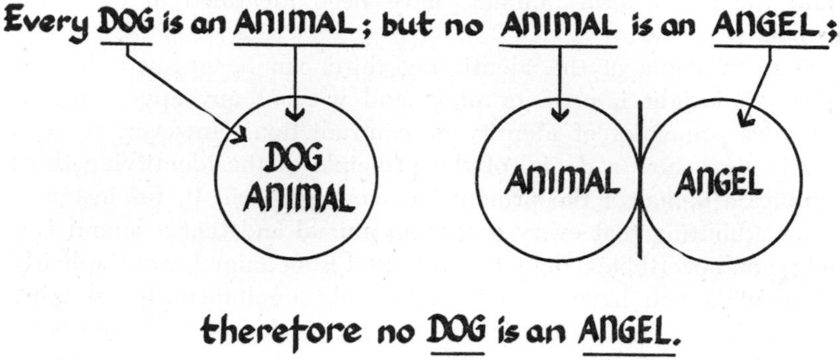
Every DOG is an ANIMAL; but no ANIMAL is an ANGEL;
DOG
ANIMAL
ANIMAL
ANGEL
therefore no DOG is an ANGEL.

What is presented to the mind under the formality of "dog" is the very same thing that is presented under the formality of "animal." But what is presented to the mind by "animal" is not the same as is presented by "angel." Let us unite the two parts of the diagram.

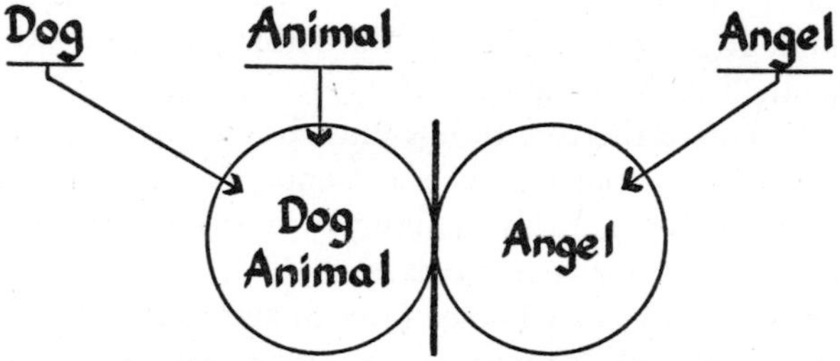
Dog
Animal
Angel
Dog
Animal
Angel

What is signified by "dog" has been shown not to be identical with what is signified by "angel," because it is identical with what is signified by "animal," whereas what is signified by "angel" is not. The middle term "animal" is the separating third because, through its union with the minor term "dog" and its separation from the major term "angel," "dog" has been separated from "angel," as explained above.

The principle of the separating third, just like the principle of the identifying third, is grasped directly through insight into an example and without any appeal to the broader principle of contradiction; yet its denial, like the denial of the principle of the identifying third, implies a denial of the principle of contradiction. If, for instance, after affirming that every dog is an animal and denying that any animal is an angel, you nevertheless affirm that a dog is an angel, you implicitly affirm what you have already explicitly denied, simultaneously asserting both an *E* and an *I* proposition. By affirming that some dog is an angel (or denying that no dog is an angel), you are implying that some animal (namely, a dog) is an angel—which is an *I* proposition; but you have already explicitly asserted that no animal is an angel—which is an *E* proposition and the contradictory of the preceding *I*.

d. The "Dictum de Omni" and the "Dictum de Nullo"

How are we to know that the middle term actually fulfills its function of identifying or separating the minor and major terms? How are we to know, for instance, that the same beings are referred to in both occurrences of the term "dog" in the example used to illustrate the principle of the identifying third, and that the same beings are referred to in both occurrences of the term "animal" in the example illustrating the principle of the separating third? The *dictum de omni* and the *dictum de nullo* ("law of all" and "law of none") are the principles that give the ultimate answer to this question.

We are by no means unfamiliar with these principles although we have never stated them explicitly. Indeed, whenever we used diagrams to display the quantitative relationship of the terms of a syllogism, our diagrams were actually a visual aid to telling whether or not the conditions required by these principles were fulfilled. Besides, many of the examples and diagrams we have already used can serve as sufficient evidence for the grasping of these principles. We shall repeat an example and a diagram that we have already used in Section 1 of the present chapter to display the quantitative relationship to one another of the syllogistic terms.[13]

Notice that these principles are not metaphysical principles at all but purely *logical principles* because they are not applicable to things as they are in themselves but only to things as they are repro-

[13] Pp. 91-92.

duced in the mind: namely, to the relationship of a logical whole to its inferiors.

1) **THE *DICTUM DE OMNI* ("LAW OF ALL").** The *dictum de omni* (or "law of all") is the principle operative in the affirmative syllogism. It is stated as follows: "What is predicated of a logical whole may be predicated distributively of each of its inferiors."

For instance, if "mortal" is predicated of *animal as such* (and therefore of every animal), it can also be predicated of "dog," since a dog is an animal.

An inspection of the following diagrams will make this perfectly clear.

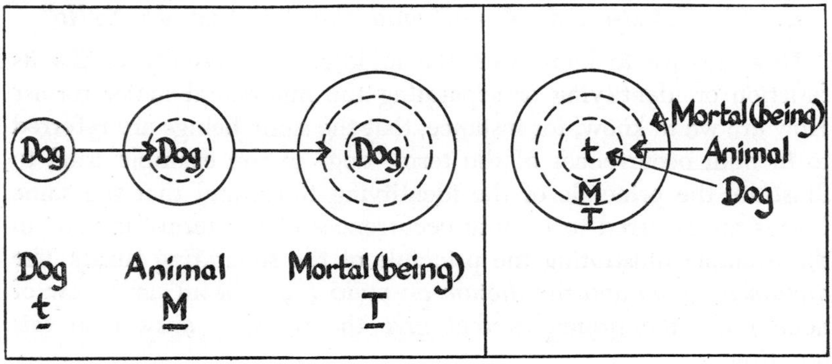

"Dog" is drawn into the extension of "animal," and "animal" is drawn into the extension of "mortal (being)." Since every dog *is* an animal, what is true of every animal must also be true of every dog. Hence, since every animal is mortal, every dog must be mortal too.

2) **THE *DICTUM DE NULLO* ("LAW OF NONE").** The *dictum de nullo* (or "law of none") is the principle operative in the negative syllogism. It is stated as follows: "What is denied of a logical whole may be denied distributively of each of its inferiors."

For instance, if "angel" is denied of *animal as such* (and therefore of every animal), it can also be denied of "dog," since a dog is an animal.

An inspection of the following diagrams will make this perfectly clear.

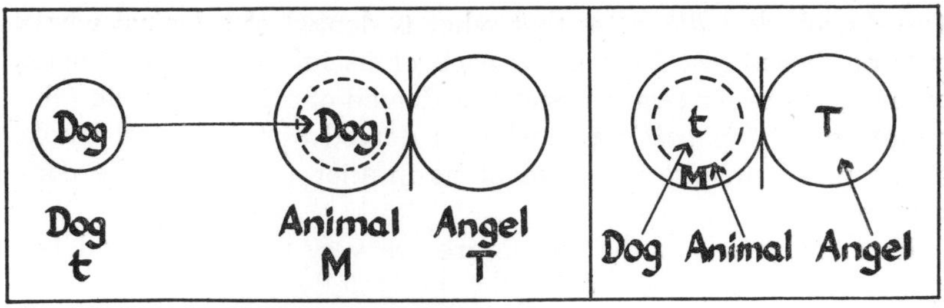

"Dog" is drawn into the extension of "animal"; "animal" is completely excluded from the extension of "angel." Since every dog *is* an animal, what is denied of every animal must also be denied of every dog. Hence, since no animal is an angel, so too no dog is an angel.

5. REDUCTION OF THE IMPERFECT FIGURES TO THE FIRST FIGURE

The first figure has special demonstrative force because the principles of the categorical syllogism regulate syllogisms of the first figure most directly and most obviously. Consider, for instance, the following *affirmative syllogism* of the first figure and reflect on the way in which the principles of the syllogism underlie it:

Every dog is an animal;
but every hound is a dog;
therefore every hound is an animal.

The *dictum de omni* states that what is predicated of a logical whole may be predicated distributively of each of its inferiors. Now in the major premise, the major term ("animal") is predicated of a logical whole (the middle term, "dog"); and what is affirmed of this logical whole in the major premise is affirmed of its inferior ("hound") in the conclusion.

Next consider the following *negative syllogism* of the first figure and again reflect on the way in which the principles of the syllogism underlie it:

No animal is an angel;
but every dog is an animal;
therefore no dog is an angel.

The *dictum de nullo* states that what is denied of a logical whole may be denied distributively of each of its inferiors. In the major premise, the major term ("angel") is denied of a logical whole (the middle term, "animal"); and what is denied of this logical whole in the major premise is denied of its inferior ("dog") in the conclusion.

Thus, syllogisms of the first figure are very obviously regulated by the *dictum de omni* and the *dictum de nullo,* which are the principles that regulate the syllogism most immediately and which enable us to see whether or not the principles of the identifying third and separating third underlie its movement.

REDUCTION consists in changing a syllogism of an imperfect figure to a syllogism of the first figure.

Its PURPOSE is twofold. Its first purpose is to show that the imperfect figures participate in the demonstrative force of the first figure. In scholastic disputation, if an opponent admitted the truth of the premises of a syllogism but denied its validity, he could be confuted by the reduction of the syllogism to a syllogism of the first figure whose validity all would immediately admit. Its second purpose is to render our knowledge of the categorical syllogism scientific by enabling us to see more clearly how the same set of principles regulates all categorical syllogisms of all figures.

Notice, however, that reduction is not required for recognizing the validity of the so-called imperfect figures. Indeed, we recognized their validity before we studied either the figures or the principles underlying the syllogism. But our knowledge was natural, not scientific.

Reduction is either DIRECT or INDIRECT.

DIRECT REDUCTION consists in changing a syllogism of an imperfect figure to one of the first figure that is the exact equivalent of the original syllogism. For instance, the syllogism "No angel is a dog; but every hound is a dog; therefore no hound is an angel," which is a syllogism of the second figure, is changed by direct reduction to the following syllogism of the first figure: "No dog is an angel; but every hound is a dog; therefore no hound is an angel."

INDIRECT REDUCTION rests on the principle "if the consequent is false, the antecedent is false" and consists in showing by a syllogism of the first figure that the denial of the conclusion of a syllogism of an imperfect figure leads to a denial of one of its premises. In the syllogism of the first figure, one premise is the contradictory of the original conclusion; the other premise is one of the premises of the original syllogism; the conclusion is the contradictory of the other premise of the original syllogism. For instance, the following example is a valid syllogism of the second figure:

All hounds are dogs;
but some animals are not dogs;
therefore some animals are not hounds.

To reduce it to a syllogism of the first figure by indirect reduction, you must: (*a*) retain the original major premise; (*b*) use the contradictory of the conclusion as the minor premise; and (*c*) use the contradictory of the original minor premise as your conclusion—as follows:

All hounds are dogs;
but all animals are hounds;
therefore all animals are dogs.

If the original syllogism were not valid, the denial of its conclusion would not involve the denial of a premise.

In all, there are nineteen valid moods of the categorical syllogism if you do not count the subalterns of the five concluding in *A* and *E:* there are four moods of the first figure, four of the second, six of the third, and five of the fourth (or inverted first).

To indicate these nineteen moods, as well as the way of reducing each mood of the imperfect figures to a mood of the first figure, logicians have composed some of the most ingenious mnemonic verses ever written. The verses are Latin hexameters. There are many variants, but the following arrangement, which is found in many English works on logic, is as convenient as any:

Barbara, Celarent, Darii, Ferio*que prioris;*
Cesare, Camestres, Festino, Baroco *secundae;*
Tertia Darapti, Disamis, Datisi, Felapton,
Bocardo, Ferison *habet; quarta insuper addit:*
Bramantip, Camenes, Dimaris, Fesapo, Fresison.

"Barbara, Celarent, Darii, Ferio" indicate the four moods of the first figure; "Cesare, Camestres, Festino, Baroco" indicate the four moods of the second figure; and so on. The vowels of every word (except of the italicized words) indicate the quantity and quality of the propositions (that is, whether they are *a, e, i,* or *o*) in the order of their occurrence in the syllogism—that is, the first vowel stands for the major premise, the second for the minor premise, and the third for the conclusion. Thus "Celarent" signifies a syllogism of the first figure whose major premise is an *E* proposition, whose minor is *A*, and whose conclusion is *E*.

All the key words in these verses begin with the letters *B, C, D,* or *F*. In the words indicating the moods of the second, third, and fourth figures, the first letter indicates the mood of the first figure to which the mood of the imperfect figure is to be reduced. Thus, for instance, "Camestres," which begins with the letter *C*, is to be reduced to "Celarent," which is the mood of the first figure beginning with *C*.

Of the remaining consonants, *s, p, m,* and small *c* have a special meaning:

S signifies that the proposition indicated by the preceding vowel is to be converted by simple conversion.

P signifies that the proposition indicated by the preceding vowel is to be converted *per accidens*—that is, by changing the quantity from universal to particular, or from particular to universal.

M means that the premises are to be interchanged so that the original major premise becomes the minor and vice versa.

Small *c*, when it occurs in the body of a word, means that the mood cannot be reduced directly but only indirectly. The contradictory of the conclusion is to be substituted for the premise indicated by the vowel after which the *c* is placed. It occurs twice: in "Bocardo" and "Baroco." Notice, however, that all moods *can* be reduced by indirect reduction and that these two receive special mention because they can be reduced in no other way.

We shall now give some examples of reduction. Examples 1 and 2 illustrate direct reduction; Examples 3 and 4 illustrate indirect reduction.

Example 1 is a syllogism in "Camestres"—that is, a syllogism of the second figure whose major premise is an *A* proposition, whose minor is *E,* and whose conclusion is *E.*

> 1. All true democracies are free countries;
> but no totalitarian states are free countries;
> therefore no totalitarian states are true democracies.

The *C* of "Camestres" indicates that the syllogism is to be reduced to "Celarent." The *m* indicates that the premises are to be interchanged, the original major becoming the minor and the original minor becoming the major. The first *s* indicates that the original minor premise must be converted by simple conversion, and the second *s* indicates that the original conclusion must be converted by simple conversion. Thus, following the instructions contained in the word "Camestres," we get this syllogism of the first figure:

> No free countries are totalitarian states;
> but all true democracies are free countries;
> therefore no true democracies are totalitarian states.

Example 2 is a syllogism in "Darapti"—that is, a syllogism of the third figure whose major premise is an *A* proposition, whose minor is also *A,* and whose conclusion is *I.*

> 2. Potassium floats on water;
> but potassium is a metal;
> therefore some metal floats on water.

Only one change need be made; it is signified by the *p* in "Darapti." The minor premise must be converted *per accidens*—that is, with a change in quantity. Thus, Example 2 is reduced to the following syllogism of the first figure, a syllogism in "Darii":

> Potassium floats on water;
> but some metal is potassium;
> therefore some metal floats on water.

Example 3 is a syllogism in "Baroco"—that is, a syllogism of the second figure whose major premise is an *A* proposition, whose minor is *O,* and whose conclusion is *O.* The *B* in "Baroco" indicates that it is to be reduced to "Barbara." The small *c* indicates that this can be done only indirectly. The position of the *c* after the second vowel of "Baroco" shows that the contradictory of the conclusion should be used as the minor premise.

3. All birds have feathers;
but some flying animals do not have feathers;
therefore some flying animals are not birds.

In order to reduce this syllogism, (*a*) keep the original major premise; (*b*) as the minor premise use the contradictory of the conclusion; and (*c*) as the conclusion use the contradictory of the minor premise—as follows:

All birds have feathers;
but all flying animals are birds;
therefore all flying animals have feathers.

Example 4 illustrates a syllogism in "Bocardo" and its indirect reduction to "Barbara."

4. Some birds cannot fly;
but all birds have feathers;
therefore some feathered animals cannot fly.

The position of the *c* indicates that the contradictory of the conclusion must be substituted for the original major premise:

All feathered animals can fly;
but all birds have feathers;
therefore all birds can fly.

Exercise

I. Examine the syllogisms in the exercises in the section entitled "Logical Form of the Categorical Syllogism: Figures and Moods," pp. 111-119. Indicate the mood of all valid syllogisms and reduce all valid syllogisms of the imperfect figures to syllogisms of the first figure.

II. Do the same to syllogisms in other exercises, as well as to syllogisms that you yourself construct.

CHAPTER 8

The Hypothetical Syllogism

A HYPOTHETICAL SYLLOGISM is a syllogism that has a hypothetical proposition as one of its premises. There are three kinds of hypothetical syllogisms, corresponding to the three kinds of hypothetical propositions: the conditional ("if . . . , then . . ."), the disjunctive ("either . . . , or . . ."), and the conjunctive ("not both . . . and . . ."). The first of these is by far the most important and—as we shall see later—the others are reducible to it. Before we take up the various kinds of hypothetical syllogisms and the rules of each of them, it will be helpful to enlarge on what we said in Chapter 4 about the relationship of an antecedent and its consequents in inference.[1]

1. THE RELATIONSHIP OF AN ANTECEDENT AND ITS CONSEQUENTS [2]

By an examination of examples we shall draw up the basic laws governing the relationship of an antecedent and its consequents in both valid and invalid inference. These laws are basic principles of all inference—of immediate and mediate inference, and of formal and material inference as well. We are taking them now because they are the immediate foundation of the rules governing the conditional syllogism.

Note that an antecedent is false when only one premise is false, as well as when both premises are false.

[1] We treated of this relationship in Chapter 4, pp. 46-47. See page 159, for a schematic synopsis of the various kinds of hypothetical syllogisms and the rules governing each of them.

[2] See the table on p. 141 for a synopsis of the relationship of an antecedent and its consequent.

Note, too, that where the sequence is invalid, there is, strictly speaking, no sequence, antecedent, or consequent at all; there is, however, an *apparent,* or *pseudo,* sequence, antecedent, and consequent. We give them these names just as we give the name "money" to counterfeit money.

Never forget that when the sequence is invalid, the apparent premises and conclusions are not related to one another at all. Consequently, in an argument whose sequence is invalid, anything can come after anything—truth after truth, truth after falsity, falsity after truth, or falsity after falsity. If the conclusion is true (or false), it is true (or false) independently of the premises.

First, we shall consider the relationship of an antecedent to its consequent and then of a consequent to its antecedent.

a. Antecedent to Consequent

1. *If the antecedent is true and the sequence valid, the consequent is true.*

This law is a particularized statement of the principle of contradiction and is the basic principle of all inference without exception. A denial of this law is an implicit denial of the principle of contradiction. If a true antecedent could have a false consequent, the antecedent would have to be both true and false at the same time—for if it were not false in any respect at all, it would be impossible to derive falsity from it.

This law has been illustrated by every example we have had of syllogisms whose premises are true and whose sequence is valid; hence, there is no need of additional examples now.

2. *If the antecedent is true and the sequence invalid, the consequent is doubtful.*

A consideration of the following two examples will make this law clear.[3] The premises of both examples are obviously true, and the sequence is obviously invalid. Yet one conclusion is true, and the other conclusion is false. If both truth and falsity can come after true premises when the sequence is invalid, the consequent must

[3] This principle may seem too obvious to require illustration. Yet year after year the author has had to write examples like these on the blackboard to clarify the principle for puzzled students; hence, he thought he would save teachers much time and effort by putting them into the book.

be doubtful (unless it can be known—as here—from some other source).

1. Every dog is an animal;
   but no cat is a dog;
   therefore no cat is an animal.

In Example 1 the premises are true; the sequence is invalid because of an illicit process of the major term; the conclusion is obviously false. Example 2 has the same defect as Example 1, but the conclusion is true *by accident.*

2. Every dog is an animal;
   but no stone is a dog;
   therefore no stone is an animal.

Because the sequence of both examples is invalid, the pretended conclusion is unrelated to the premises. It has no more connection with the premises than has the make-believe conclusion of the following pseudo syllogism.

3. Cows give milk;
   but horses pull wagons;
   therefore it will rain tomorrow.

3. *If the antecedent is false and the sequence valid, the consequent is doubtful.*

In the following examples the antecedent is false, since at least one premise is false, and the sequence is formally valid. The conclusion of the Example 4 is true *by accident;* the conclusion of Example 5 is false. This shows that either truth or falsity can flow from falsity and that therefore the consequent is doubtful unless known from some other source.

4. Every dog is an animal;
   but every cat is a dog;
   therefore every cat is an animal.
5. Every dog is a rhinoceros;
   but every cat is a dog;
   therefore every cat is a rhinoceros.

4. *If the antecedent is false and the sequence invalid, the consequent is doubtful.*

We shall now examine two syllogisms whose premises are false and whose sequence is invalid. In each example there is an illicit process of the major term. The conclusion of Example 6 is true; but the conclusion of Example 7 is false.

6. Every cat is a monkey;
   but no cat is a dog;
   therefore no dog is a monkey.
7. Every cat is a dog;
   but no cat is a terrier;
   therefore no terrier is a dog.

If both truth and falsity can come after false premises in a syllogism whose sequence is invalid, the conclusion—it is only a pseudo conclusion—is doubtful (unless it is known from some other source).

b. Consequent to Antecedent

1. *If the consequent is false and the sequence valid, the antecedent is false.*

This is a corollary of the first law on the relationship of an antecedent to its consequent. If only truth can flow from truth, every antecedent from which a false consequent can flow must itself be false. Falsity can come only from falsity (supposing, of course, that the sequence is valid).

2. *If the consequent is false and the sequence invalid, the antecedent is doubtful.*

When the sequence is invalid, anything can come after anything, since the consequent and antecedent are not related to one another at all. Consider:

1. Every cat is a dog;
   but no cat is a terrier;
   therefore no terrier is a dog.
2. No cat is a dog;
   but no terrier is a cat;
   therefore no terrier is a dog.

The consequent "no terrier is a dog" is false. The sequence of each example is invalid, since Example 1 contains an illicit process of the major term and Example 2 has two negative premises. Yet in one instance the pretended conclusion is preceded by true premises and in the other by false premises.

3. *If the consequent is true and the sequence valid, the antecedent is doubtful.*

This law is a corollary of the third law on the relationship of an antecedent to its consequent. Since a true consequent can flow from a false antecedent as well as from a true antecedent, you cannot infer that an antecedent is true because its consequent is true. The conclusion might be true only by accident; that is, for reasons other than those given in the premises. This is illustrated in the following example.

> 3. Squares have three sides;
> but triangles are squares;
> therefore triangles have three sides.

Triangles do have three sides, but not for the reason given here.

4. *If the consequent is true and the sequence invalid, the antecedent is doubtful.*

Obviously, if the antecedent of a true consequent is doubtful even when the sequence is valid, it is also doubtful when the sequence is invalid.

The results of our observations on the relationship of the antecedent and consequent as to truth and falsity in both valid and invalid inference may be tabulated as follows.

Synopsis

A. ANTECEDENT TO CONSEQUENT

	ANTECEDENT (premises)	SEQUENCE	CONSEQUENT (conclusion)
1	True	Valid	TRUE
2	True	Invalid	?
3	False	Valid	?
4	False	Invalid	?

B. CONSEQUENT TO ANTECEDENT

	CONSEQUENT (conclusion)	SEQUENCE	ANTECEDENT (premises)
1	False	Valid	FALSE
2	False	Invalid	?
3	True	Valid	?
4	True	Invalid	?

Only the first law in each group can serve as a basis of valid inference. Hence, the two basic laws with which we are especially concerned are:

1. *If the antecedent is true and the sequence valid, the consequent is true.*
2. *If the consequent is false and the sequence valid, the antecedent is false.*

2. CONDITIONAL SYLLOGISM

A conditional syllogism is one whose major premise is a conditional proposition. There are two general types: the MIXED CONDITIONAL SYLLOGISM, whose minor premise is a categorical proposition—this is the commonest and most important type—and the PURELY CONDITIONAL SYLLOGISM, both of whose premises are conditional propositions.

First we shall explain the nature of the conditional proposition; then we shall give a thorough treatment of the mixed conditional syllogism; and, finally, we shall give a brief treatment of the purely conditional syllogism.

a. Conditional Proposition

A conditional proposition is a compound proposition,[4] of which one member (the "then" clause) asserts something as true on condition that the other member (the "if" clause) is true; for instance, "If it is raining, then the roof is wet." The "if" clause or its equivalent is called the *antecedent;* the "then" clause or its equivalent is called the *consequent.* The assent in a conditional proposition does not bear on either the antecedent or the consequent taken by itself but on the connection between them—that is, on the *sequence.* Thus, if the truth of the consequent really follows upon the fulfillment of the condition stated in the antecedent, the proposition is true even if, taken singly, both the antecedent and the consequent are false. And if the truth of the consequent does not follow upon the fulfill-

[4] Compound propositions express the relationship of clauses toward one another by the use of adverbs and conjunctions, such as "therefore," "because," "if . . . , then . . . ," and so on. Compound propositions are explained in Chapter 14, pp. 286-293.

ment of the condition stated in the antecedent, the proposition is false even if, taken singly, both the antecedent and the consequent are true.

The proposition "If God exists, the world exists" is false, although each member, taken singly, is true—God does exist and the world does exist. But the existence of the world is not a necessary consequent of the existence of God, since God could exist without having created the world. On the other hand, the proposition "If God did not exist, the world would not exist" is true, although the members, taken singly, are false. The proposition is true because the non-existence of the world would really follow upon the non-existence of God.

A conditional proposition, then, is an assertion of a sequence (and nothing else), and is true if this sequence is valid. It makes no difference whether the validity is formal or merely material, as long as the truth of the antecedent necessitates the truth of the consequent.

Not every "if" proposition is a conditional proposition. Sometimes "if" is synonymous with "when," "although," "granted that," and so on. For instance, the proposition "If John is a scoundrel, his brother is a virtuous man" is equivalent to "Although John is a scoundrel, his brother is a virtuous man." Neither does every conditional proposition have an "if" or "unless." The following, for instance, are conditional propositions: "Destroy this temple, and in three days I will rebuild it," "Had I been there, it would not have happened," and "Eat too many green apples, and you'll get sick."

"Unless" is equivalent to "if . . . not." For instance, the proposition "Unless you do penance, you shall all likewise perish" is equivalent to "If you do not do penance, you shall all likewise perish."

b. The Rules of the Mixed Conditional Syllogism

The rules governing the conditional syllogism are direct applications of the laws governing the relationship of an antecedent and its consequents. As we have seen, these laws are:

1. *If the antecedent is true and the sequence valid, the consequent is true.*
2. *If the consequent is false and the sequence valid, the antecedent is false.*

Hence, to posit an antecedent is to posit its consequent, and to sublate a consequent is to sublate its antecedent. Accordingly, supposing that the major premise is a genuine conditional proposition (that is, a conditional proposition whose consequent flows from its antecedent with valid sequence), we may proceed in either of two ways:

1. *We may posit the antecedent in the minor premise and posit the consequent in the conclusion,*
2. *or we may sublate the consequent in the minor premise and sublate the antecedent in the conclusion.*

All other procedures are invalid.

To *posit* a member is to assert it as true. To *sublate* a member is to deny it by asserting either its contradictory or a proposition implying its contradictory. For instance, the proposition "Every man is seated" is sublated not only by its contradictory ("Some man is not seated") but also by its contrary ("No man is seated"). We use the words "posit" and "sublate" rather than "affirm" and "deny"

VALID AND INVALID FORMS OF THE CONDITIONAL SYLLOGISM

MAJOR PREMISE		MINOR PREMISE	CONCLUSION
Conditional proposition (If *A*, then *C*) ("If you have acute appendicitis, you are very sick.")	VALID	(1) POSIT ANTECEDENT → (But *A*) ("But you have acute appendicitis.")	POSIT CONSEQUENT (Therefore *C*) ("Therefore you are very sick.")
	VALID	(2) SUBLATE CONSEQUENT → (But not *C*) ("But you are not very sick."	SUBLATE ANTECEDENT (Therefore not *A*) ("Therefore you do not have acute appendicitis.")
	invalid	3—posit consequent - - - (But *C*) ("But you are very sick.")	posit antecedent (Therefore *A*) ("Therefore you have acute appendicitis.")
	invalid	4—sublate antecedent - - - (But not *A*) ("But you do not have acute appendicitis.")	sublate consequent (Therefore not *C*) ("Therefore you are not very sick.")

because it is inconvenient, not to say confusing, to speak of affirming a negative member by means of a negative proposition or of denying a negative member by means of an affirmative proposition.

The schema and examples on Page 144 will help us understand and remember both the valid and invalid forms of the conditional syllogism. Procedures 1 and 2 (in heavy type) are the valid forms. Procedures 3 and 4 (in light type) are invalid forms, as is clear from the examples. You can be very sick from countless other causes besides acute appendicitis—for instance, from yellow fever, ptomaine poisoning, or diphtheria. Hence, if you are very sick, it does not follow that you have acute appendicitis; and if you do not have acute appendicitis, it does not follow that you are not very sick.

With *A* (or ⬭) signifying "antecedent" and *C* (or □) signifying "consequent," the *valid* forms of the conditional syllogism are symbolized by Numbers 1 and 2 below.

1. If *A*, then *C*;	If ⬭, then □;
but *A*;	but ⬭;
therefore *C*.	therefore □.

2. If *A*, then *C*;	If ⬭ then □;
but not *C*;	but not □;
therefore not *A*.	therefore not ⬭.

The invalid forms are symbolized by Numbers 3 and 4.

3. If *A*, then *C*;	If ⬭, then □;
but *C*;	but □;
therefore *A*.	therefore ⬭.

4. If *A*, then *C*;	If ( ), then [ ];
but not *A*;	but not ( );
therefore not *C*.	therefore not [ ].

The syllogism "If he is not a thief, you will get your purse back; but he is not a thief; therefore you will get your purse back" illustrates the first form. Note that the minor premise posits the antecedent even though it is a negative proposition. We will make this clear by indicating the antecedent with an ellipse and the consequent by a rectangle.

If (he is not a thief), [you will get your purse back];
but (he is not a thief)
therefore [you will get your purse back]

Notice that conditional syllogisms do not have minor, middle, and major terms. Hence, we should not call the subject of the conclusion the minor term or the predicate the major term. This terminology is restricted to the categorical syllogism.

Notice, too, that (unless you have a disguised categorical syllogism) when you posit an antecedent in the minor premise, you must posit it in its entirety. Example 1 (below) is invalid because in the minor premise the antecedent is posited only partially.

1. If every A is a B, every X is a Y;
   but some A is a B;
   therefore some X is a Y.

"Every *A* is a *B*" is an *A* proposition. "Some A is a B" is an *I* proposition. If *I* (the minor premise) is true, *A* (the antecedent) is doubtful. If the antecedent is doubtful, its consequent is doubtful too. Hence, no conclusion can be drawn. The children of a certain grade school recognized the invalidity of this form. They got a quarter holiday when all the children were present and on time for a period of two weeks. No child ever tried to get an extra holiday by arguing as in Example 2.

2. If all were present and on time for two weeks, all will get a quarter holiday;
   but some were present and on time for two weeks;
   therefore some will get a quarter holiday.

To sublate a member, when we are proceeding from the minor premise to the consequent of the major premise, means to posit either its contradictory or some proposition implying its contradictory. In Example 3 the minor premise sublates the consequent by positing its contradictory:

3. If every A is a B, every *X* is a *Y;*
   but some X is not a Y;
   therefore some A is not a B.

In Example 4 the minor premise sublates the consequent by positing its contrary, which implies its contradictory. Notice that both Example 3 and 4 have the same conclusion.

4. If every A is a B, every X is a Y;
   but no X is a Y;
   therefore some A is not a B.

To sublate a member, when we are proceeding from the sublation of the consequent to the sublation of the antecedent, means only to posit the contradictory of the antecedent. For instance, Example 4 cannot conclude validly in the universal proposition "No A is a B," but only in the particular proposition "Some A is not a B." Let us go through Example 4 step by step. The minor premise is an *E* proposition. If *E* is true, then the consequent "every X is a Y" (A) is false. If the consequent is false, the antecedent ("every A is a B") is likewise false. If "every A is a B" is false, its contradictory, but not necessarily its contrary, must be true.[5]

Syllogisms like the one given below in Example 5 need a word of explanation, since they resemble conditional syllogisms. In the major premise a statement is made about *any* man; in the minor premise a statement is made only about *some* men, namely about *us.* What is true of any (or every) man is obviously also true about us. This syllogism does not incur the defect alluded to above where we stated that the minor premise must posit the antecedent in its en-

[5] This would be a convenient place to review the square of opposition of categorical propositions.

tirety because this is a disguised categorical syllogism—and in a categorical syllogism it is permissible to proceed from *any* (or *every*) to *some.* The syllogism given below applies a general principle to a particular instance, just as does a categorical syllogism.

5. If a *man* is convinced that virtue is rewarded and vice punished in the next world, *he* is less likely to follow every impulse;
   but *we* have that conviction;
   therefore we are less likely to follow every impulse.

"If a man is . . . , he is . . ." is equivalent to "Whoever is . . . is . . ." In spite of the fact that these are disguised categorical syllogisms, they are subject, with the qualification made above, to the general rules of the conditional syllogism.

c. The Purely Conditional Syllogism

The purely conditional syllogism, which has conditional propositions for both its premises, has exactly the same forms and the same rules as the mixed conditional syllogism except that the condition expressed in the minor premise must be retained in the conclusion. For instance,

If A is a B, then C is a D;
but if X is a Y, then A is a B;
therefore, *if* X *is a* Y, then *C* is a *D*.

Exercise

I. Complete the following where possible. If no conclusion follows from the premises, state why. When you do the exercises having quantified propositions as members, be sure to remember that, if a proposition is false, its contradictory (but not its contrary) must be true.

1. If A is B, then C is D;
   (1) but A is B; therefore . . . . . .
   (2) but C is D; therefore . . . . . .
   (3) but A is not B; therefore . . . . . .
   (4) but C is not D; therefore . . . . . .

2. If A is not B, C is D;
   (1) but A is B; therefore . . . . . .
   (2) but C is D; therefore . . . . . .
   (3) but A is not B; therefore . . . . . .
   (4) but C is not D; therefore . . . . . .

3. If A is B, C is not D;
   (1) but A is B; therefore . . . . .
   (2) but C is D; therefore . . . . .
   (3) but A is not B; therefore . . .
   (4) but C is not D; therefore . . .

4. If A is not B, C is not D;
   (1) but A is B; therefore . . . . .
   (2) but C is D; therefore . . . . .
   (3) but A is not B; therefore . . .
   (4) but C is not D; therefore . . .

5. If every A is a B, every C is a D;
   (1) but no C is a D; therefore . . .
   (2) but some C is not a D; therefore
   (3) but every A is a B; therefore . .
   (4) but some A is a B; therefore . .

6. If every A is a B, no C is a D;
   (1) but every A is a B; therefore . . .
   (2) but every C is a D; therefore . . .
   (3) but no A is a B; therefore . . . .
   (4) but no C is a D; therefore . . . .
   (5) but some A is a B; therefore . . .
   (6) but some C is a D; therefore . . .
   (7) but some A is not a B; therefore .
   (8) but some C is not a D; therefore .

7. If some A is a B, some C is a D;
   (1) but every A is a B; therefore . . .
   (2) but every C is a D; therefore . . .
   (3) but no A is a B; therefore . . . .
   (4) but no C is a D; therefore . . . .
   (5) but some A is a B; therefore . . .
   (6) but some C is a D; therefore . . .
   (7) but some A is not a B; therefore .
   (8) but some C is not a D; therefore .

8. If some A is not a B, some C is not a D;
   (1) but every A is a B; therefore . . .
   (2) but every C is a D; therefore . . .
   (3) but no A is a B; therefore . . . .
   (4) but no C is a D; therefore . . . .
   (5) but some A is a B; therefore . . .
   (6) but some C is a D; therefore . . .
   (7) but some A is not a B; therefore .
   (8) but some C is not a D; therefore .

II. Indicate the form, or procedure, illustrated by each of the following, and state whether the example is valid or invalid.

1. If A is B, C is D;
but C is D;
therefore A is B.

2. If A is not B, C is not D;
but A is B;
therefore C is D.

3. If A is not B, C is not D;
but C is D;
therefore A is B.

4. If A is B, C is D;
but A is B;
therefore C is D.

5. If the dentist is not skillful, he will cause his patient much pain;
but the dentist is skillful;
therefore he will not cause his patient much pain.

6. If his book possesses literary merit, it will be widely read;
but it will surely be a best seller;
therefore it must possess literary merit.

7. "If you have bad eyes, you'll never make the team."
"But my eyes are all right;
therefore you must admit that I will make the team."

8. If materialism is true, you would expect an intimate connection between the condition of a man's brain and his powers of thinking;
but there is such a connection;
therefore materialism must be true.

9. If a lesion of the brain affects one's thinking, there must be an intimate connection between one's body and one's mind;
but a lesion of the brain does affect one's thinking;
therefore there must be an intimate connection between one's body and one's mind.

10. If that bill passes, rents will rise;
but the bill will not pass;
therefore rents will not rise.

III. Do the same to the following. Which are disguised categorical syllogisms?

1. "Unless a man be born again of water and the spirit, he cannot enter into the kingdom of heaven." But this man has been born of water and the Spirit. Therefore this man can enter into the kingdom of heaven.

2. Eat too many green apples, and you get sick; but Jimmy ate too many green apples; so you know what's happened to Jimmy.

3. If rights have been given us by God, no government can take them away from us; but rights have been given to us by God; therefore no government can take them away from us.

4. The New Testament says: "Unless you do penance, you shall all likewise perish." But I have done penance—I gave up candy during Lent last year; therefore I shall not perish.

5. Student to dean: "You promised to admit me to the medical school and now you say I can't get in. Here's what you said: you said that I would not be eligible unless I got a "B" average; but I did get a "B" average."

6. Whatever else the huge public debt signifies, it does not mean that the United States has fallen into desperate financial straights. If it did, the American dollar would not remain, as it does remain, the most valued and sought-for currency in the world.

7. "The best way to judge a union," commented District 9 business representative Jack Manning this week, "is by its record. No union can have a good record unless it itself is good."

   "And it's easy to look at District 9's record," he added, "because it's right here on the page—the stories about how it has represented the various plants in settlement of contracts, about its success in winning best possible wages and conditions, about activities of its district and local lodges, the credit union, its own veterans organization, etc."

   "And judging by that record, a prospective member should face the future of District 9 representation with confidence."

8. If the facts established the existence of a conspiracy or agreement to restrain or to monopolize trade, or if the facts showed that a restraint of trade or of monopolization had occurred, it would be necessary to determine as a matter of law whether the situation disclosed was condemned by the statutes. However, there is no need in this case to consider that question or to discuss legal principles or precedents because there has been no conspiracy to restrain or to monopolize trade and no restriction or monopolization of the market.

9. Unless you have been bitten by an anopheles mosquito you do not have malaria; and unless you have intermittent fever, you do not have malaria. Now, since you do not have intermittent fever, you have not been bitten by an anopheles mosquito.

10. If security precautions are to be effective, the reasons for them should be understood. Although 600 to 700 scientists working on atomic bomb developments in World War II knew, of necessity, that a controlled chain reaction had been achieved—and therefore big progress made—security was very good. The reason was that the people who knew it believed it so important that they felt they shouldn't talk about it. The secret was kept from the Germans, but it wasn't kept from our Russian allies. That was because, while the danger of a leak to Germany was very plain, the danger of the Russians' knowing of it wasn't generally realized by men in the field at the time.

3. THE DISJUNCTIVE SYLLOGISM

A disjunctive syllogism is one whose major premise is a disjunctive proposition, whose minor premise sublates (or posits) one or more members of the major premise, and whose conclusion posits (or sublates) the other member or members.

a. Disjunctive Proposition

A disjunctive proposition is one that presents various alternatives and asserts that an indeterminate one of them is true. It consists of two or more members joined by the conjunctions "either . . . or." It is sometimes called an *alternative proposition.*

1) **STRICT DISJUNCTIVE.** In a disjunctive proposition in the strict or proper sense, only one member is true and the others are false. If all the members except one are false, the remaining member must be true; and if one member is true, the remaining members must be false. For instance, "Every proposition is either true or false," "Every number is either one hundred or more than one hundred or less than one hundred," and "It is either raining or not raining." A proposition and its contradictory may always be asserted in a disjunctive proposition in the strict sense.

2) **BROAD DISJUNCTIVE.** In a disjunctive proposition in the broad or improper sense, at least one member is true but more than one may be true. For instance, the proposition "Either my brother or I will go" can mean that at least one of us will go, but possibly both of us will go. Often we must decide whether a proposition is

a disjunctive in the strict or in the broad sense by a consideration of the matter and by the context.

Disjunctive propositions are reducible to a series of conditional propositions. To avoid repetition we shall postpone our treatment of the reduction of disjunctive to conditional propositions until we take the reduction of disjunctive syllogisms to conditional syllogisms.

b. Kinds and Rules

There are two kinds of disjunctive syllogisms, corresponding to the two kinds of disjunctive propositions. Each has its own rules.

1) DISJUNCTIVE SYLLOGISM IN THE STRICT SENSE. In a disjunctive syllogism in the strict sense, the *major premise* must be a disjunctive proposition in the strict or proper sense. The *minor premise* either posits or sublates one (or more—but not all) of the members of the major premise. In the *conclusion* there are two possible procedures:

a) If the minor premise posits one or more members of the major premise, the conclusion must sublate each of the other members. For instance,

> The number is either one hundred or more than one hundred or less than one hundred;
> but the number is one hundred;
> therefore the number is neither more nor less than one hundred.

b) If the minor premise sublates one or more of the members of the major premise, the conclusion posits the remaining members, one of which must be true. If more than one member remains, the conclusion must be a disjunctive proposition in the strict sense. For instance,

> The number is either one hundred or more than one hundred or less than one hundred;
> but the number is not one hundred;
> therefore the number is either more than one hundred or less than one hundred.

Every procedure besides those indicated under *a* and *b* is invalid. You may not posit one member and then posit another or sublate one member and then sublate all the others.

A diagram of the following "brain teasers" will make clear what we mean by *positing* or *sublating* a member. Note that in each example the minor posits one member, and the conclusion sublates the other.

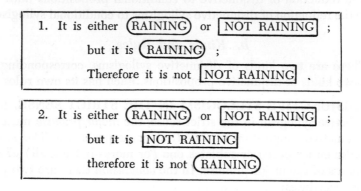

1. It is either (RAINING) or [NOT RAINING] ;
   but it is (RAINING) ;
   Therefore it is not [NOT RAINING] .

2. It is either (RAINING) or [NOT RAINING] ;
   but it is [NOT RAINING]
   therefore it is not (RAINING)

2) DISJUNCTIVE IN THE BROAD SENSE. In a disjunctive syllogism in the broad sense, the major premise is a disjunctive proposition in the broad or improper sense. There is only one valid procedure: to sublate one (or more—but not all) of the members in the minor and posit the remaining member (or members) in the conclusion. If more than one member remains, the conclusion itself must be a disjunctive proposition in the broad sense. For instance:

It is either *A*, or *B*, or *C*, or *D*—at least one of them;
but it is neither *A* nor *B;*
therefore it is either *C* or *D*—at least one of them.

Exercise

I. If possible, complete the following syllogisms. Are the major premises disjunctive propositions in the strict sense or in the broad sense?

1. He is either not speaking or lying;
   but he is not speaking;
   therefore he is . . . .

2. He is either not speaking or lying;
   but he is lying;
   therefore he is . . . .

3. John failed to pass such and such an exam, and is therefore either lazy or lacking in talent;
   but John is lacking in talent;
   therefore John is ....

4. John is either lazy or lacking in talent;
   but John is not lacking in talent;
   therefore John is ....

5. Either the men who drafted the Constitution of the United States were animated by the desire to protect their property and privileges, or they were trying to create a just government based on ethical standards of right. Historical research has shown that the members did indeed wish to protect their property and privileges. And so it is certain that they ....

II. Criticize the following. Some are valid, others are not. Examine the disjunctive propositions to see if they include all possible alternatives. Are they disjunctive propositions in the strict or in the broad sense?

1. The order in the world owes its origin either to mere chance or to an intelligent designer;
   but the order in the world cannot be due to mere chance;
   therefore it must be due to an intelligent designer.

2. He either violated the law, or else he was arrested unjustly;
   but he did violate the law;
   therefore he was not arrested unjustly.

3. Jesus Christ is either God or the world's greatest deceiver;
   but it is impossible to admit that He is the world's greatest deceiver;
   therefore we are compelled to admit that He is God.

4. THE CONJUNCTIVE SYLLOGISM

A conjunctive syllogism is one whose major premise is a conjunctive proposition, whose minor premise posits one member of the major, and whose conclusion sublates the other member of the major.

a. Conjunctive Proposition

A conjunctive proposition is one that denies the simultaneous possibility of two alternatives; for instance, "You cannot eat your cake and have it," "No man can serve both God and Mammon," "A thing cannot both be and not be in the same respect." A conjunctive proposition can be expressed in the formula "Not both A and B," as well as in the formula "Either not A or not B—and maybe neither."

b. Rule for Conjunctive Syllogism

There is only one valid procedure: to posit one member in the minor premise and sublate the other in the conclusion. Two examples will make this rule clear.

1. He cannot be in Chicago and St. Louis at the same time;
   but he is now in Chicago;
   therefore he cannot now be in St. Louis.
2. He cannot be in Chicago and St. Louis at the same time;
   but he is not in Chicago;
   therefore he is in St. Louis.

Example 1 is valid. Example 2 is invalid; obviously there are millions of places in which he might be besides Chicago and St. Louis. Hence, his not being in the one does not prove that he is in the other.

Exercise

1. You cannot be married and be single too;
   but he is married;
   therefore he cannot be single.
2. A diplomat, it is sometimes said, is either not honest or not successful;
   but John Jones is a diplomat who is not successful;
   therefore, it looks as though John Jones is at least honest.
3. It is impossible to study properly and at the same time to listen to the radio;
   but he is listening to the radio;
   therefore he cannot be studying properly.

5. REDUCTION OF DISJUNCTIVES AND CONJUNCTIVES TO CONDITIONAL

Disjunctive and conjunctive propositions are reducible to a series of conditional propositions. Notice that a disjunctive in the strict sense says all that both a disjunctive in the broad sense and conjunctive say; the negative implication ("but not both") is expressed by the conjunctive. The following schema will manifest the relationship of disjunctives and conjunctives to conditional propositions as well as to one another.

DISJUNCTIVE IN THE STRICT SENSE	DISJUNCTIVE IN THE BROAD SENSE	CONJUNCTIVE
"A is either C or D—but not both."	"A is either C or D—maybe both."	"A cannot be both C and D."—"A is either not C or not D—or neither."
This proposition is equivalent to all the following taken together.	This proposition is equivalent only to 1) and 2) taken together.	This proposition is equivalent only to 3) and 4) taken together.
1) If A is not C, A is D.	1) If A is not C, A is D.	1) ————
2) If A is not D, A is C.	2) If A is not D, A is C.	2) ————
3) If A is C, A is not D.	3) ————	3) If A is C, A is not D.
4) If A is D, A is not C.	4) ————	4) If A is D, A is not C.

Disjunctive and conjunctive syllogisms are reducible to compound conditional syllogisms whose major premises consist of the entire series of conditional propositions to which the major premises of the disjunctives and conjunctives are equivalent respectively.

Thus, the syllogism "*A* is either *C* or *D*–but not both; but *A* is *C*; therefore *A* is not *D*" is reducible to the following:

Major:————(1). If *A* is not *C*, *A* is *D*.
(2). If *A* is not *D*, *A* is *C*.
(3). If *A* is *C*, *A* is not *D*.
(4). If *A* is *D*, *A* is not *C*.
Minor:————But *A* is *C*.
Conclusion: ——Therefore *A* is not *D*.

The minor ("*A* is *C*") posits the antecedent of Number 3; hence, in the conclusion we validly posit its consequent. The same minor also sublates the consequent of Number 4; hence, in the conclusion we validly sublate its antecedent. These are the only valid procedures, and each of them gives us the same conclusion "*A* is not *D*."

The syllogism "*A* is either *C* or *D*—maybe both; but *A* is not *C*; therefore *A* is *D*" is reducible to the following:

Major:————(1). If *A* is not *C*, *A* is *D*.
(2). If *A* is not *D*, *A* is *C*.
Minor:————But *A* is not *C*.
Conclusion: ——Therefore *A* is *D*.

The minor ("*A* is not *C*") posits the antecedent of Number 1; hence, in the conclusion we validly posit its consequent. The same minor also sublates the consequent of Number 2; hence, in the conclusion we validly sublate the antecedent. Both processes give us the same conclusion.

Exercise

I. Reduce the following syllogisms to conditional syllogisms, and try to correlate the rules of the disjunctive and conjunctive syllogisms with the rules of the conditional syllogism.

1. He cannot be in New York and London at the same time; but he is now in New York; therefore he cannot now be in London.
2. He cannot be in New York and London at the same time; but he is not now in New York; therefore he must now be in London.
3. You cannot serve God and Mammon;
but many Americans, it seems, are serving Mammon;
therefore, it seems, they cannot be serving God.
4. Every triangle either has three equal sides, or only two equal sides, or no equal sides, but this triangle has no equal sides; therefore it has neither three nor only two equal sides.

II. Do the same with the exercise on disjunctive syllogisms.

SYNOPSIS OF HYPOTHETICAL SYLLOGISMS
KINDS AND RULES

KIND	MAJOR PREMISE	MINOR PREMISE	CONCLUSION
CONDITIONAL	Conditional proposition ("If . . ., then . . .")	VALID (1) POSIT ANTECEDENT	POSIT CONSEQUENT
		VALID (2) SUBLATE CONSEQUENT	SUBLATE ANTECEDENT
		invalid 3—posit consequent	posit antecedent
		invalid 4—sublate antecedent	sublate consequent
DISJUNCTIVE, STRICT	Disjunctive proposition in strict sense ("Either . . ., or . . ., but not both.")	VALID (1) POSIT ONE MEMBER	SUBLATE EACH OF THE OTHERS
		VALID (2) SUBLATE ONE (OR MORE) OF MEMBERS	POSIT OTHER(S WITH STRICT DISJUNCTIVE) [4]
		invalid 3—posit one member	posit another
		invalid 4—sublate one member	sublate all the others
DISJUNCTIVE, BROAD	Disjunctive proposition in broad sense ("Either . . ., or . . ., maybe both.")	VALID (1) SUBLATE ONE (OR MORE BUT NOT ALL) OF THE MEMBERS	POSIT THE OTHER(S WITH BROAD DISJUNCTIVE) [4]
		invalid 2—posit one member	sublate another
CONJUNCTIVE	Conjunctive proposition ("Not both, maybe neither.")	VALID (1) POSIT ONE MEMBER	SUBLATE THE OTHER
		invalid 2—sublate one member	posit the other

4 In the rules for the conclusion, the part enclosed in parentheses states what is to be done if the major premise is a disjunctive proposition of more than two members

CHAPTER 9

Special Types of Syllogism

1. ENTHYMEME

An enthymeme is a syllogism in which one of the premises or the conclusion is omitted. There are three orders of enthymemes. An enthymeme is of the first order if the major premise is omitted, of the second order if the minor premise is omitted, and of the third order if the conclusion is omitted. The enthymeme is not a distinct form of syllogism, but an incomplete statement of any of the forms we have already studied.

Let us examine some of the ways in which the following categorical syllogism can be expressed in enthymemes.

Major: What is spiritual is immortal.
Minor: But the human soul is spiritual.
Concl: Therefore the human soul is immortal.

1. *Minor:* The human soul is spiritual
   Concl: and therefore immortal.
2. *Concl:* The human soul is immortal
   Minor: because it is spiritual.
3. *Major:* What is spiritual is immortal.
   Concl: For this reason the human soul is immortal.
4. *Concl:* The human soul is immortal,
   Major: since whatever is spiritual is immortal.
5. *Minor:* The human soul is spiritual,
   Major: and whatever is spiritual is immortal.

Examples 1 and 2 are enthymemes of the first order; 3 and 4 are of the second order; 5 is of the third order.

We can recognize an enthymeme as categorical as soon as we

discover three syllogistic terms. Thus, "*A* is *B;* therefore *A* is *C*" is obviously categorical, for it has the three syllogistic terms *A*, *B*, and *C*.

An enthymeme is generally hypothetical if neither the subject nor the predicate of the conclusion occurs in the antecedent. For instance, "It is raining; therefore Peter is not working" is obviously hypothetical, the unexpressed member being "If it is raining, Peter is not working."

The enthymeme is the most natural way of applying a general principle to a particular case and the commonest expression of syllogistic reasoning. Outside of logic books you will find very few completely expressed syllogisms, but you will find enthymemes on almost every page you read.

The weakness of arguments is sometimes concealed by the suppression of false or doubtful premises. Often the only way to test the validity and truth of an enthymeme is to express the omitted member.

Since the enthymeme is not a distinct form of syllogism but merely an abridged statement of the usual forms, it has no special rules.

Notice that many "because" clauses are not intended to be a proof that a thing took place but an explanation of why it took place. The same is true of the antecedents of many "therefore" clauses.

Exercise

I. Using the following format, make complete syllogisms of the enthymemes given below. First pick out the conclusion, expressing it if it is not already given. Then fill in the other members, supplying those that are not expressed. Finally criticize the examples by applying to them the various rules of inference.

Model

The open shop is good for unions because it makes them more democratic.

Major: Whatever makes unions more democratic is good for unions.

Minor: But the open shop (is something that) makes unions more democratic.

Concl: Therefore the open shop is good for unions.

1. Communism, simply because it is a godless philosophy, contains within itself the seeds of its own destruction.
2. Teachers' unions are not desirable because they take away local control of schools.
3. "Blessed are the poor in spirit, for theirs is the kingdom of heaven." (*Mt.* 5/3)
4. "Whoever is not just is not of God; nor is he just who does not love his brother." (1 *Jn.* 3/11)
5. "Everyone who hates his brother is a murderer. And you know that no murderer has eternal life in him." (1 *Jn.* 3/15)
6. He's dangerous; every ambitious man is dangerous.
7. The weather is threatening; so I refuse to go.
8. The world cannot be self-existent; therefore it must be created.
9. He's in Boston; therefore he cannot be in Chicago.
10. We should elect Smith; he's always been an honorable man.
11. Hot summer weather is not the time for primaries or any kind of election. Too many voters are on vacation or too hot to be interested.
12. He's breathing! He must still be alive.
13. From an account of a Kentucky Derby: "Anything, of course, that attracts a crowd of 100,000 is a worthwhile spectacle."
14. If human life is important and sacred—and Christ has proved to us that it is important and sacred—then the way in which human life enters the world is most important and sacred.
15. I hold that the law regulating such-and-such is constitutional, and as proof I submit the following quotation from Chief Justice John Marshall:
    "Let the end be legitimate, let it be within the scope of the Constitution; and all means which are appropriate, which are plainly consistent with the letter and spirit of the Constitution, are constitutional."
16. Any man who works for one company for a long time becomes, in effect, part owner. This man cannot be fired as easily as the man who was hired the day before yesterday.
17. Education is impossible in many parts of the United States today because free inquiry and free discussion are impossible.
18. "I eagerly look forward to reading your editorial page even though it is obvious to any thinking and intelligent person that your viewpoint differs from that of 90% of the editors of the

country and therefore must be wrong." (From a letter to the editor)

19. John Doe does many good deeds and should therefore hold the office of dogcatcher.
20. What is thinking and how does one go about doing it? This is not an academic question because I have asked several informed friends and their answers are both confused and confusing.
21. Death is an act of God and, as such, must be respected and praised.

II. Construct enthymemes from syllogisms given in previous exercises.

III. Find examples of enthymemes in newspapers, magazines, books, and so on, and make complete syllogisms from them. Then criticize your completed syllogisms by applying to them the appropriate rules.

2. EPICHIREME

An epichireme is a syllogism in which a proof is joined to one or both of the premises. The proof is often expressed by a causal clause ("for," "because," "since," and so on). The premise to which a proof is annexed is an enthymeme. Sometimes the main syllogism is also an enthymeme.

We must be careful to distinguish the main syllogism from the proofs of a premise. In the following example the proofs of the premises are enclosed in parentheses.

Major: If man has spiritual activities, he has a spiritual soul, (because every activity requires an adequate principle).
Minor: But (since man knows immaterial things), man has spiritual activities.
Concl: Therefore man has a spiritual soul.

In the example given below, the antecedent is a proof of the unexpressed minor premise. The major premise of the main syllogism of this argument is also unexpressed because it is considered too obvious to require statement.

What atrophies those national traits which make America big, virile, and wealthy is bad; hence, we oppose all additions to federal power.

Fully expressed, this argument is as follows (the original argument is written in capital letters):

Major: We oppose whatever is bad.
Minor: But all additions to federal power are bad.
Proof: WHAT ATROPHIES THOSE NATIONAL TRAITS WHICH MAKE AMERICA BIG, VIRILE, AND WEALTHY ARE BAD;
but all additions to federal power atrophy those national traits which make America big, virile, and wealthy;
therefore all additions to federal power are bad.
Concl: HENCE, WE OPPOSE ALL ADDITIONS TO FEDERAL POWER.

Exercise

Analyze the following arguments. First, pick out the main syllogism, supplying unexpressed members where necessary; then pick out the proofs of the premises, and then—if there are any—the proofs of these proofs.

1. It looks like rain. It's overcast and the humidity is very high. But if it looks like rain, I don't care to go. It's rather silly to risk getting soaked. So count me out.
2. What is spiritual is immortal, because, since it is simple and intrinsically independent of matter, it cannot be destroyed either by resolution into parts or by separation from matter. But the human soul is spiritual. Otherwise you could not explain many of its activities: it knows spiritual things, it wills, it reflects. That's why the human soul must be immortal.
3. "This community needs Raymond Gorsch as mayor. Only a strong leader can put the city back on its feet financially. Only a willing worker can fight the forces of intolerance threatening our society. Only a true patriot can give us the real democratic government that we demand. Therefore we must elect Gorsch mayor."
4. A fair trade law is of the utmost importance to the small business man who, because he cannot buy merchandise in quantity and therefore as cheaply as large concerns, is forced either to lose business or money and in some cases both.

3. POLYSYLLOGISM

A Polysyllogism, as the name suggests (*poly* is the Greek word for "many"), is a series of syllogisms so arranged that the conclusion of one is the premise of the next. Each individual syllogism must adhere to the rules of the simple syllogism.

4. SORITES

A sorites is a polysyllogism consisting of a series of simple syllogisms whose conclusions, except for the last, are omitted. It is either categorical or conditional.

a. Categorical Sorites

A categorical sorites consists of a series of simple categorical syllogisms of the first figure whose conclusions, except for the last, are omitted. It links or separates the subject and predicate of the conclusion through the intermediacy of many middle terms.

There are two kinds of categorical sorites, the Aristotelian (or progressive) and the Goclenian (or regressive). In the Aristotelian sorites the predicate of each premise is the subject of the following premise, and the subject of the first premise is the subject of the conclusion. In the Goclenian sorites the same premises occur, but their order is reversed. Hence, the two types differ from one another only accidentally. The following diagrams reveal the differences in their construction and manner of procedure. The first diagram displays the arrangement of the premises and indicates which of them may be particular and which negative.

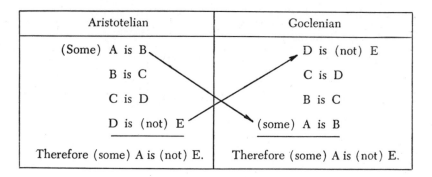

Aristotelian	Goclenian
(Some) A is B	D is (not) E
B is C	C is D
C is D	B is C
D is (not) E	(some) A is B
Therefore (some) A is (not) E.	Therefore (some) A is (not) E.

The second diagram indicates the quantitative relationship of the terms.

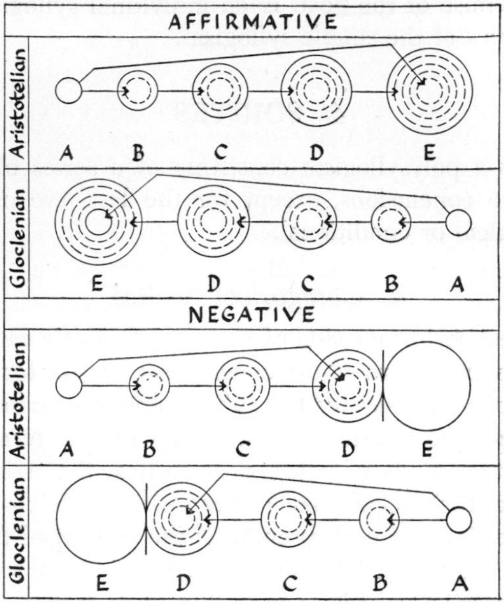

Notice (in the diagram below) how all the conclusions except the last are suppressed. In the diagram we supply the missing conclusions in the parentheses. Each simple syllogism is of the first figure, but the major and minor premises are reversed.

A is B
B is C
(therefore A is C)
C is D
(therefore A is D)
D is E
Therefore A is E.

There are TWO SPECIAL RULES FOR THE SORITES. For the Aristotelian sorites they are:

1. *All but the last premise must be affirmative. If a premise is negative, the conclusion must be negative.*
2. *All but the first premise must be universal. If the first premise is particular, the conclusion must be particular.*

Obviously, for the Goclenian sorites the rules are the reverse of these, and only the first premise may be negative and only the last particular.

If the first rule is violated, there is an illicit process of the major term. As the predicate of an affirmative proposition the term "E" is particular in the premise; but as the predicate of a negative proposition it is universal in the conclusion. (See the diagram on the left.)

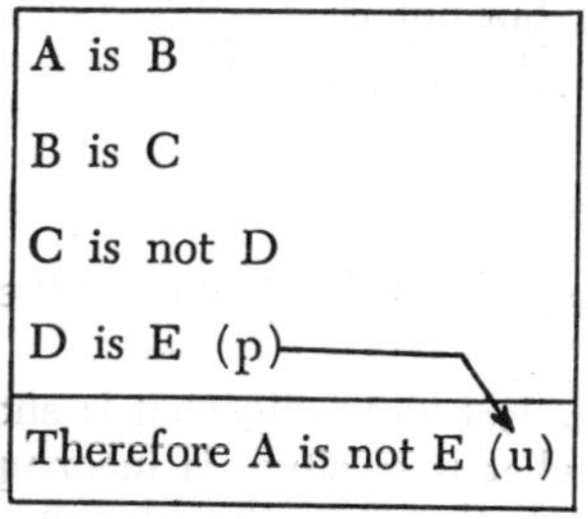

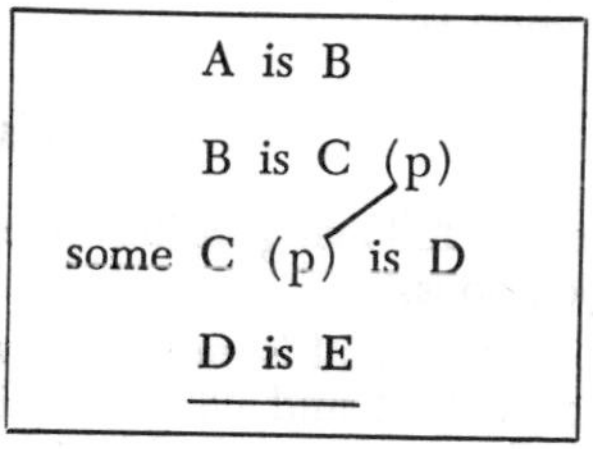

If the second rule is violated, there is an undistributed middle. (See the diagram on the right.)

These two rules are corollaries of the rules of the first figure of the categorical syllogism.

b. Conditional Sorites

A conditional sorites is one whose premises contain a series of conditional propositions, each of which (except the first) has as its antecedent the consequent of the preceding premise. Sometimes all the premises, including the last, are conditional propositions, and then the conclusion must be a conditional proposition. Sometimes the last premise is a categorical proposition, and then the conclusion must be a categorical proposition.

Keep in mind that to posit an antecedent is to posit not only its proximate consequents but also its remote consequents, and to sublate a consequent is to sublate not only its proximate antecedents but also its remote antecedents. Thus in the series "If *A*, then *B*;

if *B,* then *C;* if *C,* then *D;* if *D,* then *E,*" to posit *A* is to posit *B, C, D,* and *E;* and to sublate *E* is to sublate *D, C, B,* and *A.* Hence, we can argue in any of the following ways.

1. If A, then B;
   if B, then C;
   if C, then D;
   if D, then E;
   ———
   therefore, if A, then E.

2. If A, then B;
   if B, then C;
   if C, then D;
   if D, then E;
   ———
   therefore, if not E, then not A.

3. If A, then B;
   if B, then C;
   if C, then D;
   if D, then E;
   but A;
   ———
   therefore E.

4. If A, then B;
   if B, then C;
   if C, then D;
   if D, then E;
   but not E;
   ———
   therefore not A.

Exercise

Consider the following sorites. Are they valid, or invalid? Supply the missing conclusions.

1. The human soul is endowed with intellect and will; what is endowed with intellect and will is spiritual; what is spiritual is incorruptible; and what is incorruptible is immortal; therefore the human soul is immortal.
2. The more you exercise, the hungrier you get; the hungrier you get, the more you eat; the more you eat, the fatter you get; the fatter you get, the less you move around; therefore the more you exercise, the less you move around.
3. Peace begets prosperity; prosperity begets pride; pride begets war; war begets poverty; therefore peace begets poverty.
4. "Why, if thou never wast at court, thou never sawest good manners; if thou never sawest good manners, then thy manners must be wicked; and wickedness is sin, and sin is damnation. Therefore, thou art in a parlous state, shepherd." (*As You Like It,* Act III, Scene ii)
5. Since winesaps are apples, and apples are trees, and trees are plants, winesaps must be plants.
6. "For those whom he has foreknown he has also predestined to become conformed to the image of his Son, that he should be the firstborn among many brethren. And those whom he has predestined, them he has also called; and those whom he has called, them he has also justified; and those whom he has justified, them he has also glorified." (*Romans* 8/29-30) Therefore, those whom he has foreknown he has also glorified.

7. Education implies teaching; teaching implies knowledge; knowledge is truth; the truth is everywhere the same; hence, education should be everywhere the same.
8. The prudent man is temperate; the temperate man is constant; the constant man is imperturbed; but he who is imperturbed is without sadness; and he who is without sadness is happy; therefore the prudent man is also happy. (Seneca, *Epistle* 85)

5. DILEMMA

The dilemma is a syllogism that is both conditional and disjunctive. The major premise is a compound conditional proposition consisting of two or more simple conditional propositions connected by "and" or its equivalent. The minor premise is a disjunctive proposition that alternatively posits the antecedents (constructive dilemma), or sublates the consequents (destructive dilemma), of each of these simple conditional propositions.

In the constructive dilemma the disjunctive proposition is commonly placed first; in the destructive dilemma, however, the conditional propositions are commonly placed first. The conclusion is either a categorical or a disjunctive proposition.

If the disjunctive premise has three members, the syllogism is a trilemma; if it has many members, the syllogism is a polylemma. But the name "dilemma" is also applied to these.

a. Forms of the Dilemma

The dilemma has four forms. It is either constructive or destructive, and each of these is either simple or complex. The schema on Page 170 displays the structure of these four forms.

1) In the **SIMPLE CONSTRUCTIVE DILEMMA** the conditional premise infers the same consequent from all the antecedents presented in the disjunctive proposition. Hence, if any antecedent is true, the consequent must be true. This form is illustrated by the reflections of a man trapped in an upper story of a burning building.

I must either jump or stay—there is no other alternative.
But { if I jump, I shall die immediately (from the fall);
if I stay, I shall die immediately (from the fire);
Therefore I shall die immediately.

CONSTRUCTIVE DILEMMA (The disjunctive proposition posits the antecedents of the conditional propositions; the conclusion posits their consequents.)	
1. SIMPLE CONSTRUCTIVE	2. COMPLEX CONSTRUCTIVE
Either A or B. But { if A, then Z; if B, then Z; Therefore Z.	Either A or B. But { if A, then X; if B, then Y; Therefore either X or Y.

DESTRUCTIVE DILEMMA (The disjunctive proposition sublates the consequents of the conditional propositions, the conclusion sublates their antecedents.)	
3. SIMPLE DESTRUCTIVE	4. COMPLEX DESTRUCTIVE
If A, then X and Y. But { either not X or not Y Therefore not A.	If A, then X; and if B, then Y. But { either not X or not Y. Therefore either not A or not B.

2) In the **COMPLEX CONSTRUCTIVE DILEMMA** the conditional premise infers a different consequent from each of the antecedents presented in the disjunctive proposition. If any antecedent is true, its consequent is likewise true. But since the antecedents are posited disjunctively and since a different consequent flows from each of them, the consequents must likewise be posited disjunctively. The men who brought to Jesus the woman caught in adultery had this form of dilemma in mind.

Jesus will either urge that she be stoned to death or that she be released without stoning.

But { if he urges the first, he will make himself unpopular with the people because of his severity;
if he urges the second, he will get into trouble with the Jewish authorities for disregarding the law of Moses. }

Therefore he will either become unpopular with the people or get into trouble with the Jewish authorities.

You will recall how Jesus *slipped between the horns* of this dilemma by writing on the sand and saying, "Let him who is without sin cast the first stone." [1]

3) In the **SIMPLE DESTRUCTIVE DILEMMA** the conditional premise infers more than one consequent from the same antecedent. If any of the consequents is false, the antecedent is false. Hence, since the disjunctive sublates the consequents alternatively, at least one of them must be false, and consequently the antecedent must also be false. This type is not distinct from a conditional syllogism in which the consequent is sublated in the minor premise and the antecedent is sublated in the conclusion. Still, on account of the disjunctive premise, it is generally called a dilemma. The following example illustrates this form.

If I am to pass the examination, I must do two things—I must study all night and I must also be mentally alert as I write.

But { either I will not study all night,
or I will not be mentally alert as I write. }

Therefore I will not pass the examination.

4) In the **COMPLEX DESTRUCTIVE DILEMMA** the conditional premise infers a different consequent from each antecedent. The disjunctive premise sublates these consequents alternatively, and the conclusion sublates their antecedents alternatively. For instance:

If John were wise, he would not speak irreverently of holy things in jest; and if he were good, he would not do so in earnest.

But { he does it either in jest
or in earnest. }

Therefore John is either not wise or not good.

[1] John 8/1-11

b. Rules of the Dilemma, Answering a Dilemma

The dilemma is subject, first of all, to the general rules of the conditional syllogism. The minor premise, as in the conditional syllogism, must either posit the antecedents or sublate the consequents of the conditional propositions. If the minor premise has posited the antecedents, the conclusion must posit the consequents, either absolutely or disjunctively—depending on the type. If the minor premise has sublated the consequents, the conclusion must sublate the antecedents, and so on, as explained above.

The dilemma also has the following special rules:

1. *The disjunction must state all pertinent alternatives.*
2. *The consequents in the conditional proposition must flow validly from the antecedents.*
3. *The dilemma must not be subject to rebuttal.*

The names traditionally given to the ways of ANSWERING A DILEMMA will not puzzle us if we keep in mind that the alternatives presented in a dilemma are called "horns" and that a dilemma is sometimes called a *syllogismus cornutus* or "horned argument."

If you show that the first rule is violated, you *escape between the horns,* as in the following example:

> I must either devote myself to the interests of my soul, or to secular pursuits. If I devote myself to the interests of my soul, my business will fail; if I devote myself to secular pursuits, I shall lose my soul. Therefore either my business will fail, or else I shall lose my soul.

There is a third alternative, to devote myself both to the interests of my soul and to secular pursuits with the proper subordination of the latter to the former.

If you show that the second rule has been violated, you *take the dilemma by the horns.* For instance, in the following example you can show that at least one of the consequents does not flow from its antecedent. This dilemma is attributed to the Caliph Omar, and is quoted in many logic books.

> The books in the library of Alexandria are either in conformity with the Koran or not in conformity with it. If they are in conformity with it, they are superfluous and should be burned; if they are not in conformity with it, they are pernicious and likewise should be burned. Therefore the books in the library of Alexandria should be burned.

A book might be in conformity with the Koran and still be useful in that it can explain the Koran and treat of subjects not mentioned in the Koran.

If you show that consequents other than the unfavorable ones given in the dilemma flow from the antecedents, you *butt back* or or make a *rebuttal.* The argument of the Athenian mother who tried to dissuade her son from entering public life is a classic example. The mother argued:

> If you say what is just, men will hate you; if you say what is unjust, the gods will hate you. But you must either say what is just or what is unjust. Therefore you will be hated.

The son replied:

> If I say what is just, the gods will love me; if I say what is unjust, men will love me. But I must say either the one or the other. Therefore I will be loved.

Exercise

Criticize the following dilemmas. Supply the missing members of those that are stated incompletely.

1. A universal skeptic (that is, one who denies that anything can be known for certain) is refuted as follows:

   Either you regard it as certain that nothing can be known for certain, or else you regard it as uncertain. If you regard it as certain, you hold at least one thing as certain; if you regard it as uncertain, you also hold at least one thing as certain, namely, that you so regard it. Therefore you hold something as certain.

2. Tertullian criticizes the policy of the Emperors Trajan and Marcus Aurelius in persecuting the Christians:

   The Christians have either committed crimes, or else they have not. If they have committed crimes, your policy is unjust in that you forbid them to be hunted out: if they have not committed crimes, your policy is unjust in that you punish those who have been brought to your attention. Therefore your policy is unjust.

3. St. Augustine gave a famous dilemma to prove that the Christian religion is from God. To evaluate the argument correctly you must keep in mind the circumstances of the rapid spread of Christianity.

   The Christian religion spread throughout the pagan world either with miracles or without them. If with miracles, it is from God, for otherwise He would not have worked miracles in its favor; if without miracles, it is also from God, for spreading without miracles would itself be a great miracle. Therefore the Christian religion is from God.

4. The dilemma of Protagoras the Sophist and its rebuttal by his pupil Euathlus are among the most celebrated in history. Protagoras agreed to teach rhetoric to Euathlus on condition that half of the fee be paid at the completion of the instruction and the other half as soon as Euathlus won his first case. Euathlus delayed practicing law until finally Protagoras brought suit against him for the unpaid half of the fee. Arguing with Euathlus before the jury, Protagoras addressed him as follows:

   If you lose this case, you should pay me the remainder of the fee by the judgment of the court; if you win, you should pay according to the terms of our contract. But you will either win or lose the case. Therefore in either case you should pay me.

   Euathlus retorted:

   The judges will give their verdict either in my favor or in your favor. If in my favor, I will not have to pay, for they will have absolved me from my obligation; if in your favor, I will not have to pay because of the terms of our contract. Therefore in neither case will I have to pay.

   Perhaps Protagoras ought to have allowed Euathlus to win, and then to have sued him a second time. Then his case would have been clear.

5. When you observe that the room of another is neat and orderly, say to yourself, "This is the way he keeps his soul." When you see a room that is poorly cared for, say to yourself, "This holy man is so wrapped up in spiritual things that he has no concern for trivial, temporal matters."

   Rebutt this dilemma.

6. "Recently a union tried to organize the Southern factories. The owner did not object, but the townspeople did. That put the owner on the spot. If he didn't insist on unionization, his New York plants could be struck. If he did insist on it, he would be in bad with the townsfolk and operators of other mills in the area. A fiery cross was burned in front of the home of a plant superintendent as a reminder that some Southerners don't like unions."

7. When Alice in Wonderland finds the small cake she says: "Well, I'll eat it, and if it makes me grow larger, I can reach the key; and if it makes me grow smaller, I can creep under the door: so either way I'll get into the garden, and I don't care which happens."

8. When one of the Evangelists is alone in stating something, his testimony is to be rejected as isolated; when several say the same thing,

they must have copied from one another, and their testimony is equally worthless.

9. Either I am fated to die today or else I am not. If I am fated to die today, it is futile for me to try to avoid danger; on the other hand, if I am not fated to die today, it is needless for me to try to avoid danger. Hence, it is either futile or needless for me to try to avoid danger.

10. "As was to be expected, the President's nomination of Newbold Morris to conduct his long-promised investigation into wrongdoing in the executive establishment met with a mixed reception. In fact, Mr. Truman was taking a grave risk for himself and his party. If Mr. Morris does uncover more scandals, the Democrats will be further smirched; if he announces he has found nothing serious, the Republicans will cry "whitewash." Of course, the President's reasoning must have gone the other way: if scandals do develop, he can claim credit for cleaning them up; if nothing comes up, he can say that an honorable Republican found things all right." (*America,* Feb. 16, 1952)

CHAPTER 10

Fallacies

A FALLACY is a deceptive argument; that is, an argument that seems to be conclusive but is actually not conclusive. Either its sequence seems to be valid but is actually invalid, or else its premises seem to be true but are actually false. The word "fallacy" is derived from the Latin word *fallo,* which means "I deceive." An appearance of validity and truth is essential to a fallacy, for it would deceive no one unless it at least seemed to be valid and true. Violations of the rules of the syllogism were not traditionally regarded as fallacies because it was thought that they would deceive no one; but nowadays the term "fallacy" is also applied to them, and we speak of the fallacy of an undistributed middle, the fallacy of an illicit process of the major term, and so on. Mere errors in fact or principle are not fallacies in the Aristotelian sense.

The term "fallacy" is sometimes applied to ambiguous statements that are not actually parts of an argument. The reason for this is that they might be understood in a sense in which they are not true and thus be an occasion of deception. Strictly speaking, though, such statements are not fallacies but merely occasions of fallacies.

An intended fallacy is called a "sophism." It gets this name because it was a favorite device of the ancient Greek Sophists, who claimed to be able to prove either side of any question.

Should logic treat of fallacies? Logic is the science and art of correct thinking. Fallacies are bad thinking; consequently you might suppose that the treatment of fallacies has no place in logic. Moreover, logic treats primarily of the *formal* conditions of valid inference. Many fallacies, on the other hand, arise from the *matter* of inference rather than from defective form and might consequently seem to lie outside the scope of logic.

Yet, in spite of these objections, ever since the time of Aristotle, treatises on logic have always included a discussion of fallacies, and many good reasons can be advanced in support of this traditional practice.

In the first place, correct forms of inference are often best illustrated and explained by contrasting them with incorrect forms. Indeed, you cannot know the correct forms of thought without simultaneously knowing the incorrect forms; you necessarily know both of them together. A physician aims at procuring health but nevertheless studies diseases; so, too, a logician, who aims at attaining correctness of thought, must also study the pathology of thought. You cannot think correctly unless you avoid thinking incorrectly; and you can neither avoid incorrect thinking yourself nor detect incorrect thinking in others unless you are skilled in recognizing incorrect forms of thought.

Secondly, the study of fallacies will serve as a review of much of what we have already seen. You should not consider fallacies in isolation from the other parts of logic, but as intimately connected with them. When you study the various kinds of fallacies, you should make a special effort to note which of the general rules of inference are violated by each of them.

Thirdly, a readiness in recognizing fallacies will help you apply the principles of logic to everything you read or hear and put you on your guard against the more common sources of deception. Books, magazines, newspapers, and spoken discourse are full of fallacies; if you are skilled in recognizing them, you are less likely to be duped.

Finally, the ability to call a fallacy by name will give you a great advantage over an opponent in discussion and debate. A person unfamiliar with fallacies often has a vague suspicion that an argument is defective or even knows for certain that it has some flaw, but still cannot say exactly what is wrong with it. A person familiar with fallacies, on the contrary, can put his finger right on the flaw and thus protect himself from being embarrassed and abused by sophisms.

No classification of fallacies is entirely satisfactory. In the first place, no classification is exhaustive. Indeed, it is probably impossible to draw up a complete list of fallacies; all we hope to do is to list the more common and more important types. In the second place, the members of the classification overlap, because the same fallacious argument can generally be referred to various headings as it is considered from different points of view. This difficulty of classification springs from the very nature of fallacies. Fallacies are error, and error is multiple; the same argument can labor under manifold defects.

The following classification, which is substantially that of Aristotle, seems as satisfactory as any. It has the added advantage of having a long-established tradition behind it.

Aristotle divides fallacies into those of language and those not of language. In this classification we go beyond the confines of formal logic, and consider the thought content, as well as the form, of argumentation.

1. FALLACIES OF LANGUAGE

Aristotle lists six fallacies of language. The first five are various kinds of ambiguity and consist in using an expression in different senses in different parts of an argument but proceeding as though it were used in the same sense. A categorical syllogism in which any of these fallacies occurs has the equivalent of four terms. The middle term is the one that is most often used in two senses.

Aristotle's sixth fallacy of language is an invalid argument that infers similarity of meaning from similarity of word construction.

These six fallacies of language, with the exception of the fallacies of composition and division, are of less importance today than in ancient times when oral disputation according to set forms was more common than now. We shall treat of them very briefly.

a. Equivocation

Equivocation consists in using a word that has the same spelling or sound, but a different meaning, in different parts of an argument. The word need not be an equivocal term [1] in the strict sense; the

[1] Equivocal terms are terms that are applied to their inferiors in a completely different sense. Analogous terms are terms that are applied to their inferiors in a sense that is partly the same and partly different. Equivocal and analogous terms, as well as the supposition of terms, are explained at length in Chapter 12, pp. 224-236.

ambiguous use of an analogous term or a change in the way a term is used (that is, an illegitimate shift of supposition) can suffice. Puns illustrate this fallacy.

The essence of the fallacy consists in using a term in an acceptable sense in a premise, and thus tricking people into admitting the premise, and then drawing a conclusion as though the term had been used in that premise in an unacceptable sense.

Notice, for instance, the equivocal use of "natural" in the following example:

> What is natural is good;
> but to make mistakes is natural;
> therefore to make mistakes is good.

In its first occurrence, the word "natural" means "constituting or perfecting a nature"; in its second occurrence, it means "due to the limitations of nature." Only in the first sense of the word is it true that what is natural is good. (This syllogism also incurs the fallacy of four terms.)

Notice, too, the equivocal use of "violate a law" and of "man" in the following two examples:

> He who violates a law should be punished;
> but when we illustrate fallacies we violate many laws;
> therefore when we illustrate fallacies we should be punished.

He who violates a moral law perhaps should be punished but hardly one who violates a law of logic.

> "Man" can be predicated of many;
> but you are a man;
> therefore you can be predicated of many.

The concept "man" can be predicated of many; however, you are not the concept "man" but a real man.

b. Amphiboly

Amphiboly is syntactical ambiguity. It consists in using a phrase whose individual words are univocal but whose meaning is ambiguous because the grammatical construction can be interpreted in various ways.

When King Pyrrhus asked the oracle whether he would conquer the Romans, the oracle answered in the following Latin hexameter:

Aio te, Aeacide, Romanos vincere posse.
(Pyrrhus the Romans can, I say, subdue.)

Who was to conquer whom? King Pyrrhus made the disastrous mistake of thinking that he was to conquer the Romans rather than that the Romans were to conquer him.

Similar to this is the response that the oracle gave to King Croesus when he was planning a war against the Persians.

If Croesus wages war against the Persians,
he will destroy a mighty kingdom.

Whose kingdom? His own? Or the Persians'? The oracle did not say, but the event proved that it was to be his own.

c. Composition

The fallacy of composition consists in taking words or phrases as a unit when they should be taken separately. Cajus falls into this fallacy when he admits that thieves and murderers are excluded from the kingdom of heaven, but then denies that he himself is excluded since he is only a thief but not a murderer. In the premise, the words "thieves and murderers" are taken distributively; that is, both thieves and murderers are excluded from the kingdom, so that you are excluded if you are either a thief or a murderer (or, of course, both). But Cajus makes the mistake of assuming that only those are excluded who are both thieves and murderers. He has taken words together and as a unit when he should have taken them separately, or distributively.

A classic example of the fallacy of composition is found in John Stuart Mill's *Utilitarianism:*

> No reason can be given why the general happiness is desirable, except that each person, as far as he believes it to be attainable, desires his own happiness. This, however, being a fact, we have not only all the proof the case admits of, but all which it is possible to require, that happiness is a good; that each person's happiness is a good to that person, and the general happiness, therefore, a good to the aggregate of all persons.

The fallacy consists in arguing from the alleged fact that each individual man seeks his own happiness without any regard for the happiness of the aggregate of men to the conclusion that each individual seeks the happiness of the aggregate. From the alleged fact that *A* seeks *Ha* (happiness of *A*), *B* seeks *Hb*, *C* seeks *Hc*, *D* seeks *Hd*, and so on, he argues that *A* seeks *Habcd*, *B* seeks *Habcd*, *C* seeks *Habcd*, and *D* seeks *Habcd*.

d. Division

The fallacy of division is the converse of the fallacy of composition and consists in taking separately what should be taken together as a unit. Did one straw break the camel's back? The two-millionth straw in composition with the other 1,999,999 did break the camel's back; but the two-millionth straw in separation from the other 1,999,999 did not break it.

You fall into this fallacy when you argue:

> All in this room weigh about two tons;
> but MaryAlice is in this room;
> therefore MaryAlice weighs about two tons.

"All in this room" is to be understood collectively in the major premise; but in the conclusion you proceed as though it had been taken distributively; you divide, or separate, what is true only when taken together as a unit.

e. Accent

The fallacy of accent consists in the ambiguous use of a word that has different meanings when it is accented differently. This fallacy is the same as equivocation except that, strictly speaking, words having different accents are not the same words.

In English works on logic the name "fallacy of accent" is often applied to ambiguity that results from shifting emphasis from one word to another. For instance, in the proposition "John is not a depraved murderer," if you emphasize "depraved," you deny that John is depraved without stating whether or not he is a murderer; if you emphasize "murderer," you deny that he is a murderer without, however, stating whether or not he is depraved.

Note the change in meaning in the following example as the

emphasis is shifted from one to another of the italicized words or phrases. "Thou *shalt not bear false* witness *against* thy *neighbor.*" If you emphasize "shalt not bear," you suggest that one should not *tolerate* false witness; if you emphasize "false," you hint that it is all right to say evil things about your neighbor as long as they are true; if you emphasize "against," you suggest that it might be licit to tell lies in his favor; and if you emphasize "neighbor," you suggest that it might not be forbidden to tell lies about men who are not your neighbors.

The fallacy of accident in this second sense is a kind of amphiboly.

f. Figures of Speech

The fallacy of figures of speech is a special type of false analogy that consists in wrongly inferring similarity of meaning from similarity of word structure. Note the words "immaterial," "insoluble," and "inflammable" in the following example.

> What is immaterial is not material
> and what is insoluble is not soluble;
> therefore what is inflammable is not flammable.

In "immaterial" and "insoluble" the prefix "im-" or "in-" is a negative particle; but in "inflammable" it is an intensive particle. The argument proceeds, though, as if the prefix must have the same meaning in its third occurrence that it had in the first and second.

One of the most famous examples of this fallacy is found in Mill's *Utilitarianism:*

> The only proof capable of being given that an object is visible is that people actually see it. The only proof that a sound is audible is because people hear it; and so of the other sources of our experience. In like manner, I apprehend, the sole evidence it is possible to produce that anything is desirable, is that people do actually desire it.

This fallacy rests on the false assumption that, in the word "desirable," the suffix "-ible" (or "-able") must mean "capable of being . . ." since it has this meaning in "visible" and "audible."

In order to avoid the fallacy of figures of speech, you must know the meanings of words.

2. FALLACIES NOT OF LANGUAGE

Aristotle lists seven fallacies not of language. They have this in common, that all of them arise from some kind of confusion about the things that are spoken of. Either what is essential to a thing is confused with what is merely accidental to it, or what is true absolutely and without qualification is confused with what is true only with a qualification or limitation, or what is against a thesis is confused with what is not against it—and so on, as we shall explain in connection with each fallacy. After treating of these Aristotelian fallacies we shall add a few others that seem important enough to deserve special attention.

a. Accident

The fallacy of accident consists in affirming or denying of a thing what has been affirmed or denied only of some accidental modification or condition of the thing, or vice versa. This fallacy rests on a confusion of what is essential or necessary to a thing and what is merely accidental to it.

The sophist's dialogue with the acquaintance of Coriscus illustrates this fallacy.

> "Do you know Coriscus?"
> "Yes."
> "Do you know the man who is approaching with his face muffled?"
> "No."
> "But he is Coriscus; you have both affirmed and denied that you know Coriscus."

To have his face muffled is an accident in Coriscus; it is possible to know Coriscus without knowing him according to this particular accidental condition. (You can *know* him without always *recognizing* him.) You illustrate the same fallacy when you argue:

> "You say that you ate what you bought;
> but you bought raw meat;
> therefore you must have eaten raw meat."

You did not intend to assert a complete identity between what you ate and what you bought. All you wanted to say is that they were substantially the same; you did not intend to deny that the accidental condition of the meat was changed by cooking.

A common form of this fallacy consists in arguing that a thing itself should be forbidden or destroyed because its use sometimes leads to abuse. The abuse should be eliminated, of course; but it does not follow from this that the use should also be eliminated.

> Alcoholic drinks lead to drunkenness
> and should therefore be forbidden.

You can construct a parallel argument which is obviously absurd.

> Good food leads to overeating
> and should therefore be forbidden.

You might have a valid argument, though, if you show that the use of a thing is inseparable from its abuse and that the abuse always has serious evil consequences.

b. Confusion of Absolute and Qualified Statement

Under this heading we shall treat of two distinct but closely related fallacies. The first of these consists in using a principle that is restricted in its applicability as though it were an absolutely universal principle, and thus applying it to cases for which it was not intended. What is true only with qualification or limitation is taken to be true absolutely or without any qualification or limitation. We illustrate this fallacy when we argue:

> Water boils at 212° Fahrenheit;
> therefore water boils at 212° Fahrenheit on the top of Mount Everest.

The premise is not true absolutely but only with the limitation "under an atmospheric pressure corresponding to 760 mm. of mercury." Hence, when we use this premise to infer that water boils at 212° Fahrenheit on the top of Mount Everest, we are applying a principle to a case that it was not intended to cover. We do the same when we argue:

> Germans are good musicians; therefore this
> German is a good musician.

The premise is true of Germans as a group or in general, but not of each individual German. (This example, if expressed in a complete syllogism, would incur the fallacy of undistributed middle since the middle term "German" would be particular in each occurrence.)

The other form of this fallacy consists in assuming that an absolute statement is implied in a qualified, or limited, statement when it is actually not implied therein. Compare the following propositions:

1. John is a good doctor;
   therefore John is a doctor.
2. He gave me $1000 of counterfeit money;
   therefore he gave me $1000.

"John is a good doctor" implies the absolute statement that John is a doctor; but "He gave me $1000 of counterfeit money" does not imply the absolute statement that he gave me $1000.

c. Ignoratio Elenchi

The fallacy of *ignoratio elenchi* consists in proving a conclusion other than the one that should be proved. It is called by various names; for instance, "the fallacy of irrelevant conclusion," "ignorance of the question," "ignoring the issue," "missing the point," and so on.

The fallacy gets its name from the Latinized form of the Greek word *elenchos,* which means "refutation." In order to refute a statement, you must establish its contradictory. Now if you establish something other than the contradictory of the statement to be refuted, you are said to be "ignorant of the refutation."

Suppose, for instance, that someone uses the following argument to refute the Catholic claim that the pope is infallible.

> There have been bad popes;
> therefore the pope is not infallible.

Suppose, too, that this opponent of papal infallibility has proven that there were a few bad popes. The question is, Is the fact that there have been a few bad popes really inconsistent with the pope's infallibility? Does this fact really involve the contradictory of "The pope is infallible"? Or can a pope be bad and still be infallible? Now, anyone who knows the exact technical sense in which Catholics claim infallibility for the pope will immediately see that the fact that there have been a few bad popes is irrelevant to the point at issue. The fact proves that the pope is not *impeccable;* but it does not prove that the pope is not infallible. In this example, as in many others, an *ignoratio elenchi* could have been avoided by clarifying the exact point at issue through precise definition.[2]

The following argument of the young lad who denied the guilt of his adult friend who had been sent to prison for murdering his wife also incurs an *ignoratio elenchi:*

> He wasn't guilty. He was nice to all the kids and very athletic. We played basketball and water-skied with him and had wonderful times. He'd do anything for anybody.

He could have been "nice to all the kids," and so on, and nevertheless have murdered his wife. The question was not, Was he a pleasant companion, and so on, but, Did he, or did he not, murder his wife?

The prosecutor at a trial for murder commits this fallacy if he expatiates on how terrible murder is instead of proving that the accused is guilty.

The *ignoratio elenchi* is very common and assumes many minor forms. The following are the most important.

The *argumentum ad hominem* ignores the issue and attacks the person of an opponent instead. It includes such things as personal abuse, attacks on a man's character or nationality or religion, "mud slinging," "name calling," "poisoning the wells," charges of inconsistency, retorting an argument, and so on. Sometimes, of course, it is legitimate to question the credibility of a witness; for instance, if he has a criminal record, if he has perjured himself in the past, or if his testimony is inconsistent. Sometimes, too, it is legitimate to point out that a man's present testimony is inconsistent with his conduct or with what he held in the past. Thus, Christ used a legitimate *argumentum ad hominem* when He silenced those who found fault with Him for healing on the Sabbath by asking, "Which of you

[2] Notice that on the assumption that no bad person can be infallible even by the special favor of God, the antecedent ("there have been bad popes") would not be irrelevant to the conclusion ("therefore the pope is not infallible"). If the person using the argument would not admit that this assumption is false, he would incur, not the fallacy of *ignoratio elenchi,* but the non-Aristotelian fallacy of false assumption.

shall have an ass or an ox fall into a pit, and will not immediately draw him up on the Sabbath?"

The *argumentum ad populum* ("appeal to the people") is an appeal to popular prejudices rather than to reason. Every election year supplies altogether too many examples of this fallacy.

The *argumentum ad misericordiam* ("appeal to pity") ignores the point at issue and appeals, instead, to our instinct to have compassion on the unfortunate. For instance, instead of proving that an accused person is innocent, the argument may be aimed at winning sympathy for him by portraying how unfortunate he has always been, how much his innocent and poverty-stricken family will suffer if he is convicted, and so on. Many arguments favoring divorce, contraception, abortion, euthanasia, and so on, illustrate this fallacy. They obscure the issue by playing on our emotions. Note, for instance, the following plea for euthanasia.

> I have watched three loved ones and a dear friend die slowly and horribly of cancer. I saw their flesh turn yellow and shrivel into a hanging mass of vicious sickly design. I watched the light of reason die in their eyes and a haunting madness take its place. I heard their shrieks of agony and their desperate plea for death when opiates ceased to deaden their pain. . . . The Bible says, "Blessed are the merciful, for they shall obtain mercy." Let the law-makers take this page and apply it in their courtrooms.

The question is not, Is a lingering death from cancer a terrible thing? All admit that it is. To dwell at length on the sufferings of the incurably ill is to befuddle the issue. The question is, Does God alone have dominion over the lives of innocent people? If he has, the direct killing of an innocent human being by another human being is always a serious crime.

The *argumentum ad verecundiam* (literally, "appeal to shame") is an appeal to misplaced authority. It aims at overawing people by appealing to the dignity of those who hold an opinion rather than to their special competence in the matter under discussion. A mathematician, for instance, might be a genius in mathematics and still be an ignoramus in *aesthetic matters;* to accept his opinion in aesthetic matters on account of his pre-eminence in mathematics is to fall into this fallacy. This fallacy is a common device of advertisers who urge you to smoke a certain brand of cigarettes or drink a certain kind of whiskey because some famous person does. It is often introduced by phrases like "scientists say," "informed people will tell you . . . ," "surely you know . . . ," "everyone knows," and so on.

The *argumentum ad baculum* ("appeal to the stick") is an appeal to physical force or moral pressure.

d. Begging the Question

The fallacy of begging the question, or *petitio principii,* consists in assuming under some form or other the conclusion that should be proved and then using it as a premise to prove the very same conclusion. This fallacy occurs in two forms.

The first form consists in using the same or an equivalent proposition as both premise and conclusion, as in the following examples.

> Whiskey causes drunkenness because it is intoxicating.
> The soul is immortal because it cannot die.
> Morphine induces sleep because it has soporific effects.

Both the premises (the "because" clauses) and the conclusions state exactly the same thing and differ from one another only verbally.

The second form consists in using a premise that cannot be known to be true unless the conclusion is first known to be true, as in the following example:

> All in this room are wearing shoes;
> but Martha is in this room;
> therefore Martha is wearing shoes.

The major premise is an enumerative universal and cannot be known to be true unless the conclusion is first known to be true. You cannot know that all in this room are wearing shoes unless you first know that Martha is wearing them.

The "vicious circle," or "arguing in a circle," is a special type of the fallacy of begging the question and consists in proving a proposition by a second proposition and then proving the second by the first. You have a vicious circle, for instance, if you prove that man has free will because he is responsible for his actions and then—

generally a few pages later—prove that man is responsible for his actions because he has free will.

The fallacy of begging the question is incurred by the use of "question-begging epithets," which imply that what is to be proved has already been proved. The prosecutor who refers to the man accused of murder as a murderer assumes precisely what he is supposed to prove. Or suppose that so-and-so, belonging to such-and-such an organization, has informed the police of its illegal activities. If you report his action by calling him a stool pigeon, you do more than merely report a fact; you insinuate a conclusion by using a *weighted word* with an unfavorable innuendo.

Akin to this is the practice of insinuating interpretations and conclusions into what is claimed to be an objective and impartial presentation of facts. An example of this can be found in Joseph P. Kamp's *We Must Abolish the United States.*[3] At the beginning of the book Mr. Kamp says:

> Here then are the results of our researches. We present the facts as we find them, and our own conclusion as to their meaning. We have tried to be objective.

On the next page he continues:

> Under the Constitution of the United States they [the American people] have the unalienable right to believe in, and to fight for, any idea, no matter how visionary, impractical, far-fetched, phony or screwball it may be.
>
> Accordingly, since World War II an increasing number of forthright Americans, *and some who call themselves Americans,* have been spending their time, energy and money in furthering programs for World Government that are all of these things . . . and *worse.*

He has already told us what to think of certain programs although he has not yet given us a single fact about them. A page later, after presenting an outline "stripped of all pretense" of the position of his opponents, he adds to his list of derogatory epithets, or unfavorably weighted words, by asking:

> Is such a sinister program too far-fetched, too asinine, and too plainly disloyal to win any real measure of public support?

[3] Pp. x-12.

The program may indeed be "visionary," "impractical," "far-fetched," "phony," and "screwball"; it may involve "pretense" and be "sinister," "asinine," and "disloyal"; nevertheless, this does not belong to the facts as facts but is a conclusion rightly or wrongly inferred from the facts. Mr. Kamp, of course, did not say that he would *first* present the facts and *then* his conclusions about them; still, by mingling his interpretations and conclusions with his presentation of the facts in such a way as to confound the two, he argues in a manner that is objectively fallacious.

e. False Cause

We must distinguish between the Aristotelian fallacy of false cause (*non causa pro causa*) and the much more important fallacy to which later logicians give the same name.

The Aristotelian fallacy of false cause consists in drawing an absurd conclusion from an assumption that is falsely imputed to an opponent or wrongly assumed to underlie a thesis. What is not the cause or reason for a thesis is assumed to be its cause or reason. Suppose, for example, that a sophist's opponent has made the statement that the death penalty for murder is just, and the sophist argues as follows:

> The claim that the death penalty for murder is just leads to an absurdity. If the death penalty for murder is just and if, moreover, punishment is just precisely insofar as it is an effective deterrent from crime, it would follow that it would be equally just to inflict the death penalty for pocket-picking.[4]

The claim that the death penalty for murder is just actually rests on the principle that punishment should be proportionate to the gravity of a crime. But the sophist pretends that it rests on the assumption that punishment is just only insofar as it is an effective deterrent from crime, and then he draws his absurd conclusion from this falsely imputed assumption.[5]

Later logicians give the name of "false cause" to various fallacies arising from a confusion of causal with non-causal relationships. Its

[4] This example is adapted from George Howard Joyce's *Principles of Logic* (London: Longmans, Green and Co. [1923]) p. 281.

[5] The Aristotelian fallacy of false cause often involves the additional fallacy of sublating the antecedent.

commonest form is the *post hoc, ergo propter hoc* ("after this, therefore because of this"), which consists in mistaking a purely temporal sequence for a causal relationship.

> Night comes before day;
> therefore night causes day.
>
> I got well after taking a certain medicine;
> therefore I got well because I took that medicine.

The fallacy of false cause is also incurred by mistaking a mere condition or occasion of an event for its cause, as in the following example.

> A man cannot think without his brain;
> therefore a man's brain is the cause of his thought.

The fallacy of false cause in this modern sense is usually an *ignoratio elenchi;* sometimes, however, it rests on a false assumption and is not an Aristotelian fallacy at all.

f. Consequent

The fallacy of the consequent consists in inferring that an antecedent is true because its consequent is true, or that a consequent is false because its antecedent is false. This fallacy is based on the mistaken opinion that the relationship of an antecedent and its consequents in regard to truth and falsity is always reciprocal.

The best known forms of this fallacy are the invalid moods of the conditional syllogism. The first of these is called "positing the consequent" and is incurred by positing a consequent in the minor premise and then positing the antecedent in the conclusion; the second is called "sublating the antecedent" and is incurred by sublating the antecedent in the minor premise and then sublating the consequent in the conclusion. We treated of these adequately when we discussed the conditional syllogism.

The fallacy of the consequent can also be incurred in categorical syllogisms. Any notion included in the comprehension of a concept —whether as a constitutive note (genus and difference) or as a derived note (logical property)—is a consequent of that concept, and in relation to its consequents the concept itself is an antecedent. In this sense the notions "animal," "organic," "material," and so on, are consequents of the antecedent "dog." In the minor premise of the following syllogism the term "animal," which is a consequent of "dog," is predicated of the minor term "Moby Dick" and in the conclusion its antecedent ("dog") is predicated of the same term:

> A dog is an animal;
> but Moby Dick is an animal;
> therefore Moby Dick is a dog.

This example not only incurs the fallacy of positing the consequent but also the formal fallacy of an undistributed middle term.

In the minor premise of the following syllogism the term "dog," which is an antecedent of "animal," is denied of the minor term "Moby Dick" and in the conclusion its consequent is denied of the same term.

> A dog is an animal;
> but Moby Dick is not a dog;
> therefore Moby Dick is not an animal.

This example not only incurs the fallacy of sublating the antecedent ("dog" is sublated with reference to Moby Dick) but also the formal fallacy of an illicit process of a major term.

We must be on our guard against three common ways of incurring the fallacy of the consequent. First, we should not reject a thesis merely because one or the other of its proofs is inconclusive. The reason for this is that an antecedent can be false (or the sequence invalid) while the consequent is nevertheless true. Secondly, we should not assume that the arguments advanced in proof of a thesis must be conclusive because the thesis itself is known to be true. A true consequent can flow from a false antecedent. Thirdly, we should not assume that a hypothesis or theory must be true simply because its consequents have been verified. A hypothesis or theory is not proved conclusively by the mere verification of its consequents but only by showing that it is the only antecedent from which the verified consequents can flow.

g. *Many Questions*

The fallacy of many questions consists in asking either a multiple question as though it were a single question—or a question involving a supposition as though it involved no supposition—and then demanding a simple yes or no for an answer and thus tricking someone into making admissions he did not intend to make.

Consider the following multiple question which is proposed as though it were a single question.

Is he a democrat with socialistic tendencies?

If he is both a democrat and a man of socialistic tendencies, the question should be answered by a simple yes. If he is neither a democrat nor a man of socialistic tendencies, the question should be answered by a simple no. If he is the one but not the other, the question cannot be answered by a simple yes or no but *must be distinguished.* You must answer, "He is a democrat but does not have socialistic tendencies" or "He does have socialistic tendencies but is not a democrat."

The following example is a favorite illustration of a question that has suppositions.

Have you stopped beating your wife?

Both yes and no will involve you in embarrassing admissions. The question rests on two suppositions; first, that you have a wife; and, second, that you have beaten her. If you have no wife, or if you have one but have never beaten her, you should *deny the suppositions* that are not fulfilled in your case.

h. Other Fallacies

The following fallacies are not included in Aristotle's list of fallacies, but are important enough to merit a brief notice.

1) **NON SEQUITUR** is the Latin for "it does not follow." In a sense every invalid argument is a *non sequitur,* just as every invalid argument is also an *ignoratio elenchi;* but the name "non sequitur" is generally restricted to a series of true but unrelated propositions that simulate the structure of a syllogism; for instance,

Cows give milk;
but sheep have wool;
therefore goats chew cud.

Most examples are rather trivial. We mention this fallacy only because its name is in rather common use and is included in most lists of fallacies.

2) The **ARGUMENTUM AD IGNORANTIAM,** or **APPEAL TO IGNORANCE,** infers that a statement is false because it cannot be proved, or true because it cannot be refuted. The assumption that a man is guilty until he proves himself not guilty is an example of this fallacy, as illustrated by a pamphleteer who lists a series of charges and then exclaims:

> This is evidence that must be accepted
> because it cannot be refuted.

3) The fallacy of **SUPPRESSING THE FACTS** consists in selecting only the facts that favor an opinion and suppressing, or ignoring, all facts that are against it. By a careful selection of quotations you can often give the impression that a writer holds an opinion that is just the opposite of what he really holds.

4) The **ARGUMENT FROM SILENCE** infers that an alleged fact did not take place because it is not recorded in writings in which it would surely have been recorded if it had taken place. This argument can be legitimate, but is often misused. To know for certain that, if an event had taken place, it would have been recorded is often difficult and frequently impossible.

5) The **FALLACY OF FALSE ASSUMPTION** consists in using a false principle or false statement of fact as an unexpressed premise (or at least as a presupposition) of an argument. It is not a fallacy at all in the Aristotelian sense but an error. The fallacy of false assumption is incurred most frequently in enthymemes whose unexpressed member is false, as in the following example:

> No one has ever seen a soul;
> therefore you cannot know for certain that you have a soul.

This argument rests on the false assumption that you cannot know anything for certain unless you can see (hear, touch, smell, or taste) it, and this false assumption is the reason for assenting to the conclusion. Unless the false assumption "causes" the conclusion, the fallacy of false assumption is not incurred.

6) Fallacies of **ILLICIT GENERALIZATION** consist in making a generalization on insufficient evidence. These fallacies are incident to induction.

7) The **FALLACY OF FALSE ANALOGY** will be treated in connection with induction. Actually it is an *ignoratio elenchi.*

How to Handle Fallacies: Some Sample Answers

The following sample answers will serve as models for the handling of fallacies. They will likewise clarify the differences between certain fallacies that are often confused with one another, and illustrate how the same fallacy can often be classified under various headings when considered from different points of view.

SAMPLE 1. If there were no time, there would be no day;
if it were not day, it would be night;
but if it were night, there would be time;
therefore, if there were no time, there would be time.

EQUIVOCATION. The word "day" is used in two senses: in its first occurrence it signifies a period of twenty-four hours; in its second occurrence it signifies "day" as opposed to "night."

DIVISION. The argument starts with the condition "if there were no time"; but then it proceeds as though this condition had not been made, "dividing" the rest of the argument from the first portion. On the supposition that there were no time, it would not be true that it would be night if it were not day, because on this supposition there would be neither day nor night.

SAMPLE 2. The American worker shouldn't kick; he's much better off than his European brother.

IGNORATIO ELENCHI. The American worker could be much better off than his European brother and nevertheless have just grounds for complaint. Hence, the antecedent ("He's much better off than his European brother") is irrelevant to the conclusion ("The American worker shouldn't kick"), and an *ignoratio elenchi* is incurred.

Is a so-called FALLACY OF FALSE ASSUMPTION incurred? Let us complete the argument, supplying a major premise that will render the argument formally valid:

Major: No one who is better off than anyone else can ever have just grounds for complaint;
Minor: but the American worker is better off than someone else (namely, his European brother);
Concl: therefore the American worker has no just grounds for complaint (shouldn't kick).

If the principle expressed in the major premise were true, the evidence adduced in the minor premise would not be irrelevant to the conclusion but would clearly prove it. However, the major premise is obviously false. Now if this false principle actually caused the assent to the conclusion, the non-Aristotelian fallacy of false assumption would be incurred. However, in all likelihood the person using the argument in Sample 2 does not even advert to the general principle behind his argument and would promptly reject the principle if it were brought to his attention. In this case, the false principle would not cause the assent to the conclusion; and the fallacy incurred is not FALSE ASSUMPTION, but *IGNORATIO ELENCHI*. But if the person using the argument would think that the principle in the major premise were true, he would incur the non-Aristotelian fallacy of false assumption.

SAMPLE 3. Labor unions cause strikes and should therefore be abolished.

If we supply the missing parts and set up the argument in logical form, we get the following arrangement:

Major: Whatever causes strikes should be abolished;
Minor: but labor unions cause strikes;
Concl: therefore labor unions should be abolished.

The argument is formally valid but fallacious. The major premise is true only when two qualifications are added: that the strikes are UNJUST and that they are caused, not PER ACCIDENS, but PER SE. Passing to the minor premise, where the major is applied to labor unions, we find that labor unions cause, not unjust, but JUST strikes (at least from the point of view of the union) or, if they cause unjust strikes, they do this, not PER SE, but PER ACCIDENS.

Two fallacies are incurred: the fallacy of confusion of ABSOLUTE AND QUALIFIED STATEMENT, because a principle (the major premise) that is true only with the qualification made above is used as though it were true without qualification; and the fallacy of ACCIDENT, because the argument concludes that the very existence of labor unions should be abolished, although all that has been proven is that their abuse (an accident) should be abolished.

SAMPLE 4. Capital punishment is un-Christian, because the death penalty falls for the most part on obscure, impoverished, friendless or defective individuals and rarely on the well-to-do and educated.

If we supply the missing parts and set up the argument in logical form, we get the following syllogism:

Major: That punishment is un-Christian which falls for the most part on obscure, impoverished, friendless or defective individuals and rarely on the well-to-do and educated;
Minor: but the death penalty (or capital punishment) is such a punishment;
Concl: therefore capital punishment is un-Christian.

The evidence aims directly at proving that such punishment is unjust and only indirectly that it is un-Christian. Hence, we must supply the following syllogism as a proof of the major premise given above:

Major: What is unjust is un-Christian;
Minor: but a punishment that falls for the most part on obscure, impoverished, friendless or defective individuals and rarely on the well-to-do and educated is unjust;
Concl: therefore that punishment is un-Christian which falls for the most part on obscure, impoverished, friendless or defective individuals and rarely on the well-to-do or educated.

The syllogisms are both formally valid, but fallacies occur in the syllogism given as a proof of the main syllogism.

ACCIDENT. That such a punishment is unjust may be due to its faulty administration (an accident) rather than to its very nature. In other words, injustice might not be essential to capital punishment but accidental to it: if the accidental abuses would be eliminated, capital punishment would cease to be unjust.

IGNORATIO ELENCHI. Perhaps the obscure, impoverished, friendless or defective individuals commit more crimes that merit capital punishment than the well-to-do and educated. If this is true, then, not injustice, but the fact that more of them commit such crimes would be the reason why more of them receive capital punishment. In this case, the given antecedent is irrelevant to the conclusion, and the fallacy of *ignoratio elenchi* is incurred.

Exercise

Criticize the following passages from as many points of view as possible.

1. First, decide whether a passage is argumentative or merely expository.
2. Then, pick out the conclusion and the premises of the argumentative portions, and supply the missing members of all the enthymemes.
3. Next, apply the general rules of inference.
4. Finally, decide what fallacies are incurred. Refer each example to as many headings as possible and explain why you are referring it to each. If you cannot refer an example to any of the headings given above, explain what is wrong with it in your own words.

Some of the examples are rather trivial and are included only because they are very obvious examples of the various kinds of fallacies. Most of the examples are adapted from newspapers, magazines, or books and illustrate the kinds of arguments in common use today.

1. Lopez undertook the struggle single-handed against a powerful Brazil, joined with Argentina and Uruguay as allies.

2. He obviously lacks the qualifications requisite for the position and is therefore clearly not fit for the job.
3. His opinion is absolutely worthless; why, he didn't even finish high school.
4. "Three times six plus two equals twenty."
"You are wrong; it equals twenty-four."
5. Three and two are odd and even; but three and two are five; therefore five is odd and even.
6. Lost: an umbrella by an old lady with two broken ribs.
7. Miracles are impossible because they simply can't happen.
8. Teacher to pupil: "Your essay is very good and very original." The pupil beams.
Then the teacher continues: "The only trouble is that the very good parts are not very original and that the very original parts are not very good."
9. "The farm laborer doesn't get near the pay check the industrial worker gets; but still he manages to live quite well."
10. "Are you in favor of extending federal aid to parochial schools and thereby violating the first amendment of the Constitution by breaking down our traditionally American separation of church and state?"
11. "If all get 100% in today's quiz, we'll not have a quiz tomorrow. But it's impossible for all to get a 100 today. Therefore, as sure as night follows the day, we'll have a quiz tomorrow."
12. "In the early days our ancestors came to America in boatloads. They were poor men but willing workers. They saluted the Statue of Liberty, spit on their hands, grabbed a shovel and pick ax, and built our railroads. America belongs to the worker!"
13. "For sale: combination stove and baby buggy."
14. "And if the Congressmen who object to the President's European relief were to visit the hovels of Europe, would they be so calculating in their appraisals of human misery?"
15. To call you a man is to speak the truth; but to call you a stupid idiot is to call you a man; therefore to call you a stupid idiot is to speak the truth.
16. "Should you worry about your motives? No; it is usually what you do that determines whether or not you are useful and accepted."
17. "No sane person can reasonably object to euthanasia, for it is only an act of pity to put incurable sufferers out of their misery by killing them painlessly."
18. X disinfectant kills 50,000,000 germs in 3½ seconds; therefore use X.

19. Christianity and the capitalistic system are inseparable, because only in a free country do we have a free church.
20. Capital punishment should be abolished because it does not help the criminal to amend his ways.
21. On a street car, sitting man to standing woman: "If you can vote like a man, you can stand like a man."
22. State-owned industries should be done away with; in featherbedding and absenteeism they lead all others.
23. Only fine tobacco gives you both mildness and rich taste; and Lucky Strike means fine tobacco.
24. No cat has nine tails; but one cat has one more tail than no cat; therefore one cat has ten tails.
25. Could not the Post-Dispatch repudiate the perverse doctrine it saw fit to print?
26. The more you study, the more you learn;
the more you learn, the more you know;
the more you know, the more you forget;
the more you forget, the less you know;
the less you know, the more ignorant you are;
therefore, the more you study, the more ignorant you are.
27. The more you forget, the less you know; but old men have forgotten more than newly born babies; therefore old men know less than newly born babies.
28. People should not smoke cigarettes because smoking them makes their fingers dirty.
29. It is silly to say that modern killer-diller comic books hurt youngsters; they are just the modernized dime novel.
30. Of course hydrogen burns; it's combustible; isn't it?
31. "How about drafting only college youths? Since it seems to be necessary for our boys to fight, let's not give privileges to any particular group."
32. "Thou seest I have more flesh than another man; and therefore more frailty." (Falstaff in *Henry* IV)
33. If gasses were composed of tiny particles of matter in constant motion, they would exert pressure. But, as we can readily see, gasses do exert pressure. Thus, we are justified in saying that gasses are composed of minute particles of matter in constant motion.
34. "We have seen more than once that the public welfare may call upon the best citizens for their lives. It would be strange if it could not call upon those who already sap the strength of the State for these lesser sacrifices, often not felt to be such by those concerned, in order to

prevent our being swamped with incompetence. It is better for all the world, if instead of waiting to execute degenerate offspring for crime, or to let them starve for their imbecility, society can prevent those who are manifestly unfit from continuing their kind. The principle that sustains compulsory vaccination is broad enough to cover cutting of the Fallopian tubes." (U. S. Supreme Court upholding the Virginia Sterilization Law [274 U. S. 200] in the year 1927. The opinion was expressed by Justice Holmes)

35. "Since a married woman is not a serf but a citizen, her right to abandon her husband and to decide on her own future cannot be questioned." (Justice McCardie)

36. "To learn that such practices as the killing of children, human sacrifice, abandoning of the aged to starvation, homosexuality, masturbation, lying, and stealing may be accepted mores in certain primitive tribes is shattering to the notion that truth [moral standards] is fixed, eternal, and universal."

37. "If the murder of one man is one mortal sin, the murder of 40,000 men is 40,000 mortal sins."

38. Universal truth is not possible because every truth we adhere to contains within itself some part of our aims, and aims are never unanimous. (From a sociology textbook)

39. No science proves its own principles; therefore the starting points of all the sciences are accepted blindly.

40. Why does a fish weigh less heavily in water while it is alive than after it is dead? (This question is reputed to have been proposed by King Charles II to his Royal Society.)

41. A baby monkey was reared with a group of human children. At first the monkey's intelligence developed as fast as the children's. Only as they began to talk, did the children leap ahead. Talk, therefore, is what makes us human.

42. I am an ex-soldier and have voted Republican all my life, but I agree with President Truman on his socialized medicine law. What else do we have with our big armies? ("Letters to the Editor")

43. "I agree with Senator Byrd that a woman Vice-President would be a good idea. The male Presidents and Vice-Presidents haven't stopped wars."

44. White lies are all right because everybody tells them.

45. As a matter of fact, most of those who would become eligible to vote under the reduced voting age would be high school graduates who have had recent courses in government or civics, or at least history. With political problems in mind, these would be more discriminating voters than the rutbound, thoughtless, careless voters already too

much in evidence. (From an argument in favor of reducing the age requirement for voting.)

46. The Air Force, because of its pre-eminent position, must continually change its ideals.

47. The policy of towing away automobiles which are illegally parked should be discontinued. The damage to and interference with property, the inconvenience, and the unusual expense which such action entails cannot but cause anger and resentment. (Letters to the Editor)

48. I was certainly amazed to see that officials of this institution permitted the premises of this university to be dishonored by the presence of a United Nations propaganda display.
Referring, of course, to the model U. N. which was held in the gym Oct. 19, it appears that the university has joined the unholy crusade to betray our great nation to its avowed enemies.
This fact is extremely disturbing to a student who still has great faith in his country; and is not willing to have America surrender its sovereignty to a totally alien organization.
I can't see how St. Louis U., which proclaims such noble beliefs, can support a movement which, if fully developed, will result in the destruction of such places as St. Louis U. (The Mail Bag)

49. If the transit service is considered good, then why do the company's employees use autos to and from work when they can ride free? (Letter to Editor)

50. "...inasmuch as men do not bear children they have no right to vote, going to war possibly being necessary and possibly not, but perpetuity of the state demanding that someone bear children." (A statement in defense of woman's suffrage)

PART IV

SIMPLE APPREHENSION, THE CONCEPT, AND THE TERM

In Part I, Chapter 2, as a prerequisite to the study of inference, we treated of the term in its role of subject and predicate. We gave a preliminary definition of a term as a word or a group of words that can serve as the subject or predicate of a proposition. Then we explained the notions of comprehension and extension, and treated of two divisions of terms—(a) into distributive and collective and (b) into singular, particular, and universal.

Part IV is to a great extent a development and completion of what was said in a summary fashion in Chapter 2.

CHAPTER 11

Simple Apprehension and the Concept

IN CHAPTER 2 we spoke briefly of the term. In the present chapter we shift our point of view from the term itself to the mental operation by which we grasp the meaning of a term and to the concept, which is immediately signified by the term. In the first section we shall define simple apprehension and explain the nature of the concept, and in a second section we shall describe a few of the many kinds of concepts.

1. NATURE OF SIMPLE APPREHENSION AND THE CONCEPT

a. Definition of Simple Apprehension

To show its connection with what we have already had, we shall first define simple apprehension as *the operation by which we grasp the meaning of a term.* Suppose, for instance, that you hear the word "chiliagon," which means "thousand-sided figure," and that you advert to its meaning: the operation by which you know the meaning of this term is an example of simple apprehension.

However, simple apprehension precedes our use of terms and frequently we know what a thing is without being able to call it by a suitable term. Hence, it is better and more philosophical to define simple apprehension without reference to terms.

Without reference to terms, simple apprehension is defined as *the operation of the mind by which we mentally grasp a thing, making it present in and to our minds but without affirming or denying anything about it.*

The words "operation of the mind" express the proximate genus [1] of simple apprehension; that is, what simple apprehension has in common with the things that resemble it most closely. These words differentiate simple apprehension from non-mental operations such as those of the will and the sensory faculties but not from judgment and reasoning, which are also mental operations.

The words "by which we mentally grasp a thing . . ." express the specific difference of simple apprehension; that is, what differentiates simple apprehension from the things that resemble it most closely. These words differentiate simple apprehension from other mental operations by expressing its special function, which is merely to lay hold of, seize, grasp, reproduce, express, or represent the essences, or quiddities, of things, thus making things present in and to our minds, but without affirming or denying anything about them. To affirm or deny is the specific function of judgment.

We can define simple apprehension more briefly as the *operation by which we grasp the essences of things.* You will understand the propriety of this definition more clearly when we have taken up the formal object of simple apprehension.

b. The Object of Simple Apprehension

First we shall explain the general notion of object, of material object, and of formal object; then we shall apply what we have said about object in general to the object of simple apprehension.

1) **GENERAL NOTION OF OBJECT.** An OBJECT, in the technical sense in which the word is commonly used in philosophy, is a thing inasmuch as this thing is the terminus of a cognitive or appetitive faculty. Antecedently to its being known (at least potentially), a thing is not an object; but on becoming known, it becomes an object. To the notion of "thing," the notion of "object" adds a relationship to a cognitive or appetitive faculty—that is, to an intellect, a will, or a sense faculty. However, at present we shall speak only of the objects of cognitive faculties.

Philosophers distinguish between the *material object* and the *formal object.* This distinction is not only of great importance in our analysis of simple apprehension but also in the definitions of the various sciences.

[1] Proximate genus and specific difference are explained in Chapter 13.

A MATERIAL OBJECT is the whole object just as it is in itself, together with all its attributes and relationships.

A FORMAL OBJECT is the special aspect of the material object that a faculty or operation grasps directly and immediately. It is what we know about the material object through the use of some faculty or by means of some operation. Notice that the formal object is the material object itself but only insofar as the material object enters directly into cognition.

An example may help to clarify the notions of material and formal object.

Suppose you are standing on a hilltop and see an object at a great distance. At first, let us say, you know it merely as something; but as it comes closer, you know it successively as an animal, as a man, as a big man, as a well dressed man, and finally as John Smith. Now the material object of each act of cognition was the same—it was all of John Smith, as he is in himself, together with all his attributes and relationships; but the formal object, or what you knew about John Smith, increased progressively with each successive act.

2) **APPLICATION TO SIMPLE APPREHENSION.** We shall now apply what we have just said of the general notion of object, material object, and formal object to the object, the material object, and the formal object of simple apprehension.

The OBJECT of simple apprehension is what we grasp by simple apprehension. This object is always something distinct from the mental operation by which we grasp it and belongs either to the real order of actual (or possible) existence, to the imaginary order of fiction and fairy tale, or the purely mental order.

The MATERIAL OBJECT of simple apprehension is the *whole thing* that is known by simple apprehension: it is the thing as it is in itself, together with all its attributes and relationships. The material object of simple apprehension includes not only *what we know about* the thing grasped by simple apprehension (that is, its formal object), but also all else that is knowable in the thing.

The FORMAL OBJECT of simple apprehension is *the essences, or quiddities, of things.* In other words, simple apprehension does not grasp *whether* a thing is—which is the function of judgment—but only *what* a thing is. If we grasp *what a thing is,* no matter how vaguely or indeterminately, even if we grasp it only as a vague and indeterminate "something"—or as "something big," "something colored," "something far away," and so on—we grasp its essence, or quiddity, in the sense in which we understand these words here.[2]

It is extremely important to bear in mind that the object or simple apprehension is not merely the sensible qualities of a thing—such as what it looks like, sounds like, feels like, tastes like, or smells like—and that simple apprehension is not like taking a little photograph or a sound-recording of a thing. Simple apprehension, rather, is an *intellectual* grasping of what a thing is.

c. *The Concept*

A CONCEPT is the mental expression of an essence or quiddity. It is the product that simple apprehension produces within the mind as a means of knowing the essences of things. It is a pure "image," or sign, whose whole essence is to be only a sign and nothing else, and whose sole formal function is to give knowledge of whatever it signifies. For this reason it is called a formal sign.[3]

Now, you do not know a formal sign first and then the thing it signifies; you know both of them simultaneously. First you direct your attention primarily to the thing it signifies, and you know the sign concomitantly; then, if you direct your attention to the sign itself, you know the thing concomitantly. It is impossible to know either of them without knowing the other.[4]

[2] We are here using "essence" in its broadest meaning; later, in Chapter 13 we shall use "essence" in its strict and proper sense in which it signifies the *basic* intelligible elements of the comprehension of a concept.

[3] In contrast to the formal sign, an *instrumental* sign is not a pure sign. It is something else first and only secondarily a sign. You can know an instrumental sign without knowing what it signifies, and you must know it in itself before it can lead you to the knowledge of the thing that it signifies. The sound of an automobile horn is an instrumental sign. It is something in itself independently of its being a sign that an automobile is approaching; you can know it without knowing what it signifies; and you must know it in itself before it can lead you to the knowledge that an automobile is approaching.

[4] Perhaps the relationship of our knowledge of a formal sign to our knowledge of the thing it signifies can be clarified by the following analogy. Suppose a man is shaving in front of a mirror. His image in the mirror is for him a means of seeing his face. Ordinarily he directs his attention primarily to his face, and knows the image in the mirror only concomitantly. However, if he should direct his attention primarily to the image itself, he knows his face concomitantly, since it is impossible to know an image without simultaneously knowing the thing whose image it is.

Charlie

The study of concepts belongs to many branches of philosophy. Insofar as concepts are modifications of a thinking subject and physical accidents inhering in the soul, their study belongs to the philosophy of human nature. Insofar as they are representations of things, their study belongs to epistemology, criteriology, and to some extent to metaphysics. Only insofar as they are genera, species, specific differences, and so on, and insofar as they are the subjects and predicates of propositions and the terms of syllogisms, are concepts the concern of logic.[5]

2. KINDS OF CONCEPTS

Of the innumerable classifications of concepts, we shall take only those that have some bearing on logic. Carefully note the point of view from which each classification is made. This point of view is called the basis of classification or division. If you understand this basis, it will be very easy for you to understand and remember the following definitions.

a. First and Second Intentions

For medieval philosophers, "intention" signified an act of the mind as representative of things. By a first act of the mind we merely grasp the essence, or nature, of a thing; we do not advert to the special mode of existence that the thing has as it exists in the mind and gets as a result of being known. By a second, reflective act we become aware of the attributes that an essence, or nature, has as it exists in the mind but does not have in the real order.

Hence, a FIRST INTENTION is a concept by which we grasp what a thing is according to its own proper being and without our adverting to the special mode of existence that the thing has as it exists in the mind and gets as a result of being known. Thus, when

[5] The concept, as we have defined it above, is sometimes called the formal, or mental, concept. It is often contrasted with the *objective concept,* which strictly speaking is not a concept at all but a thing known by a concept precisely insofar as it is known. The objective concept is the same as the formal object of an act of simple apprehension.

Things, of course, are individual. Yet the objective concept of a thing is universal (in the sense of abstract) because it is the thing only insofar as the thing is known, and the thing is known by simple apprehension only according to its universal attributes abstracted from individual differences.

I say "Man is mortal," "man" is a first intention, because man is mortal as he exists or can exist in the real order. Man is mortal whether we think of him or not. Similarly, in the proposition "A dog is an animal," "dog" is a first intention, because a dog's existence as an animal does not depend on our thinking of him.

A SECOND INTENTION is a concept in which, after grasping what a thing is according to its own proper being, we also advert to the special mode of existence that the thing has as it exists in the mind. Thus when I say "Man is a universal concept," "man" is a second intention, because man exists as a universal concept only as a result of being thought of. Man is not a universal concept as he exists in the real order, but only as he exists in the mind. In "Man is a species" "man" is also a second intention, because man does not exist as a species except in the mind.[6]

Exercise

Classify the subject term as a first intention or a second intention, and give the reason for your answer. Ask yourself, Does the predicate belong to the subject as it exists, or can exist (or is conceived of as existing), in the real order, or only as it exists in the mind?

1. *Man* is a rational animal.
2. *Man* is the middle term of a syllogism.
3. *Man* is the subject of the last proposition.
4. *Man* is a social being.
5. *Man* is a being composed of an organized body and a rational soul.
6. *Man* is a species.
7. *Man* has greater comprehension than "animal."
8. *Man* has less extension than "animal."
9. *Man* has lived for many thousands of years.
10. *Man* has an eternal destiny.
11. *Animal* is particular in "A dog is an animal."
12. *Man's soul* is spiritual.
13. *Angels* really do not have wings.
14. *Jupiter* is the king of the gods.
15. In the last proposition *the king of the gods* is singular.

[6] The notion of second intention will be explained at length in Chapter 16, in which we define logic as the science of second intentions.

b. Concrete and Abstract Concepts

Abstraction consists in considering one aspect of a thing while omitting other aspects.

In one sense, all conceptual knowledge is abstract because it expresses certain aspects of its material object while leaving other aspects unexpressed.[7] The concept "man," for instance, is abstract in the sense that it expresses only the essence "man" and omits innumerable differences (for instance, sex, race, weight, height, social status, and so on). As opposed to abstract in this sense, terms like "this man" and "John Smith" are concrete, since they stand for an individual being and include all his attributes (at least indeterminately).

However, in the classification we are about to take up, we shall call a concept concrete or abstract from a different point of view. We shall call it concrete if it expresses a "subject" and a "form" but abstract if it expresses a "form" only and omits the "subject" in which this form inheres. We shall now explain this classification.

Compare "animal" with "animality," "long" with "length," and "white" with "whiteness." If you have an animal, that animal has animality; and the concept "animality" expresses what it is that makes the animal an animal. If you have a long thing, that long thing has length; and "length" expresses what it is that makes the long thing long. If you have a white thing, that white thing has whiteness; and "whiteness" expresses what it is that makes the white thing white. If a thing *has* animality, it *is* an animal; if it *has* length, it *is* long; and if it *has* whiteness, it *is* white.

Whatever has, or is looked upon as having, a perfection or attribute embodied in itself is called the *subject* of that perfection or attribute. Previously we spoke of the subjects of propositions. Now we are speaking of subjects as possessing perfections. A perfection, or attribute, is looked upon as inhering in (embodied in) the subject that possesses it. The perfection, or attribute, itself is called *form*. Thus, "animality" is the form that makes its subject an animal; "length" is the form that makes its subject long; and "whiteness" is the form that makes its subject white.

[7] This meaning of "abstract" will be clearer when we have studied "Universal as Abstract" in Chapter 13, pp. 239-241.

1) **A CONCRETE CONCEPT** is one that presents to the mind a form as inherent in a subject. It presents to the mind both a form (that is, a perfection or attribute) and the subject in which that form (perfection or attribute) is embodied. "Animal," "long," and "white" are concrete. They present to the mind the forms "animality," "length," and "whiteness" together with the subjects in which these forms inhere.

(The demonstrative pronouns "this," "that," and so on, are concrete *terms* that present only a subject to the mind without expressing a form at all. But such pronouns, strictly speaking, do not signify concepts because they do not express what a thing is but merely point out a subject of perfection.)

All adjectives signify concrete concepts. Even if an adjective modifies an abstract noun, what is signified by the adjective is regarded as concrete, because it is looked upon as inhering in what is signified by the abstract noun. Thus, what is signified by "great" in "great height" is looked upon as a form inhering in the subject "height."

2) **AN ABSTRACT CONCEPT** is one that presents to the mind a form (perfection, or attribute) as separated from its subject (such a concept as "animality," "whiteness," and "length"). It does not express what a subject is, but that which makes a subject what it is. "Animality," for instance, expresses the perfection that makes an animal an animal.[8]

c. Absolute and Connotative [9]

Is a thing presented to the mind as a substance, or as an accident inhering in a substance? If as a substance, the concept is absolute; if as an accident inhering in a substance, the concept is connotative.

[8] A complete understanding of the division of concepts into concrete and abstract, as well as of the following division into absolute and connotative, presupposes an understanding of the notions of substance and accident. The study of these belongs to metaphysics.

[9] Many English logicians use "connotative" and "nonconnotative" in a different sense. According to them a connotative concept is one that denotes a subject and implies an attribute ("man," "dog," "cowardly"), and a nonconnotative concept (term) is one that either denotes a subject ("John") or an attribute ("animality") but not both.

1) AN ABSOLUTE CONCEPT (as opposed to a connotative concept)[10] is one that presents its object to the mind as an independent reality, either as a substance or as though it were a substance. It either expresses the subject in which the form that it sets before the mind inheres ("man," "animal," and "sun"), or else it abstracts from the subject altogether ("humanity," "animality," "kindness"). All abstract concepts are absolute in this latter sense. Absolute concepts are also called "nonconnotative concepts."

2) A CONNOTATIVE CONCEPT is one that presents its object to the mind as an accident actually inhering in, and therefore implying, a substance. It directly sets before the mind a form and merely "connotes," but does not express, the subject in which the form inheres. "Long," "acrobat," "rider," and "weak" are connotative concepts.

All adjectives signify connotative concepts; so do nouns like "orator," "teacher," "pupil," and so on, which express accidental modifications of a being (a man) that is substantially complete.

The following synoptic diagram shows the relationship of concrete and abstract, as well as of absolute and connotative, concepts to both form and the subject in which form inheres.

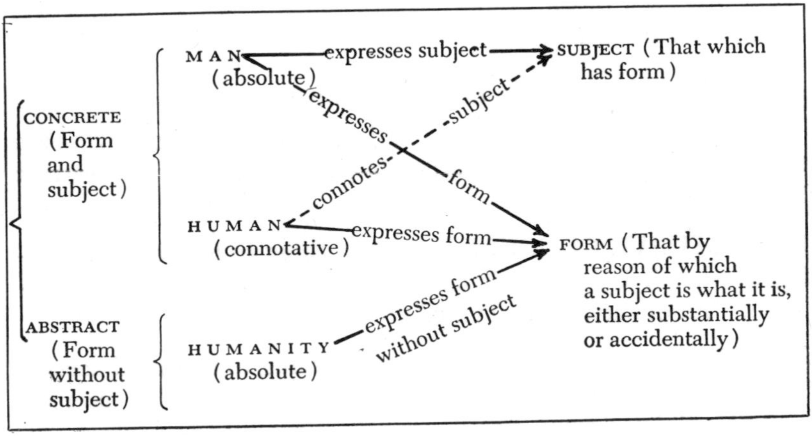

[10] "Absolute concept" is also opposed to "relative concept." In this sense it means a concept that (unlike a relative concept) can be thought of and defined without reference to anything else.

Exercise

I. First classify each of the following as concrete or abstract; then as absolute or connotative.

1. God.
2. Size.
3. Energy.
4. Shape.
5. Yellowish.
6. Good.
7. Goodness.
8. Dimensions.
9. Rational animal.
10. Soul.
11. Powerful.
12. Orator.
13. Man.
14. King.
15. Voltage.
16. Presidency.
17. Student.
18. Resistance.
19. Democracy.
20. Kindness.

II. The following propositions illustrate a confusion of concrete and abstract terms, and of absolute and connotative terms, in their use as subjects and predicates. Explain exactly what is wrong with each.

1. The top of Mount Everest is height.
2. He is a tall.
3. Humanity is a rational animal.
4. Kind is a virtue.
5. Gasoline is energy.

d. Positive and Negative Concepts

Does a concept present a thing to the mind according to what the thing is or what it has, or according to what the thing is not or what it lacks?

1) **A POSITIVE CONCEPT** presents a thing to the mind according to what it is or what it has; for instance, "being," "man," "rational," "rationality," and "living."

2) **A NEGATIVE CONCEPT** presents a thing to the mind according to what the thing is not or what the thing lacks; for instance, "non-being," "non-man," "irrational," "irrationality," and "dead."

No concept is entirely negative in all respects; for every concept must, in some way or other, be an expression of "something," and "something" must be positive in at least some respect. Even "non-being" is positive insofar as the mind gives it a kind of mental being.

Negative concepts are called infinite or indefinite concepts if they include in their extension everything not expressed by the corresponding positive concept. Thus, "non-man" is an infinite, or indefinite, concept because it includes in its extension all that is not man —"man" and "non-man," together, embrace the whole of both the real and the conceptual orders.

We shall treat of negative concepts in greater detail in the next section where we take up contradictory, privative, and contrary concepts.

e. Classifications Based on Mutual Relationships

The following classifications are based on the various relationships that two concepts can have towards one another.

1) **UNCONNECTED CONCEPTS** are so related that the absence or presence of one in a subject neither implies nor excludes the presence of the other in the same subject; for instance, "flat-footed" and "bald," "tall" and "cold," "little" and "white." A man can be both flat-footed and bald, neither flat-footed nor bald, flat-footed but not bald, or bald but not flat-footed. The absence or presence of flat-footedness in a man neither implies nor excludes baldness in the same man, and vice versa. There is simply no connection between flat-footedness and baldness, tallness and coldness, littleness and whiteness.

2) **CONNECTED CONCEPTS** are so related that the absence or presence of one of them in a subject either implies or excludes the presence of the other in the same subject, and vice versa. In other words, connected concepts either must be, or cannot be, simultaneously realized in the same thing. Briefly, they either include one another or exclude one another.

a) **Concepts That Include One Another** are either convertible or non-convertible.

1—CONVERTIBLE CONCEPTS have the same comprehension and extension; for instance, a concept and its definition ("man" and "rational animal"), a species and a specific property ("living organism" and "mortal"), and so on. Convertible concepts are also called reciprocal, interchangeable, or identical concepts. (You will recall that an *A* proposition whose subject and predicate have identical comprehension can be converted by a materially valid conversion.)

2—Non-convertible Concepts are so related that the one includes the other in its comprehension but is not included in it. A genus and species, for instance, are non-convertible, as "animal" and "dog." "Dog" has the entire comprehension of "animal" and, besides that, whatever attributes make a dog a dog rather than some other animal. Every dog is an animal; but it does not follow from this that every animal is a dog. Non-convertible concepts are also called non-reciprocal concepts.

A knowledge of convertible and non-convertible concepts is necessary for making materially valid conversions of propositions.

***b*) Concepts That Exclude One Another** are relative, opposed in the strict sense, or disparate. The following classifications of concepts are of importance in obversion, contraposition, inversion, oppositional inference, and certain types of material eduction.

1—Relative Concepts [11] are mutually exclusive and so related that neither of them can be thought of without reference to the other. Both of two relative concepts must be understood simultaneously, and each belongs to the definition of the other; for instance, "husband" and "wife," "master" and "servant," "subject" and "ruler," and "cause" and "effect." It is impossible for each of two relative concepts to be realized in the same subject, at least in the same respect. A parent, for instance, cannot be its own offspring—although a parent is offspring in relation to its own parent. Such concepts are often called "correlatives."

Concepts like "big," "small," "heavy," and so on, are *relative in a different sense*. Their very notion implies a reference, or comparison, to a standard. For instance, an elephant is a big or small elephant in comparison with the normal size of elephants; and a mouse is a big or small mouse in comparison with the normal size of mice. An elephant can be a small elephant and still be bigger than a big mouse.

2—Strictly Opposed Concepts include contradictories, privative concepts (as opposed to the perfections whose absence they express), and the two kinds of contrary concepts.

[11] See Note 10 on p. 213 for the meaning of "absolute concept" as opposed to "relative concept."

a—*Contradictory Concepts* are so related that the one is the simple negation of the other; for instance, "man" and "non-man," and "being" and "non-being." Such concepts, taken together, include in their extension all beings of all orders (real and mental, possible and even impossible—for even impossible things are conceived of in imitation of what is or can be.) Absolutely everything is either the one or the other of two contradictory concepts. Thus, anything you can think of is either a man or a non-man. Whatever is not a man—whether it is a lion, a house, a number, or absolute nothing—is a non-man.[12]

b—*Privative Concepts* include concepts like "dead," "blind," "deaf," "defective," and the corresponding abstract concepts, "death," "blindness," "deafness," and "defect." A concept is privative if it presents a thing to the mind according to what the thing was, or had, or would be expected to have, and without which the thing is defective; and, secondly, a concept is privative if it expresses such a defect in the abstract.

The word "privative" is derived from the Latin word *privo*, which means "I deprive." Now, a thing can be deprived only of what it has or ought to have. Thus, blindness is the lack of sight in a subject that ought to have it; deafness is the lack of hearing in a subject that ought to be able to hear; and dumbness is the lack of the ability to speak in a subject that is defective if it lacks this ability. A stone can neither see nor hear nor speak, but is not therefore blind, deaf, and dumb. The reason for this is that to lack the power to see, hear, and speak is not a defect in a stone. Similarly, a mole is not blind but sightless, because nature does not endow this animal with the power to see. A mole can have all that a mole is supposed to have and still be unable to see.

In inference, the relationship of a privative concept and the corresponding perfection is similar to the relationship of immediately opposed contraries to one another. We shall study immediately opposed contraries in the next few paragraphs.

c—*Contrary Concepts* belong to the same genus but differ from one another as much as possible within that genus. For instance, "hot" and "cold" are at the extremes of the genus of temperature;

[12] Concepts like "non-man" depend on previous judgments. We get them by obverting a proposition (for instance, "A dog is not a man" to "A dog is a non-man") and then considering just the predicate.

"expensive" and "cheap" are at the extremes of the genus of price; and "first" and "last" are the extremes of every series within the genus of both spatial and temporal order.

If one of two contraries is in a subject, the other is excluded; for instance, a thing cannot be both hot and cold, expensive and cheap, first and last, white and black, and so on, in the same respect.

Contrary concepts are IMMEDIATELY OPPOSED if there is no middle ground between them and if collectively they embrace the entire extension of the genus to which they belong. For instance, "mortal" and "immortal" are immediately opposed contraries belonging to the genus of "living being." Every living being is either mortal or immortal: if a living being is mortal, it is not immortal; and if it is not mortal, it is immortal. Non-living beings, however, are neither mortal nor immortal, for they do not belong to the genus of things of which mortality and immortality can be predicated. "Mortal" means "having life that is subject to death"; "immortal" means "having life that is not subject to death." A stone, since it does not have life, is neither mortal nor immortal. The use of immediately opposed contraries in inference is similar in many ways to that of contradictories.

Contrary concepts are MEDIATELY OPPOSED if there is a middle ground between them. In the genus of color, for instance, various shades of gray intervene between black and white; and in the genus of both spatial and temporal order an indefinite number of units may intervene between the first and the last of a series. Both of two mediately opposed contraries can be absent from a subject even if the subject belongs to the genus of things in which they are sometimes found. For instance, it is possible for a colored thing to be neither black nor white, but gray; for a unit in a series to be neither the first nor the last, but somewhere in between; for a thing susceptible of heat to be neither hot nor cold, but lukewarm.

Some concepts that on first consideration might seem to be privative are generally regarded as contraries; for they are not looked upon as mere negations of perfections that ought to be present, but as expressions of something positive at the opposite extreme of the same genus as the perfection that they negate. "Sickness," for instance, is generally not looked upon as a mere negation of health in a subject that ought to have health but as something that positively interferes with health. Similarly, "insanity" is not considered a mere negation of sanity but a positive force within an insane person.

Some concepts that from their verbal expression might seem to be contradictories are actually contraries; for the one is not the mere negation of the other, but each is something positive at the opposite extreme of the same genus—for instance, "kind" and "unkind," "holy" and "unholy," "just" and "unjust." "Unkind" is not the same as "not kind." A stone is not kind, but it cannot be unkind.

3—DISPARATE CONCEPTS are incompatible and simply diverse. They are concepts of things that belong to the same genus (either proximate or remote) but differ at least specifically, yet not as contraries; for instance, "square" and "circle," both of which belong to the genus of plane figure; "dog" and "cat," both of which belong to the genus of animal; and "apple" and "peach," both of which belong to the genus of fruit.

In inference disparate concepts are similar to contraries and for this reason are sometimes called contrary concepts.

Exercise

I. What kind of opposition is exemplified in each of the following pairs? Give the reason for your answer.

1. Kind and not-kind.
2. Kind and unkind.
3. Alive and dead.
4. Alive and lifeless.
5. Parent and offspring.
6. Corporeal and incorporeal.
7. Being and non-being.
8. Big and small.
9. Friendly and unfriendly.
10. Mortal and immortal.
11. Mortal and not-mortal.
12. Expensive and inexpensive.
13. High and low.
14. Cabbage and potato.

15. High and heavy.
16. Ruler and subject.
17. Hot and cold.
18. Expensive and cheap.
19. Perfect and defective.
20. Endowed with sight and blind.
21. High and not-high.
22. Brother and sister-or-brother.
23. Avaricious and prodigal.
24. Grandparent and grandchild.
25. North and south.
26. Peach and lemon.
27. Rational and irrational.
28. Finite and infinite.
29. Creator and creature.
30. Cause and effect.

II. Are the following inferences valid or invalid? Give the reason for your answer.

1. It is white; therefore it is not black.
2. It is not white; therefore it is black.
3. It is not alive; therefore it is dead.
4. It is not alive; therefore it is lifeless.
5. It is not expensive; therefore it is cheap.
6. It is not endowed with sight; therefore it is blind.
7. He is not very friendly to me; therefore he must be somewhat unfriendly to me.
8. It's a peach; therefore it's not a lemon.
9. It's not a peach; therefore it is a lemon.
10. He is not kind to me; therefore he is unkind to me.

CHAPTER 12

The Term

THOUGHT IS INVISIBLE, imperceptible to the senses, and strictly personal. It is a vital act, and cannot exist except in the thinker's mind. We cannot put a thought bodily—so to speak—into someone else's mind, as we put a goldfish into a bowl; thought cannot pass directly from one mind to another. We can communicate our thoughts only indirectly and through the intermediacy of various kinds of sensible signs.

The principal means of communicating thought is language.[1] We think; then we express our thought in suitable language; and then, if our hearers rightly interpret what they hear, they rethink our thoughts for themselves and thus make our thoughts their own personal possession.

In Chapter 2, as a preliminary to the study of inference, we treated briefly of the term in its role of subject and predicate, defining it as a word or group of words that can serve as the subject or predicate of a proposition. In the present chapter we shall first inquire further into the nature of the term and its relationship to what it signifies.

[1] Language has the fourfold function of expressing, communicating, facilitating, and preserving thought and emotion. The ability to speak follows necessarily from the nature of man. Because man is rational (unless his mental powers are undeveloped or accidentally impeded), he has something to say; and because he is an animal, he has the mechanism to say it with.

Man not only has the ability, but also the exigency, to speak. He is a social being; and the proper physical, mental, and moral development of each individual man requires the cooperative efforts of many other men. Now, without language such cooperation would be impossible. Man needs language, too, because it is the medium by which much of his cultural heritage is handed down to him. Man's need for language also follows from the nature of his cognitive faculties. The connection between thinking and the expression of thought is so intimate that thought is greatly impeded in persons whose command of language is deficient.

Then we shall treat of the division of terms into univocal, equivocal, and analogous. Finally we shall study the supposition of terms.

Notice that we shall treat principally of the oral term. Written terms, however, signify oral terms; [2] and oral terms signify concepts (or mental terms), which are formal signs of things.

1. DEFINITION OF "TERM"

An oral term is an articulate sound that serves as a conventional or arbitrary sign of a concept.

We saw in Chapter 2 that a term consists either of one word or of an entire group of words that signify a concept when they are taken together as a unit. We shall now explain each part of the definition given above.

a. "An Articulate Sound"

Only an articulate sound can be a term; that is, a sound formed in the mouth and consisting of one or more distinct syllables. A fire siren, a shriek, and a groan are not articulate sounds and therefore are not terms. (There are other reasons, too, why these are not terms.)

b. A "Sign"

A sign is anything that leads to the knowledge of something distinct from itself. A red traffic light at a street corner is a sign leading me to the knowledge that I must stop; the sound of a horn is a sign leading me to the knowledge of an approaching automobile; a certain arrangement of ink on a page, "m-a-n," leads me to the knowledge of man; smoke is a sign of fire; and a groan is a sign of pain.

c. "A Conventional or Arbitrary Sign"

What is the *source of the connection* between a sign and what it signifies? The answer to this question is the basis of the division of signs into natural, on the one hand, and conventional or arbitrary, on the other.

[2] The sign language of deaf-mutes and certain types of written characters, such as hieroglyphics, ideograms, and diagrams, directly signify concepts. Written language, however, directly signifies thought, which in turn signifies things.

A NATURAL SIGN is one whose connection with what it signifies is from nature, independently of human conventions and the arbitrary will of man. Smoke is a natural sign of fire; the connection between smoke and fire does not arise from the arbitrary will of man, but is determined by nature itself. A groan is a natural sign of pain; a blush, of emotion; a scream, of fright; thunder, of lightning; and a low barometer, of unsettled weather.

A CONVENTIONAL OR ARBITRARY SIGN is one whose connection with what it signifies arises either from convention or custom or from the arbitrary will of man. Except for a few onomatopoeic words that are formed in imitation of certain sounds ("bow-wow," "moo," "meow," "ping-pong," "crash," "slap," "pop"), there is nothing in the make-up of a given word that requires it to have a particular meaning. At least ultimately, all words (with the exceptions noted above) get their meaning solely from convention. Even imitative words like "bow-wow," and so on, are conventional more than natural. Their resemblance to the sound they signify is so slight that you would not know their meanings from the words alone. The words for animal cries vary considerably, too, in different languages; but if they were purely natural signs, they would have to be the same in all languages. A dog, for instance, says "bow-wow" in English, "guáu guáu" in Spanish, "wauwau" in German, and "bau bau" in Italian.

Terms are conventional or arbitrary signs.[3] It does not follow from this, however, that we are free to give them any meaning we want to without any limitation. We cannot, for instance, use "wolf" to signify the animal commonly called "sheep," or "nitwit" to signify "beloved." The meanings of these words are already fixed by usage. In order to communicate our thoughts to others we must use words in accordance with their commonly accepted meanings. Otherwise, our words will stand for one set of concepts for us, and for a different set of concepts for our hearers.

[3] Oral terms are instrumental (not formal) signs. They exist as sounds first and only secondarily as signs of the things that they present to our minds. You can know them as sounds without knowing them as signs, as you do when you hear an unknown foreign language. And you must know them as sounds before they can lead you to the knowledge of the things that they signify. For an explanation of the nature of instrumental and formal signs, see p. 208, Notes 3 and 4.

To some extent, of course, we must coin words to signify concepts for which there is no suitable word. To some extent, too, we can give words the meanings that we want to. We shall recur to this point when we take up nominal definition.

d. "Sign of a Concept"

Terms signify concepts directly and immediately; indirectly and through the intermediacy of concepts they also signify things.

Exercise

Basing your answer on the definition and explanation of oral term, give as many reasons as you can why the noise that a cat makes when you step on its tail is not a term.

2. KINDS OF TERMS: UNIVOCAL, EQUIVOCAL, AND ANALOGOUS

The classifications given in Chapter 11, pp. 209-220, are primarily classifications of concepts; but the same names are applied in a secondary sense to the terms by which the concepts are signified. A term signifying a first intention is called a term of first intention; a term signifying an abstract concept is called an abstract term; terms signifying contrary concepts are called contrary terms; and so on. To enumerate all of them again would involve needless repetition.

The classification of terms into singular, particular, and universal (given in Chapter 2) and the following classification into univocal, equivocal, and analogous are primarily classifications of terms.

Is a term applied to at least two of its inferiors in exactly the same sense, in an entirely different sense, or in a sense that is partly the same and partly different? The answer to this question is the basis of the division of terms into univocal, equivocal, and analogous. Note that before you can tell whether a term is univocal, equivocal, or analogous, you must consider it (at least implicitly) in relation to more than one inferior. The question "Is *man* univocal, equivocal, or analogous?" does not make sense unless at least two uses of the word "man" are referred to. You must compare the meaning of "man" in one use with its meaning in another. If it has the same meaning in both uses, it is univocal; if it has an entirely different meaning, it is equivocal; if it has a meaning that is partly the same and partly different, it is analogous.

The same word is sometimes univocal in one context, equivocal in another, and analogous in still another. For instance, "pen" is univocal in "Parkers and Shaeffers are pens," but equivocal in "Pens are instruments for writing and enclosures for pigs." "Pens" has exactly the same sense when it is predicated of Parkers and Shaeffers, but a sense that is completely different when it is predicated of instruments for writing and enclosures for pigs.

a. Univocal Terms

Univocal terms are applied to their inferiors in *exactly the same sense.* In other words, a term is univocal if it signifies exactly the *same concept,* or essence, in (at least) two occurrences of the term. When I say "James, John, and Peter are men," I use "men" univocally because I apply it to three subjects in exactly the same sense; "man" stands for the same concept, or essence, with reference to each of them. When I say "Napoleon was a man; a scarecrow is a man," "man" is not univocal because it has a different meaning in each occurrence.

b. Equivocal Terms

Equivocal terms are applied to their inferiors in a *completely different sense.* They stand for *different concepts,* or essences, in each of (at least) two occurrences of the term; it is a pure accident that the same term is applied to different kinds of inferiors (or else we have lost sight of, or no longer advert to, an original similarity of meaning). Equivocal terms signify as many concepts as they have completely different meanings. There are no equivocal concepts.

"Pen" is equivocal when applied to the enclosure for animals and the instrument for writing; "pitch," when applied to the black, tenacious substance and the delivery of a ball to a batter; "page," to the page in court and the page of a book; "bark," when applied to the bark of a dog and the bark of a tree.

Some terms are equivocal both when they are spoken and when they are written; for instance, the examples given in the preceding paragraph. Some terms are equivocal only when spoken; for instance, "yolk," signifying the yellow of an egg, and "yoke," signifying the frame that joins two oxen. Some terms are equivocal only when they are written; for instance, "incense," signifying to make angry, and "incense," signifying the aromatic substance.

c. *Analogous Terms*

Analogous terms are applied to their inferiors in a sense that is *partly the same and partly different.*

The inferiors of an analogous term are called analogues, or analogates. A primary analogue is one to which a term is applied primarily and absolutely. A secondary analogue is one to which a term is applied secondarily and relatively. Thus "health" is applied primarily and absolutely to a living organism; secondarily and relatively to food, climate, exercise, work, complexion, and so on. These latter are called healthy (or healthful) only secondarily and because of their relationship to health in living organisms—they are either a cause, an occasion, or a sign of health in a living organism.

Analogy is divided into (1) intrinsic and extrinsic analogy, and (2) analogy of proportionality and attribution.

1) **INTRINSIC AND EXTRINSIC ANALOGY.** Is the concept that is signified by an analogous term realized in each of its analogues, or is it extrinsic to one of them? The answer to this question is the basis of the division of analogy into intrinsic and extrinsic.

a) **Intrinsic Analogy.** Analogy is intrinsic if the concept that is signified by an analogous term is realized in each of the analogues of the term. "Being," for instance, is analogous by intrinsic analogy with reference to all its analogues. The perfection signified by "being" is actually in everything that we call a being. We do not call things beings merely because of some similarity we fancy them to have towards other beings or because they stand in certain relationships towards other beings. We call things beings because they *are* beings intrinsically and in their own right.

b) **Extrinsic Analogy.** Analogy is extrinsic if the concept signified by an analogous term is realized only in its primary analogues. The term is applied to the other analogues on account of their relationship to the primary analogue; but the perfection signified by the term is not actually in them. "Healthy," for instance, is predicated of a living organism and, as well, of food, climate, exercise, work, complexion, and so on. But notice that only a living organism is the subject of health; it is the only thing that has health intrinsically and the only thing of which health is predicated primarily and absolutely. Food, climate, and so on, are not healthy intrinsically. Health is attributed to them as being merely causes, occasions, or signs of health in some other being. They do not have health within themselves, but are *called* healthy because of the relationship that each of them has towards health in a living organism. They are healthy by *extrinsic denomination;* that is, because of their relationship to health in something outside of, or extrinsic to, themselves.

The base of a mountain, to take another example, is not a foot intrinsically; it is merely called a foot because of a similarity that we conceive it as having. All metaphors exemplify extrinsic analogy. Thus, we say that a meadow *smiles* (although it does not really smile), bread is a *staff* (although it is really not a staff), the sky *glowers,* and the sea is *angry.*

For all practical purposes, terms that are analogous only by extrinsic analogy are *equivalent to equivocal terms.* In fact, some authors (including Aristotle) call them equivocal.

2) ANALOGY OF PROPORTIONALITY AND ATTRIBUTION.[4] Is the application of the term to various analogues based on a *similarity of two relationships,* or is it based on a *relationship* of a secondary analogue to a primary analogue? The answer to this question is the basis of the division of analogy into analogy of proportionality and analogy of attribution.

a) **Analogy of Proportionality.** Analogy of proportionality is based on a *similarity of two relationships.* Two examples will make this clear.

A pen is good in proportion to its fitness to fulfill its function of writing; ink eradicator is good in proportion to its fitness to fulfill its function of removing ink. To write and to remove ink are very different functions, and for a thing to be good for writing is very different from a thing's being good for removing ink. Yet the two uses of "good" are partially alike in meaning in one respect at least:

[4] Analogy of proportionality and attribution are of great importance in metaphysics, in which analogy of being is studied at length.

both a pen and an ink eradicator are called good in proportion to the fitness of each to do its job well. The proportion of the one to its function is similar to the proportion of the other to its function. Hence, "good" is predicated by analogy of proportionality. In other words, *the relationship* of a good pen to the proper fulfillment of its function *is similar to the relationship* of good ink eradicator to the proper fulfillment of its function. This *similarity of two relationships*, or proportions, accounts for the partial likeness in the meaning of "good" when it is predicated of a good pen and of good ink eradicator. The diversity of functions accounts for the difference in meaning. Hence, the meaning of "good" in each case is partly alike and partly different.

To take a second example, "foot" is predicated of what a man stands on and of the base of a mountain by analogy of proportionality. The base of a mountain has no direct resemblance whatsoever to the foot of a man. But *the relationship* of a mountain to its base is *similar to the relationship* of a man to his feet. On the basis of this similarity of relationships, the term "foot," which is applied in its primary sense to the foot of a man, is applied in a secondary sense to the base of a mountain. Except for this similarity of relationships, the sense of "foot" is completely different in each occurrence. But the meaning is partly alike in at least this one respect.

***b*) Analogy of Attribution.** Analogy of attribution (or proportion) is based on a *relationship* of a secondary analogue to a primary analogue. "Healthy," for instance, is predicated of a living organism and, as well, of food, climate, exercise, work, complexion, and so on, because of the relationship in which each of the latter stand toward health in the living organism: healthy food, climate, exercise, and work are related to health in the human organism as its cause or occasion; a healthy complexion is related to health in the human organism as its sign; and so on.

Again, when we read "Macbeth" or "Hamlet" we say that we are reading Shakespeare. We are using the name of an author for his works because of the relation of authorship in which he stands towards them. We call a stay in the country a "rest" because it is an occasion of rest. We call a legislative body a "house" because it meets in a house.

Notice that the same term can sometimes be predicated by both analogy of proportionality and by analogy of attribution. "Being," for instance, is predicated by analogy of proportionality in some contexts and by analogy of attribution in others.

Exercise

I. Classify the underlined terms as (1) univocal, (2) equivocal, (3) analogous by analogy of proportionality, or (4) analogous by analogy of attribution. If the underlined terms are analogous, state if the analogy is intrinsic or extrinsic. Explain all your answers.

1. *Triangles* are scalene, isosceles, or equilateral.
2. His *taste* for fried chicken is more developed than his *taste* for poetry.
3. *Good* robbers are rarely *good* men.
4. People do too much *lying*—some in their beds, and some in their conversation.
5. Cabbages and potatoes are *vegetables.*
6. A nurse must have *patience* with her *patients.*
7. Both Russia and the United States of America are *democracies.*
8. Both have *freedom of religion.*
9. Newly born babies weigh anywhere from two to a dozen pounds; therefore it is false that all men are created *equal.*
10. The *eye* of the intellect sees many things that the *eye* of the body cannot see.
11. Both God and creatures are *beings.*
12. Both cats and dogs are *animals.*
13. Both the carpenters and the musicians are *skillful.*
14. He *ran* as he *ran* the power mower.
15. He's not *free* to go out because he's confined to his bed; but one who is not *free* is a slave; therefore he is a slave.

II. Study the meanings of "man" in the following examples.

1. Man is a rational animal.
2. He belongs to the men's division.
3. He's a real man.
4. The picture on the wall is a man.
5. The child is father to the man.
6. Are you a mouse or a man?

III. Study the meanings of "body," "organism," and other words in various contexts, and decide whether they are univocal, equivocal, or analogous.

3. SUPPOSITION OF TERMS

We shall now consider supposition of terms (*suppositio terminorum*), which is the most important of the properties that terms acquire from their use in propositions. First, we shall define supposition; then we shall explain and illustrate its principal kinds.

a. Notion of Supposition

Supposition is the property (that terms acquire from their use in a proposition) by which a term stands for a definite one of the various things that it can stand for.

We must carefully distinguish between the *meaning,* or definition, of a term and its *supposition.* Terms have meaning by themselves, outside of a proposition (for instance, the words that are defined in a dictionary); but terms have supposition only from their function in discourse. Notice that a term can have the same meaning (signification or definition) in various occurrences and still stand for very different things. The term "man," for instance, has exactly the same meaning in each of the following examples—in each case it signifies "rational animal"; yet in each example "man" stands for something very different. What "man" stands for is determined in each instance by the nature of the predicate attributed to it.

1. *Man* has three letters.
2. *Man* is a species.
3. *Man* is mortal.
4. A *man* is running down the street.

In Example 1, "man" stands for the mere material make-up of the word "man" without any regard for its meaning. Only in the material make-up of the word, does "man" have three letters. In Example 2, "man" stands for the essence "man" as it exists only in the mind; for man cannot exist as a species except in the mind. In Example 3, "man" also stands for the essence "man." But here we prescind from his actual existence in the real order, neither affirming nor denying it.

In Example 4, however, "man" stands for an actually existing man. Yet in all four examples "man" has exactly the same meaning, signification, or definition. Its comprehension does not vary, in spite of the fact that in each instance it stands for a different thing.

The notion of supposition is not entirely new to us. We have alluded to it several times in previous chapters. For instance, when we spoke of the collective *use*, of a term, as opposed to its distributive, or divisive, use, we were actually treating of supposition. (In the proposition "All the ducks cover the entire pond," "all the ducks" is used collectively, since all of them are taken together as a unit. However, in the proposition "All the ducks are flying," "all the ducks" is used distributively, or divisively, since each individual duck is flying.) The division of terms into singular, particular, and universal is also a division of supposition, since it is based on the *application* of terms to their inferiors. We also alluded to supposition in connection with the fallacy of equivocation. For instance, the syllogism "Man is a species; but you are a man; therefore you are a species" is invalid because of an illegitimate change in the supposition of "man."

The meaning of supposition will be clearer after we have studied its various kinds.

b. Kinds of Supposition

We shall explain only a few of the many kinds of supposition. First, we shall treat of an important classification of the supposition of terms insofar as they are the subjects of propositions. Much of what we say in this connection will be applicable, as well, to other terms. Then, we shall give a brief account of several other kinds.

1) SUPPOSITION OF SUBJECT TERMS. The supposition of subject terms—indeed, of all terms—is either material or formal, and formal supposition has several subdivisions.

a) **Material Supposition.** Material supposition is the use of a term for the spoken or written sign itself, but not for what it signifies. In the following example the supposition of "man" is material: "*Man* rimes with *ban*," "*Man* is the first word of this sentence," and "*Man* is nothing but a little ink on a page." In all these examples "man" actually signifies "rational animal." Nevertheless, man's nature as a rational animal has nothing to do with the fact that *man* rimes with *ban,* and so on. *Man* would still rime with *ban* even if it had a different meaning. In each example, the nature of the predicate attributed to "man" is such that "man" must stand for the spoken or written sign itself, but not for what it signifies.

b) **Formal Supposition.** Formal supposition is the use of a term for what it signifies. The supposition of "man" is formal in the proposition "Man is a rational animal." Not the word "man" but what the word "man" signifies is a rational animal. Formal supposition is logical or real.

1—LOGICAL SUPPOSITION. Logical supposition is the use of a term for a second intention.[5] The supposition of "man" is logical in the following examples: "*Man* is a species," "*Man* is the middle term of a syllogism," "*Man* is a universal concept," and "*Man* has less extension but greater comprehension than *animal.*" Man cannot exist as a species, as the middle term of a syllogism, as a universal concept, and so on, except in the mind. Supposition is logical whenever a term stands *merely for the concept* that it signifies. Thus, the *concept* "man" is a species, the *concept* "man" is the middle term of a syllogism, and so on.

2—REAL SUPPOSITION. Real supposition is the use of a term for a first intention. The supposition of "man" is real in the following examples: "Man is a rational animal," "Man is mortal," and "A man is running down the street." When we say that man is a rational animal, and so on, we are using the term "man" for the essence "man," not only as this essence exists in our minds but also as it exists (or can exist) in the real order. Man exists (or can exist) as a rational animal, as something mortal, and as something running down the street, whether we think of him or not.

Real supposition is, on the one hand, either absolute or personal and, on the other hand, either essential or accidental. To some extent these divisions overlap.

a—*Absolute and Personal Supposition.* Does a term stand directly for an essence as such, or does it stand directly for a subject in which an essence is realized and only indirectly for the essence? The answer to this question is the basis for the division of real supposition into absolute and personal.

[5] For an explanation of first and second intentions see pp. 209-210 and 308-309.

(1) ABSOLUTE SUPPOSITION [6] is the use of a term for an essence as such, prescinding from, but not excluding, actual existence in the real order. The supposition, for instance, of "man" in "Man is mortal" and of "triangle" in "A triangle is a plane figure bounded by three straight lines" is absolute.

Absolute supposition does not directly set before the mind the individual subjects in which an essence is realized; but it does do this indirectly, because what is true of an essence as such must be true of every individual subject having the essence. Hence, absolute supposition is *virtually* universal. For instance, if *man as such* is mortal, then *every* man is mortal. We considered this use of the subject term when we studied the indeterminate proposition.

Absolute supposition is always also essential supposition, but not vice versa.

(2) PERSONAL SUPPOSITION is the use of a term, not for an essence as such, but for the subject in which the essence signified by a term is realized. The supposition, for instance, of "the brown horse" in the proposition "The brown horse is more valuable" is personal. It is not the essence "brown horse" that is more valuable but the subject having this essence.

The subjects of all quantified propositions have personal supposition; and personal supposition is singular, particular, or universal, depending on what portion of the extension of a term it sets before the mind and on whether or not this portion is designated definitely.

b—*Essential and Accidental Supposition.* Does a term stand for a subject inasmuch as it is the subject of essential attributes—that is, of attributes that cannot be absent from it—or does it stand for a subject only inasmuch as it is the subject of nonessential, or accidental, attributes? The answer to this question is the basis for the division of real supposition into essential and accidental.

(1) ESSENTIAL SUPPOSITION is the use of a term for a subject inasmuch as this subject is the subject of essential, or necessary, attributes. The supposition of "man" in each of the following propositions is essential: "Man is mortal" and "Every man is mortal."

[6] Notice that absolute supposition is *real* supposition only in the very negative sense that it does not exclude existence in the real order, whereas logical supposition does. Inasmuch as absolute supposition does not positively assert the existence of what a term stands for, it is sometimes called logical supposition. See "Direct Universal," p. 241.

Notice, however, that the supposition of the first "man" is absolute; of the second, personal.

(2) ACCIDENTAL SUPPOSITION is the use of a term for a subject inasmuch as this subject is the subject of accidental, or unnecessary, attributes. For instance, the supposition of "the man" in "The man has a dirty face" is accidental (and also personal). To have a dirty face does not belong to the nature of man as such, as it is possible for the man not to have a dirty face.

A Note on Existence. Supposition, as we have seen, is a property that terms acquire from their use in a proposition. In a proposition, the existence of the subject is always asserted: sometimes this existence is only in the mind; sometimes it is also in the real order. A proposition asserting the existence of something in the *real* order is an existential proposition.

Now when we consider a term by itself and outside of a proposition, we prescind entirely from the actual existence of what it signifies. But when we consider a term in the context of a proposition, we do not prescind from actual existence, since we are using the term as actually standing for an existent thing—it always stands for a thing as having at least mental existence and sometimes for a thing as also having real existence. Hence, in treating of the supposition of terms, we must make at least a few remarks on the relationship to existence of absolute and personal, and of essential and accidental, supposition.

Absolute supposition is never existential, since (as the very name "absolute" suggests) it prescinds from all orders of existence. Accidental supposition, on the other hand, is always existential (at least conditionally). The reason for this is that the copula directly affirms or denies an accidental attribute in a subject whose existence is presupposed. For instance, when we say "He is seated," we presuppose that he *is;* but when we say "A mammoth is an elephant-like animal," we do not presuppose that a mammoth *is*. In regard to both essential and personal supposition, we must determine from the context whether or not they are existential.

Exercise

I. Which of the kinds of supposition treated in this section are illustrated by "man" (or "men") in each of the following propositions? Explain and defend your answer.

1. *Man* is a rational animal.
2. *Man* is one syllable.
3. *Man* is a universal concept.
4. *Man* is predicable of many in exactly the same sense.
5. *Man* is a creature.
6. All *men* are mortal.
7. *Man* is mortal.
8. This *man* is mortal.
9. *Man* exists and has existed for many thousands of years.
10. Take *man* away from *woman* and all you have left is *wo*.
11. Some *men* are singing.
12. "Some *men*" is the subject of the last proposition.
13. A *man* is a weak and sinful creature.
14. A *man* made those footprints.
15. *Man* has three letters.

II. Criticize the following syllogisms by calling attention to illegitimate changes in supposition. Notice, too, whether or not the real existence of the subject is asserted.

1. Man is a species of the genus "animal."
   But John is a man.
   Therefore John is a species of the genus "animal."
2. Man has one syllable;
   but you are a man;
   therefore you have one syllable.
3. A man is speaking too loudly;
   but you are a man;
   therefore you are speaking too loudly.
4. God is a self-existent being;
   but a self-existent being must exist;
   therefore God must exist.
5. God is that being than which no greater can be thought of;
   but what exists in reality as well as in the mind is greater than what exists only in the mind;
   therefore God must really exist.

2) SOME OTHER KINDS OF SUPPOSITION. We have already called attention to the fact that some of the classifications of terms and concepts are in reality classifications of supposition. We shall now briefly indicate and illustrate a few other kinds of supposition.

The supposition of "dog" is *proper* in the proposition "A dog is an animal," but *improper* or *metaphorical* in the proposition "The dog! He ought to be locked up in jail."

The supposition of "a horse" is *determinate* in "Lost: a horse." In this example, "a horse" stands for a definite horse, although it indicates this horse indefinitely. However, in the example "Wanted: a horse," the supposition of the term "a horse" is *indeterminate.* In this proposition, "a horse" does not stand for a definite horse, but for any horse that will suit the man who advertises for a horse.

The supposition of the term "five men" is *distributive* of *divisive* in the proposition "Five men are walking," since each individual man is walking. But in the proposition "Five men make up a basketball team," the supposition of "five men" is *collective;* the predicate "making up a basketball team" is not applicable to each of the five men taken alone, but only to all five of them taken together as a unit.

There are innumerable other kinds of supposition, but we have studied enough of them to realize the necessity of examining a context very closely in order to tell exactly what a term stands for.

Exercise

I. Classify and compare the supposition of the underlined terms in each pair of propositions.

1. *a. The members of this class* weigh about two tons.
   b. The members of this class are university students.

2. *a.* For sale: a *horse.*
   b. Wanted: a *stenographer.*

3. *a.* A *whale* is a mammal.
   b. Whales are swimming two miles north of us.

4. *a.* I am looking for *a good place to sleep.*
   b. The Sea View Hotel is *a good place to sleep.*

5. *a.* He is a *wolf* in *sheep's* clothing.
   b. A *wolf* sometimes hunts *sheep.*

II. Show how we have considered supposition of terms in various parts of logic that we have already studied—for instance, in connection with the following topics: the quantity of propositions, indeterminate propositions, conversion, the rules of the syllogism, fallacies, and so on.

CHAPTER 13

Further Analysis of the Concept

IN THE PRESENT CHAPTER we shall first explain the notion of essence and the nature of universals. The terms "essence" and "universal" recur frequently in philosophical treatises, and an understanding of them will serve both as a background for general readings in philosophy and as a prerequisite to the study of the predicables, the categories, and definition. Then we shall treat successively of the predicables, of the Aristotelian categories, of definition, and of logical division. To a great extent, the present chapter is a development of the notions of comprehension and extension, which we treated briefly in Chapter 2.

1. ESSENCE

In connection with the predicables and definition, the term "essence" has a more restricted sense than it often had in previous chapters. We have often used "essence" in a broad sense, in which it signifies "what a thing is" in any way whatsoever. According to the broad meaning of "essence," if we grasp what a thing is, no matter how vaguely or indeterminately, even if we grasp it only as a vague and indeterminate "something"—or as "something big," "something colored," "something far away," and so on—we grasp its essence or quiddity. For instance, if we know a horse only as "something brown," we know what the horse is at least insofar as it is something brown; hence, we grasp its essence in this broad sense of the word.

But in connection with the predicables and definition we use "essence" in the strict or proper sense, in which it includes only *the basic intelligible elements of the comprehension of a concept* but does not include the derived elements. For instance, the essence, in this sense, of "triangle" includes "figure bounded by three straight lines meeting by twos on a plane" but does not include "enclosing three interior angles." The three lines of a triangle are looked upon as prior to the three angles and more basic than they. If you think of the three lines meeting by twos at three points on a plane, you think of what a triangle is primarily and necessarily; as a consequence of having this essence—as a consequence, that is, of the three lines meeting by twos at three points on a plane—a triangle has three interior angles. We do not think of the three angles as the reason why a triangle has three straight lines as sides, but of the three straight lines as the reason why it has three angles.

Similarly, the essence (in the strict sense) of "man" is "rational animal" rather than "speaking animal" or "tool-using animal," although the notes "speaking" and "tool-using" suffice to differentiate man from all other kinds of animals. The reason for this is that "rational animal" is looked upon as prior to, and more basic than, "speaking animal," "tool-using animal," and so on. Man is not a rational animal because he can speak and use tools; rather, he can speak and use tools because he is a rational animal. Speaking and using tools may be reasons *for our knowing* that he is a rational animal—since we can reason from man's properties and activities to his essence—but they are not the reason for his being a rational animal.

Our explanation of universals, of the predicables, and of definition will throw further light on the nature of essence.

2. UNIVERSAL AS ABSTRACT

In previous chapters we often used the word "universal" as synonymous with "distributed" and as opposed to "particular" and "singular." A term and concept are universal in this sense if they stand for each of their inferiors (that is, if they stand for each of the subjects that they can be applied to). We shall now use the word "universal," not as synonymous with "distributed," but as synonymous with one meaning of "abstract" (except that "universal," unlike "abstract," is used both as a noun and an adjective).

Abstraction, as we saw in Chapter 11,[1] consists in considering one aspect of a thing while omitting other aspects. Now a UNIVERSAL, as we understand the word in the present chapter, is a concept that expresses the essence (quiddity, or nature) of many really distinct individual subjects but leaves their differences entirely unexpressed. It expresses just an essence, and nothing else. The concept "man," for instance, is a universal; and what is signified by "man" is such an essence. The essence "man" is found simultaneously in Peter, Paul, John, and Mary—Peter is a man, Paul is a man, John is a man, and Mary is a man (at least in the sense that she is a subject having a human nature). Peter, Paul, John, and Mary are four (many) completely distinct individual subjects—Peter is not Paul, Paul is not John, and so on. They not only differ from one another in being each a different individual but by innumerable other differences as well. They differ, for instance, in sex, age, height, and weight; in ability, virtue, and attainments; in race, place of residence, and social status. "Man" expresses the essence (nature, or quiddity) of each of them insofar as they are rational animals and nothing more, and leaves innumerable common attributes, together with all their individual differences, entirely unexpressed. The concept "man," then, is universal, because it expresses only what can exist concretely and at the same time in each of many distinct individual subjects; and, however much these subjects differ from one another in other respects, the essence "man" can be predicated of each of them in exactly the same sense.

Universals, as understood here, must be distinguished from transcendental concepts such as "being," "good," and "true." Transcendental concepts are similar to universals in that what they signify can be realized concretely and at the same time in each of many subjects—there are, for instance, many beings, many good things, and so on. Transcendental concepts differ from universals, however, in that they express the differences among things, as well as their similarities, and consequently are never predicated of two things in exactly the same sense.

Let us compare the way the transcendental concept "being" is predicated of Peter, Paul, John, and Mary with the way "man" is

[1] See p. 211.

predicated of them. We have already seen that "man" has *exactly the same sense* when it is predicated of each of them, although they differ from one another in age, sex, height, weight, and so on. These differences are attributes of men, but none of these differences is man, and consequently none of these differences is expressed by the concept "man." The concept of "being," however, expresses all that is in its inferiors; it expresses not only the notes in which they are similar to one another, *but also their differences.* These differences are being—since they are something—and consequently they are expressed by the concept "being." Now, since things actually are different from one another, and since "being" expresses their differences, the meaning of "being" shifts according to the differences among things.[2]

From this it is clear that "being" is analogous in relation to its inferiors, whereas "man" is univocal.

The distinction between DIRECT and REFLEX UNIVERSALS is of importance in logic and in other branches of philosophy as well. It is a special case of the more general division of concepts into first and second intentions.

A DIRECT UNIVERSAL is a concept signifying an *absolute essence*—that is, an essence (nature, or quiddity) *as such,* abstracted from all individualizing conditions, and considered without reference to the mode of existence it has either in the mind or in things. You grasp the absolute essence "man," for instance, if you think of "man" and nothing else—not of Peter or Mary, or this man or that man, or some man or all men, but just "man"—completely prescinding from all orders of existence and expressing only the comprehension of the essence "man" without any consideration of its extension.

Nothing but individual, fully determined natures can exist in the real order. Consequently, direct universals, or absolute essences, cannot exist as such except in the mind. Nevertheless, *all that a direct universal signifies* can exist in the real order; all that it signifies has been abstracted from things and can therefore be realized in things and predicated of them.

A direct universal, as we have seen, is considered without refer-

[2] The meaning of "being" is explained at length in metaphysics. Notice that the expression "human being" is synonymous with "man."

ence to its inferiors. It *can* be referred to its inferiors, but its meaning is independent of any such reference. Suppose, now, that we go one step further and actually refer it to its inferiors; suppose we consider an essence as capable of being realized in many subjects and of being predicated of them. What we grasp then is a reflex universal. A REFLEX UNIVERSAL, therefore, is an essence, nature, or quiddity, considered with reference to the individuals in which it is verified and to its potential predicability. It includes not only the comprehension of an essence but also its multiplicability and its predicability (that is, its extension).

3. THE PREDICABLES

Before studying the predicables it will be helpful to review pages 17-19 on comprehension, on the distinction between basic and derived notes, on the meaning of absolute extension, and on the inverse ratio of comprehension and extension. To a great extent, the treatment of the predicables is nothing but an elaboration of these notions.

The predicables [3] are a classification of reflex universals based on the five ways in which they express the nature of subjects of which they are predicated. They are listed as species, genus, specific difference, logical property, and logical accident. These names primarily signify the relationships of universals to their inferiors, or the five ways in which they are used as predicates; but these names also signify the universals themselves. Thus, we not only say that "man" is predicated of John as his species, but also that "man" is his species.

The predicables are a classification of *reflex* universals, since we are here viewing universals with reference to their inferiors (with reference, that is, to the subjects in which the essence they signify can be realized and of which they can be predicated); we are considering not only their comprehension, but their extension and predicability as well.

First we shall give a general survey of the predicables, defining each of them very briefly and explaining why there are five predi-

[3] In this context the word "predicable" is a noun. We have often used the word as an adjective meaning "able to be predicated."

cables and only five; then we shall give a detailed explanation of each of them.

a. General Survey

The following analysis contains brief definitions of each of the predicables [4] and shows why there are exactly five predicables:

Every universal predicate expresses the nature of the subject of which it is predicated in one of the following ways. Either it expresses its essence (in the strict sense), or else it does not. If it expresses the essence of the subject, it either expresses all the basic constitutive notes (that is, the fully determined essence) and is predicated of the subject as its (1) SPECIES; or else it expresses only some of the basic constitutive notes (that is, the partially determined essence). If it expresses only some of the basic constitutive notes of the essence, it expresses either a determinable constitutive element and is predicated of the subject as its (2) GENUS; or else it expresses the determining constitutive element that distinguishes the essence from other essences belonging to the same genus and is predicated of the subject as its (3) SPECIFIC DIFFERENCE. Suppose, now, that the universal predicate does not express the essence of the subject it is predicated of. Then it either expresses an attribute that belongs to the subject necessarily (and convertibly) and is predicated of the subject as a (4) PROPERTY; or else it expresses an attribute that does not belong to the subject necessarily but only contingently and is predicated of the subject as a (5) LOGICAL ACCIDENT.

The following schema displays the structure of this analysis and sets off certain key words that will help us understand and remember the definitions of each of the predicables. This schema also emphasizes two very important distinctions—(*a*) the distinction between the notes that constitute an essence and those that do not constitute it but merely accompany it and (*b*) the distinction be-

[4] Note that the meaning of "genus" and "species" in logic is not the same as in the *biological sciences.* In them "species" means a group, or class, of animals or plants supposed to have descended from common ancestors and to be indefinitely fertile in breeding among themselves. "Genus" is the next higher class. We shall see that "genus" and "species" have a far more flexible meaning in logic.

tween the first four of the predicables, which are necessary to the subject, and the fifth predicable, which is not necessary to it. An understanding of these distinctions is an absolutely necessary prerequisite to an understanding of definition and of the very important division of propositions into necessary propositions and contingent propositions.

SYNOPTIC SCHEMA

	Every universal predicate expresses the nature of the subject of which it is predicated in one of the following ways:	(EXAMPLE)	The predicable that is exemplified when the adjoining member of the disjunction is verified:	
ESSENTIAL OR CONSTITUTIVE NOTES	*either* AS CONSTITUTING THE ESSENCE of the subject			
	either WHOLLY	("man," "rational animal")	(1) SPECIES	NECESSARY NOTES
	or PARTIALLY			
	either as a DETERMINABLE constitutive element	("animal")	(2) GENUS	NECESSARY NOTES
	or as a DETERMINING constitutive element	("rational")	(3) SPECIFIC DIFFERENCE	NECESSARY NOTES
NONESSENTIAL OR NONCONSTITUTIVE NOTES	*or* NOT AS CONSTITUTING THE ESSENCE of the subject but as ACCOMPANYING THE ESSENCE:			
	either NECESSARILY	("risible," "able to speak")	(4) LOGICAL PROPERTY	NECESSARY NOTES
	or NOT NECESSARILY BUT CONTINGENTLY	("white," "actually speaking")	(5) LOGICAL ACCIDENT	NOT NECESSARY

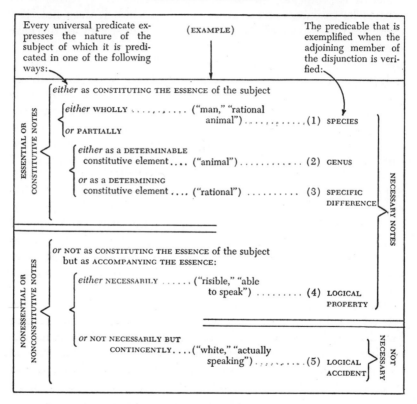

b. Detailed Explanation of Each Predicable

We shall prefix a schema of the category of substance to our detailed explanation of each of the predicables. This will help us see the relationship of species, genus, and difference among one another and understand various distinctions made in the definitions given below.

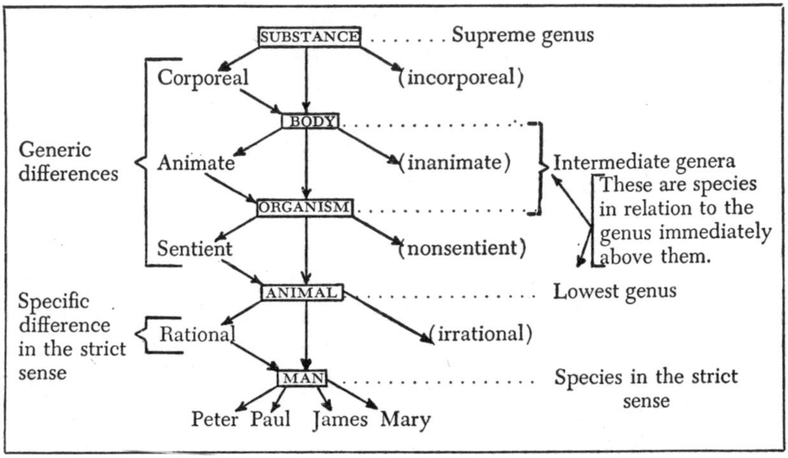

All the predicables are universals. Consequently all of them express the nature of many really distinct individuals and can be predicated of each of these individuals in exactly the same sense. This is taken for granted in the following definitions.

1) SPECIES. *A species, in the strict and proper sense, is a universal that expresses the completely determined essence of its inferiors and only that.* It gives a complete answer to the question, What is a thing essentially? but does not express attributes by which individuals having the same essence differ from one another.

The words "completely determined essence" must be understood correctly. They do not refer to the determinations that an essence, or nature, must have in order to exist in the real order. They refer, rather, to the basic notes involved in the intelligible structure of various kinds of things. The concept "man," for instance, is a species in relation to all individual men. It expresses only what a thing has to be in order to be *thought of* as a man, but does not express the innumerable attributes—such as nationality, parentage, place of birth, place of residence, sex, height, weight, age, and so on—that belong to a man because he is *this* or *that* man rather than because he is simply man.

A species in the strict and proper sense is predicated directly of individuals but (unlike a genus) only of individuals that do not differ from one another essentially. Between a species in the strict sense and the individuals of which it is predicated no other species in the strict sense can intervene. No species, for instance, intervenes between "man" and Peter, Paul, James, Mary, and so on.

In a broader sense, each genus beneath the supreme genus of a category (for instance, beneath "substance") is called a species in relation to the genus immediately above it. Thus, "animal," which is the genus of the species "man" is itself a species in relation to the genus "organism." Subdivisions of universals (both of genera and species) based on the presence or absence of accidental attributes are likewise called species in a broad sense. In this sense, "green triangle" and "non-green triangle" are species of "triangle."

Up to the present, we have considered species only from the point of view of comprehension. We can also consider it from the point of view of extension. Viewed under this aspect, "species," both in the strict and in a broader sense, is defined as *a class of things that is a sub-division of a broader class (that is, of a genus).*

Since "species" includes both "genus" and "difference" as its constitutive elements, our understanding of it will be more perfect after we have studied them.

2) GENUS. *A genus is a universal that expresses the incompletely determined essence of its inferiors, giving an incomplete answer to the question, What is a thing essentially?* A genus expresses the essence of its inferiors so indeterminately that what it signifies can be predicated of things that differ from one another specifically (of things, that is, that belong to different species). Thus, "animal," which is the genus of "man," expresses the nature of man so indeterminately that what it signifies can be predicated not only of men, but also of dogs, horses, elephants, whales, and so on, which differ from man specifically. "Organism," again, expresses the nature of "animal" so indeterminately that it can be predicated alike of animals and plants.

Considered from the point of view of extension, "genus" is defined as *a broader class made up of narrower classes (that is, of more than one species).*

A genus must be either a supreme genus, an intermediate genus, or a lowest genus. A *supreme genus* is one that is not a subdivision of any other genus (for instance, "substance"). A *lowest genus,* or *genus infimum,* has no other genus intervening between it and a species in the strict sense (for instance, "animal," in relation to "man"). An *intermediate genus* is one that intervenes between a supreme genus and a lowest genus ("body" and "organism"). (Refer to the schema on p. 245.)

From another point of view, genus is divided into proximate and remote. A *proximate genus* is directly above a species or another genus. Thus, "animal" is the proximate genus of the species "man," and "organism" is the proximate genus of the lower genus "animal." ("Proximate" is derived from *proximus,* the Latin word for "nearest" or "closest.") A *remote genus* is one that has one or more other genera intervening between it and the species or lower genus in relation to which it is being considered. Thus, "organism," "body," and "substance" are remote genera of "man." (See the schema on p. 245.)

Note that what a genus signifies cannot exist in the real order unless it has essential attributes that are not expressed by the genus. "Triangle," for instance, is the genus of "equilateral triangle," "isosceles triangle," and "scalene triangle." Now a triangle that is only triangle and nothing more, cannot exist; if a triangle is to exist, it must be either equilateral, isosceles, or scalene. The relationship of a genus with a species is not like that of "barn" with "painted barn." A barn can exist without paint and without any other determination in place of paint. Hence, "barn" is not the genus—at least not in the strict sense—of "painted barn."

3) **DIFFERENCE.** *A difference is a universal that expresses the constitutive note that distinguishes a species from its genus or a genus from a higher genus.*

A *specific difference* is a difference that distinguishes a species from its proximate genus, as "rational" distinguishes "man" from "animal."

A *generic difference* is a difference that distinguishes a species or a lower genus from things that differ from it generically but belong to the same higher genus. Thus, "sentient," "animate," and "corporeal" are generic differences of "man," since each of them distinguishes a genus that man belongs to from the next higher genus.

We must not think that a difference is added to a genus as paint is added to a barn or cream to coffee. We do not have an "animal" in us that is somehow or other overlaid with "rational," so that the two of them together make the "man" in us, as "barn" plus "paint" makes a painted barn. There is a *real distinction* between a barn and the paint on it, as well as between coffee and cream. A barn and paint—as well as coffee and cream—are different things. We do not just think of them, the one without the other, but they are two distinct things independently of our thought. There is, however, *no real distinction* between a genus and logical difference but only a *mental distinction.* A genus does not express the nature of one real thing, and a difference the nature of another real thing; but both express the nature of the same real thing—the genus and difference together expressing it more completely than does the genus alone. For instance, when we say "John is a rational animal," we give a more complete answer to the question, What is John? than when we say "John is an animal," since we not only state that he is an animal but also what kind of animal he is. But we do not imply that one part of John—say his head—is rational and the rest animal but not rational, or that what is signified by "rational" is mixed with what is signified by "animal," as cream is mixed with coffee. The very same concrete reality that is signified by "animal" is likewise signified by "rational animal," and vice versa. This reality ("John") is signified by each of them whole and entire; but its nature, or intelligible structure, is expressed more determinately and completely by "rational animal" than by "animal" alone.

Let us consider another example. The genus of "equilateral triangle" is "triangle" and its difference is "equal-sided." We can think of the number of the sides without thinking of their equality. Hence, there is a mental distinction between the two. Nevertheless the equal sides are really the same as the three sides, and vice versa.

4) **LOGICAL PROPERTY.** In an earlier chapter, when we treated of the comprehension of terms and concepts, we distinguished between the basic, constitutive notes of an essence and the notes that are implied in and deducible from these. The basic, constitutive

notes, as we have seen, are the genus and specific difference of an essence. The notes that are implied in and deducible from the genus or specific difference, or from both of them together, are called properties. Thus, "animal" and "rational" are the genus and specific difference of man; "capable of speech," "social," "risible," "tool-using," and so on, are properties.[5]

A logical property is a universal that expresses, not the essence of the subject of which it is predicated, but an attribute that accompanies this essence necessarily. A property in the strictest sense is connected with its subject conceptually—in such a way, that is, that its subject cannot even be thought of, without contradiction, as not having the property. In this sense, "three-angled" is a property of "triangle." The essence of triangle, as we explained above, is "figure bounded by three straight lines meeting by twos in a plane." Because its three straight lines meet by twos in a plane, a triangle must likewise have three interior angles. A triangle without three interior angles involves a contradiction and is therefore absolutely impossible. In other words, the very notion of a triangle requires that a triangle have three interior angles, and a triangle without three interior angles not only cannot exist but cannot even be thought of.

We shall refer to the necessity arising from such a conceptual connection as logical necessity.

A logical *specific property* (in the strictest sense) expresses an attribute that results with logical necessity from the completely determined essence of the subject of which it is predicated. It arises from the combined genus and specific difference but not from the genus alone. It is therefore realized concretely in *every* individual having the specific nature and *only* in such individuals. "Capable of speech," "social," "risible," and so on, are specific properties of man.

A *generic property* (in the strictest sense) expresses an attribute that results with logical necessity from the incompletely determined essence of the subject of which it is predicated. It arises from the basic, constitutive elements that one species has in common with other species (that is, from its generic nature). "Mortal," for in-

[5] See pp. 18-19 for the explanation of how "capable of speech" is implied in "rational animal."

stance, is a generic property of man. "Mortality" flows from man's nature insofar as man is a living organism; mortality is not distinctive of man but common to all living organisms. The grounds, in other words, for the possibility of dying in both animals and plants is in their generic nature as organisms. Since organisms consist of parts, they can be resolved into them; and such resolution is death. Similarly, to be "three-angled" is a generic property of the species "equilateral triangle." An equilateral triangle is not three-angled because it is equilateral but because it is a triangle—that is, because of its generic nature of "triangle." It shares the attribute of "three-angled" with "isosceles triangle" and "scalene triangle," the other species of the genus "triangle."

We often hear the term "physical property" used with reference to the various chemical elements and compounds and to the various kinds of animals and plants. A *physical property* is an attribute that belongs to its subject with physical necessity but is not conceptually connected with it—or at least, if it is conceptually connected with it, we are unable to see the connection.

Physical properties are both specific and generic. Atomic weight, atomic number, boiling point, and so on, are specific properties of the various chemical elements and compounds. To be subject to the law of gravitation is a generic property of all species of bodies. To be white is a generic property of common salt—common salt has to be white, but there are many other things that also are white. Inasmuch as physical properties are not conceptually connected with the subjects of which they are predicated, they are not logical properties in the strict sense but logical accidents.

The term "property" is also applied to attributes that are realized concretely in individuals of only one species (or genus), but not in every individual or at all times. To write poetry, to play the piano, to give speeches, and so on, are properties of man in this sense. Only men do these things but not all men; and even the men who do them are not doing them all the time. Note that the basic ability of a man to do these things is a specific property in the strict sense; but the actual doing of them is a property only in a broader sense, since a man can be thought of, without contradiction, as not doing them.

5) LOGICAL ACCIDENT.[6] *A logical accident is an attribute that is not conceptually connected with the essence of the subject that it is predicated of.* It is compatible with the subject—for otherwise it could not be predicated of it at all—but the subject can be thought of, without contradiction, as not having the attribute. To be white, standing, an American, six feet tall, and so on, are logical accidents in relation to the essence "man." A man can be white, standing, an

SYNOPTIC SCHEMA

THE QUESTION	EXAMPLES	THE PREDICABLES
1) What is John essentially? Give a complete answer.	A man, a rational animal	(1) SPECIES
2) To what immediately more general class of beings does John belong?	Animal	(2) GENUS
3) What kind of animal is John? What is the basic note that distinguishes his kind from other kinds?	Rational	(3) DIFFERENCE
4) What are some attributes that John has, and must have, simply because he is a man?	Risible, able to speak and to use tools, social	(4) PROPERTY
5) What are some other attributes that John has but can be conceived of as not having; attributes, that is, that are compatible with his essence (since he has them), but do not necessarily accompany it?	Tall, heavy, white, residing in St. Louis, actually walking, actually talking	(5) LOGICAL ACCIDENT

[6] Logical accidents must be distinguished from the accidents that are categories, or predicaments. These will be discussed in the next section.

American, six feet tall, and so on; but a man can be thought of, without contradiction, as not being any of these.

The schema on Page 251 throws further light on the nature of the predicables. Pay special attention to the questions. They suggest the key words in the definitions of each of the predicables. Notice that "rational" is not the specific difference of John, but *of the kind of being he is.* Similarly, "risible," "able to speak," and so on, are not properties of John as an individual but rather of the kind of being he is (that is, of "man").

When you do the exercises, remember that the same universal can be classified variously as it is considered in relation to various subjects. "Animal," for instance, is a genus in relation to "man" but a logical accident in relation to "organism" (since an organism can be thought of, without contradiction, as not being an animal—a plant, for instance). Consequently, a question like "To which of the predicables is 'animal' to be referred?" does not make sense unless you are told the subject in relation to which you are to consider the concept "animal."

Exercise

To which of the predicables is each of the predicates to be referred? Notice that a few of the predicates are not universals and are therefore not to be referred to any of the predicables. Distinguish between properties in the strict sense and properties in the broad sense, between the various kinds of properties in the broad sense, and between specific and generic properties.

1. John is

(1) a man,
(2) a rational animal,
(3) an animal,
(4) rational,
(5) able to speak,
(6) subject to the law of gravitation,
(7) mortal,
(8) six feet tall,
(9) in America,
(10) on the earth,
(11) two-legged,
(12) an organism,
(13) animate,
(14) playing tennis,
(15) endowed with an intellect,
(16) a good piano player,
(17) a social being,
(18) laughing loudly,
(19) risible,
(20) a corporeal substance.

2. Man is
   (1) a being,
   (2) a creature,
   (3) larger than a mouse but smaller than an elephant,
   (4) a substance,

3. A triangle is
   (1) a rectilinear plane figure,
   (2) bounded by three lines,
   (3) enclosing three angles,
   (4) either equilateral, isosceles, or scalene,
   (5) a figure.

4. THE ARISTOTELIAN CATEGORIES OR PREDICAMENTS

A brief treatment of the Aristotelian categories, or predicaments, will complete our background for the study of definition and logical division. It will do this by clarifying the notion of "genus" and by deepening our understanding of the law of the inverse ratio of comprehension and extension, showing how we abstract from differences as we rise from individual beings through species and genera to a supreme genus and how we unify our knowledge of things by referring them to a minimum number of univocal concepts. A study of the categories will likewise throw light on the function of the copula by revealing how its meaning varies according to variations in the meaning of the predicate. A final fruit of our study of the categories will be an acquaintance with certain very important philosophical terms which we simply must understand in order to read Aristotelian or Thomistic philosophy intelligently.

First we shall treat of the categories insofar as they express modes of being; then we shall treat of them insofar as they are orderly classifications of individuals, species, and subgenera under a supreme genus—which is the special point of view from which logic considers them.

a. The Categories as Expressing Modes of Being

The categories are a classification of predicates, each of which expresses some mode of being of its subject while omitting other modes of being. There are ten categories: substance and the nine accidents. Our first step in explaining the nature of each of the categories will be to list various predicates, or modes of being, of John; then we shall indicate the category illustrated by each of these predicates, adding in parentheses either the question to which each category gives the ultimate and logically irreducible answer or else the key words of a descriptive definition of the category. Finally we shall give brief definitions of substance and accident and of the first three of the accidents—quantity, quality, and relation. The treatment of the categories as expressing modes of being belongs to metaphysics, not to logic; still, since these modes of being are the intelligibilities expressed by the supreme genus of every category, logic cannot ignore them entirely.

Let us now examine the following illustrations of substance and the nine accidents: "John is: (1), (2), (3), and so on," on Page 255.

Each of these predicates or groups of predicates declares what (or how) John is but each in a different way. The first predicates ("man," "animal," and "organism") declare what he is substantially; the others declare what he is accidentally. John is necessarily, permanently, and constitutively a man; he cannot exist at all without being a man or without having "man" as predicable of him. But many of the accidents express a perfection that he may have at one time and not have at another. Although John cannot exist without having at least some accidents predicable of him, the way in which he has many of them will vary from day to day and moment to moment; once sick, he is now healthy; once shorter than James, he is now taller; although he must be in some place, he is not necessarily in the street; and so on.

SUBSTANCE is that which exists in itself and for itself, without requiring another being as a subject of inherence. A man, a tree, and an angel are substances, since they exist in and for themselves and not as mere modifications or further perfections of a subject in which they inhere. However, a smile, a wink, and a thought are not substances (but accidents) since their nature is such that they cannot exist except as perfections or modifications of a subject that has existence directly in itself and for itself (that is, of a substance).

A concrete individual thing is called FIRST SUBSTANCE. It cannot be a predicate in the strict and proper sense but is the ultimate subject of all perfections and of all predication. Universal concepts belonging to the category of substance are called SEC-

JOHN IS:

1—*a man, an animal, an organism* . .	SUBSTANCE	(What?)
2—*short, bulky, and broad*	QUANTITY	(How much? How big? How many?)
3 { *healthy* . . . . Disposition . . . / *able to do much* Capacity . . . . . / *white* . . . . Passive Quality / *square* . . . . Figure . . . . . . }	QUALITY	(What further determinations characterize his nature from within?)
4—*taller than James and a son of James*	RELATION	(Being ordered to other persons or things)
5—*pushing a cart*	ACTION	(Doing something)
6—*being shoved and kicked*	PASSION	(Receiving something from an agent)
7—*now*	TIME	(When?)
8—*in a street of the city of St. Louis*	PLACE	(Where?)
9—*standing and leaning forward* . . .	SITUS [7]	(Arrangement of parts among themselves and with reference to contiguous space)
10—*well dressed and wearing glasses.*	HABITUS [8]	(Being equipped with clothing, arms, tools, ornaments, etc.)

[7] We retain the Latin word *situs* because there is no exact English equivalent. "Posture" is not adequate because it includes only the relationship of parts to one another but not their relationship to contiguous space.

[8] "Habitus" must be distinguished from various determinations of operative

OND SUBSTANCES; all of these can be predicates, and all but the highest can likewise be subjects.[9]

A predicamental ACCIDENT (that is, any of the accidents of the categories or predicaments) expresses being—or, more accurately, a perfection or mode of being—that cannot exist in and for itself but whose nature is such that it must exist in another as in a subject of inherence. Ultimately every accident must exist in a substance. Accident presupposes substance and cannot even be defined without bringing the notion of substance into its definition. A smile, height, weight, skill, power, place, superiority, inferiority, and similarity are examples of accidents.

We must carefully distinguish the kind of accident we are treating here from the kind we treated in the previous section. The accidents of the categories are first intentions, expressing the nature of things according to their own proper being—what they signify can be predicated of things themselves and not just of concepts—whereas the accidents of the predicables are second intentions. Now, when we reflect on some of the accidents of the categories, considering them in relation to the subjects whose predicates they are, we find that they are also logical accidents because they can be absent from their subject without destroying its nature. However, many accidents of the categories are referred to the predicable of logical property. For instance, man's intellect is an accident inasmuch as it is a perfection inhering in man's soul; however, to have an intellect is a logical property of the concept "man," since it is a necessary consequent of his essence "rational animal."

Notice that the notion "accident" (like "being") is predicated analogously, not univocally, of the various kinds of accidents, and is therefore not their supreme genus. The reason for this is that the differences among the various accidents, as well as their similarities, are formally "being that inheres in another as in a subject."

We shall now give very brief definitions of the three most important kinds of real accidents: quantity, quality, and relation. The

---

powers that are called habits ("good habits," "bad habits," various acquired skills, etc.). These latter belong to the category of quality.

[9] Even a supreme genus can be a subject when its supposition is personal (for instance, "Some substance (actually) is a man") but not when the supposition is absolute or essential.

other accidents will be understood sufficiently for our present purpose from the examples and the words in the parentheses in the schema given above.

QUANTITY is that by which a material substance has parts outside of parts and on account of which it is big or small, long or short, thick or thin, and so on. A line, a surface, and a solid are continuous quantity; a number is discrete quantity.

QUALITY is the accident that characterizes, from within, a nature that is already substantially complete.

RELATION is the order that one thing has towards another.

Notice that an existing thing (for instance, a man) *is* a substance but *has* quantity, quality, relations, and so on.

b. The Notion of a Logical Category

Now that we have considered the categories as expressing modes of being—that is, from the point of view of metaphysics—we are ready to consider them as orderly classifications of concepts and from the point of view of logic. To prepare ourselves for the definition of "category" we shall build up the category of substance; and then, with an eye on the arrangement of genera, subgenera, species, and individuals as displayed in our schema of this category, we shall give a descriptive definition of category itself.

To build up the category of substance, let us ask the question, What is John essentially? Let us first give the narrowest answer to this question ("man"), then the next broader answer ("animal"), and so on, until we work our way up to the broadest answer short of "being" (which is a transcendental concept and therefore pervades all the categories, without being limited to any one of them). We shall place the word "John" at the bottom of our schema and the narrowest answer ("man") directly above the word "John" but beneath the other answers. We shall now place the broadest answer ("substance") on top and the other answers in between, arranging all of them in the order of increasing extension and decreasing comprehension. This gives us the series of terms directly above "John" in the schema given on Page 258.

Our next step will be to add the difference that narrows down each genus to the genus below it, beginning at the top and working down, until we come to the species "man" and, under it, to the enumeration of individuals (Peter, Paul, John, and so on). To the right of these differences we shall add terms ("incorporeal," "inanimate," and so on) that include all the differences that might narrow down each of the genera to lower genera or species.

Now we have the fully worked out category of substance. Every substance, except God, can be fitted into this schema.

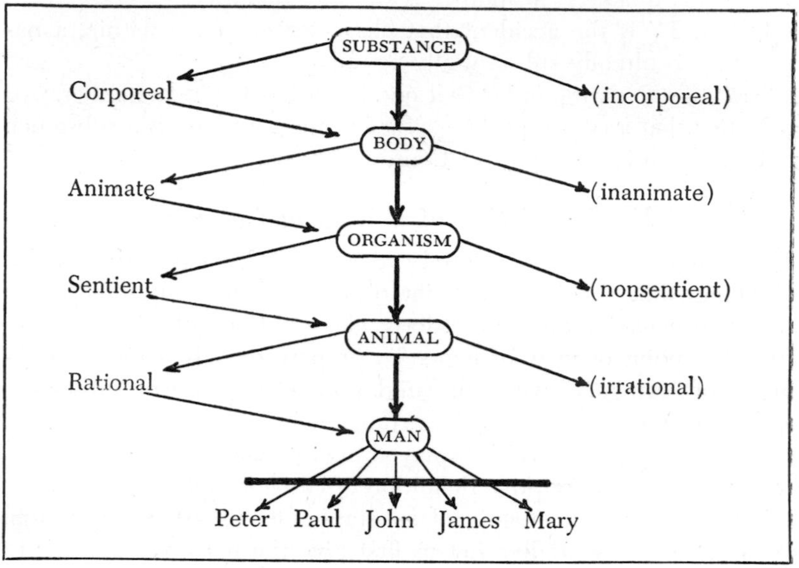

THE CATEGORY OF SUBSTANCE [10]

[10] This is the so-called Porphyrian Tree as it has appeared in logic books since the early Middle Ages. In connection with the Porphyrian Tree we must make a few important observations that may save us from much confusion later on.

First it seems that "material substance," or "body," is the highest genus reached by simple abstraction. It is true, of course, that "substance" is somehow common to both "angel" and "body"; yet this common "substance" is reached by a rather complicated process, which is not abstraction, and this common concept would seem to be analogous rather than univocal.

Secondly, although God is substance, the notion "substance" is not predicated univocally of God and other substances. Hence, God is not the substance of the categories.

Thirdly, we wish to call attention to the fact that the relationship of individual beings ("Peter," "Paul," and so on) to a species is far different from the relationship of a species to a genus, and so on. We do not get to the knowledge of an individual being by a mere aggregation or addition of notes.

With an eye on this schema of the category of substance, we shall now give a descriptive definition of "category." A category, as the word is usually understood in logic, is *an orderly classification of genera, species, and individuals under a supreme genus,* all of them so arranged that each of the universal terms can be predicated univocally and essentially of everything under it. For instance, "substance" is predicated univocally and essentially of "body," "organism," "animal," and "man," of Peter, Paul, and so on, as well as of every animal, every plant, and every body. Similarly, "body" is

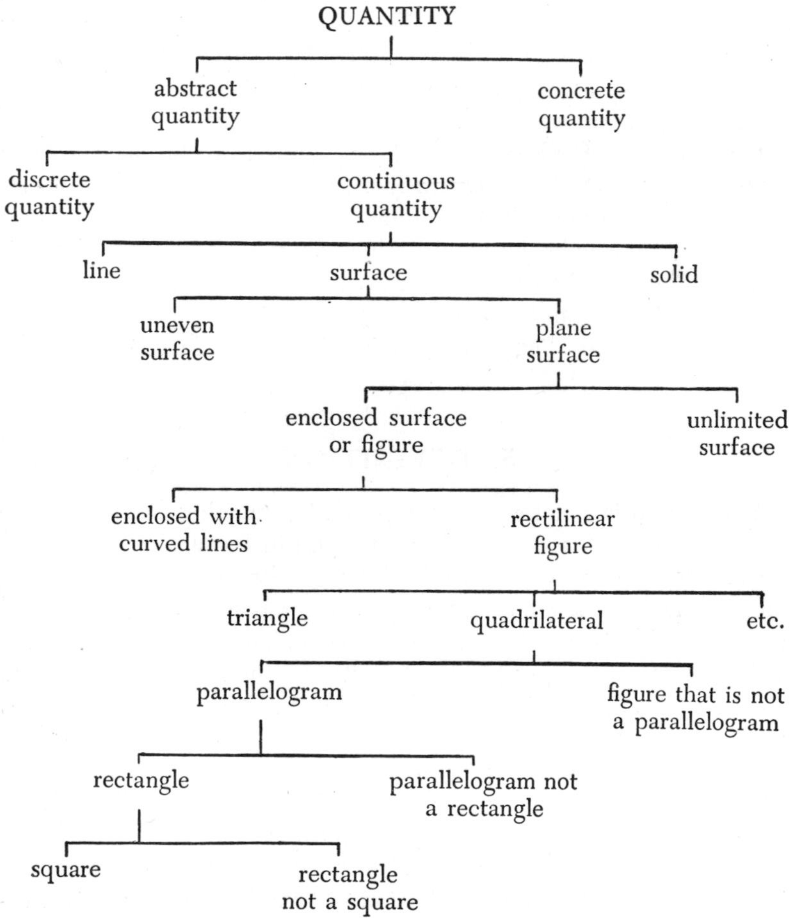

predicated univocally and essentially of everything under it; and so on. Sometimes, especially in metaphysics, the name "category" signifies only the supreme genus, without explicitly including its inferiors.

The supreme genus, then (not only of substance but of each category), gives the ultimate and logically irreducible answer to the question, What is a thing essentially and in the last analysis? Asked what John is essentially, you reply "A man." And that? "An animal." And that? "An organism." And so on, until you come to "substance," which is at once the broadest and the simplest concept that can be predicated univocally of John and other beings. Or asked what white is, you reply "A color." And that? "A kind of quality." Shortness and bulkiness are essentially and in the last analysis quantities; standing is a *situs;* and so on.

The category of substance has been worked out in much greater detail than any of the other categories. Above (on Page 259) we have indicated a possible arrangement of the category of quantity. All quantities can be fitted into this schema. Many of the headings can be further divided—for instance "line" can be divided into "straight line" and "curved line"; "triangle" can be divided into "isosceles triangle," "equilateral triangle," and "scalene triangle," and so on.

5. DEFINITION

A definition is a statement that gives the meaning of a term. The word "definition" is derived from the Latin word *definire,* which means "to enclose within limits." Originally, *definire* meant "to mark boundaries or limits" as of a field. Later it came to be applied to the act of stating the meaning of a term. The boundary of a field is defined by indicating the limits within which a field is confined and by which it is marked off from other fields; similarly, a term is defined by indicating the limits within which it is used and by which it is marked off from other terms.

"Definition" signifies the act of defining, as well as the finished statement in which the meaning of a term is given.

Notice that a definition is not a proposition but a term, generally a *complex term.* Thus, the definition of "man" is not "Man is a rational animal," but simply "rational animal." A definition is generally expressed by the predicate of a proposition whose subject is the term or thing to be defined. Often, too, a definition is expressed by a formula such as " 'Man' means 'rational animal'," or "The definition of 'man' is 'rational animal'."

First we shall treat of the kinds of definition—of nominal and real definitions and of various subdivisions of each—and then of the rules governing definition.

a. Kinds of Definitions

Does a definition merely indicate what thing is signified by a term, without declaring the nature of that thing, or does it also declare its nature? The answer to this question is the basis for the very important division of definitions into nominal and real.

1) NOMINAL DEFINITION. A nominal definition (*definitio nominis,* "definition of a name") merely indicates what thing is signified by a term, without declaring the nature of that thing. Its purpose is merely to give the meaning of a term—either its current meaning or a special meaning within some context—so that hearers or readers will know the sense in which the term is used. If you are asked "What does *anthropos* mean?" and you answer "*Anthropos* means 'man'," you are giving a nominal definition. By substituting a word that your questioner knows for the one that he does not know, you indicate for him what thing is signified by the word *anthropos*. However, if you are then asked "But what's a man?," you will be expected to give a real definition (supposing, of course, that the person asking the question knows English).

Nominal definitions are commonly given at the beginning of debates to ensure agreement among the disputants as to the exact point at issue. Nominal definitions, again, are used to call attention to the equivocal use of terms. To show that a term is used equivocally, you need only show that it signifies a different kind of thing in each of (at least) two occurrences; there is no need of declaring what the essences of these things are. Nominal definitions are also used to introduce new terms or to indicate a special sense in which a speaker or writer intends to use a term that is often used in other senses.

On the basis of the various ways in which they indicate the thing signified by a term, nominal definitions are either etymological definitions, definitions by synonym, definitions by description, or definitions by example.

a) **Etymological Definition.** An etymological definition defines a word by giving the meaning of the word or words from which it is derived. "Philosophy" is derived from *philos,* a Greek word meaning "loving," and *sophia,* which means "wisdom." Consequently, the etymological definition of "philosophy" is "love of wisdom." The etymological definition of "martyr" is "witness."

The meaning of many words is so different from the meaning of their parent words that giving their etymology throws little or no light on their present meanings and is therefore really not a definition at all. For instance, the etymological meaning of "scruple" is "small sharp rock," which is far removed indeed from the uneasiness of conscience that the word "scruple" signifies today.

b) **Definition by Synonym.** A nominal definition can be made by giving a synonym (either of the same language as the word to be defined or of a different language) that is better known than the word to be defined; for instance, *anthropos* means "man," and "to confect" means "to put together."

c) **Definition by Description.** A nominal definition can be made by describing the thing signified by the term, not for the purpose of revealing its nature, or essence, but merely to indicate what thing it is that is being spoken of. "Chalk," for instance, can be defined by this sort of definition as "the material of which is made the little stick that a teacher uses to write on the blackboard."

d) **Definition by Example.** A nominal definition can also be made by indicating an example of the thing signified by the term to be defined. For instance, if a child asks "What is chalk?" and you show him a piece of chalk and say "This is chalk," you are giving him a nominal definition by example.

Notice that many nominal definitions are, to some extent, also real definitions. The purpose of the person giving the definition sometimes determines whether a definition is to be regarded as nominal or real. If his purpose is merely to indicate what thing is signified by a term, a definition is to be regarded as nominal even if it throws some light on the nature of the thing. On the other hand, if the person giving a definition assumes that his hearers or readers already know what things are signified by a term and intends to declare the nature, or essence, of those things, his definition is to be regarded as a real definition, or a *definitio rei* ("a definition of the thing").

Except for words that are better known than any words we could use to define them, all words can be defined by nominal definitions.

2) **REAL DEFINITION.** A real definition (*definitio rei,* "definition of a thing") not only indicates what thing is signified by a term but also declares the nature of that thing. It manifests the intelligible structure of the thing by *explicitly* setting before the mind various notes that are expressed only obscurely by the term that is to be defined.

A real definition is always a complex term, consisting of at least two parts—one part giving the note that the thing has in common with similar kinds of things; the other, the note that differentiates it from them. For instance, in the definition of man as a rational animal, the term "animal" (man's proximate genus) expresses what man has in common with the kinds of things that resemble him most closely, and the term "rational" (man's specific difference) expresses the note that differentiates him from them.

Limits of Real Definition. Only *common terms*—and not all of them—can be defined by real definitions.

Individuals are identified rather than defined. Thus, if you say "Mary is the girl in the front row nearest the window," you are not defining Mary but merely pointing her out. Again, if you say "John is a rational animal," you are defining the nature he possesses, but not John himself.

Transcendental concepts (such as "being," "thing," "something," and so on) cannot be defined by a strict definition but can only be described. Such concepts transcend the limits of all genera and express the differences among things as well as their similarities. The transcendentals are studied at length in metaphysics. To explain them at length now would take us too far afield.

The *supreme genera* of the categories ("substance," "quantity," "quality," "relation," and so on) are also incapable of definition in the strict sense. Since they are supreme, there is no higher genus to which they can be referred.

Simple qualities that are the *immediate data of sense experience* do not admit of definition in the strict sense, but can be known (properly) only by direct experience. If you do not already know what red is, you will still not know what it is if you are told that it is a color that manifests itself by vibrations varying from 350 to 500 billions per second. No description can convey the meaning of taste to one who never had taste buds, or of light to one who was always blind.

***a*) Definition by Genus and Specific Difference.** The notion of real definition is verified most perfectly in a definition that defines by stating a thing's genus and specific difference. These, as we saw when we treated of the predicables, are the notes or intelligibilities that constitute the intelligible structure or essence of a thing, the genus giving an incomplete answer to the question, What is a thing essentially? and the specific difference indicating the note or intelligibility that distinguishes the thing to be defined from other things of the same genus. The definition of "man" as "rational animal" is such a definition, "animal" expressing man's genus and "rational" expressing man's specific difference.

A definition by genus and specific difference in the strict sense is the ideally perfect type of definition. It is the briefest, fullest, and most precise answer to the question, "What is that (kind of) thing?" In the first place, it expresses the notes that are the grounds for the other attributes of a thing. We saw this when we studied genus, specific difference, and species and the relationship of properties to them. The grounds, for instance, of man's ability to speak, to use tools, to laugh, and so on, lie in his being a rational animal. A man is not a rational animal because he can speak, use tools, and so on; rather, he can speak, use tools, and so on, because he is a rational animal. In the second place, a definition by genus and specific difference is perfectly convertible with the thing defined. For instance, a thing that is a man but not a rational animal, or a rational animal but not a man, would involve a contradiction. Some of the other kinds of definition, however, are not perfectly convertible with the thing defined. Take the definition of "man" as a "two-handed, featherless biped that holds its head erect," which is not a definition by genus and specific difference but a descriptive definition. There is no conceptual repugnance—no contradiction—in the thought of a man that is not a two-handed, featherless biped holding its head erect, or of a two-handed, featherless biped holding its head erect that is not a man. This will be clearer after we have taken the other kinds of real definitions.

Only a few things can be defined by stating their genus and specific difference in the strict sense. Still, this type of definition is very important because it is a model that we should imitate as closely as possible in other types of definitions.

Notice that "genus" and "specific difference" are frequently used in a broad sense in which "genus" signifies whatever a thing has in common with other kinds of things that resemble it most closely and "specific difference" signifies whatever differentiates a thing from other kinds of things.

Since "genus" and "specific difference" constitute the essence of a thing, a definition made by stating a thing's genus or specific difference is often called an essential definition.

***b*) Definition by Substitutes for Genus and Specific Difference.** Most definitions define by stating the genus or quasi genus of a thing together with some substitute for a specific difference in the strict sense. This substitute may be a description or a cause, as explained below. As opposed to definition by genus and specific difference in the strict sense, these are called nonessential definitions.

1—DESCRIPTIVE DEFINITIONS. A descriptive definition states the genus or quasi genus of the thing defined and uses a description in place of the specific difference. The following classification is based on the various relationships that nonessential attributes have towards the subjects of which they are predicated.[11]

a—*Descriptive Definition by Properties.* Some descriptive definitions give one or more logical properties in place of the specific difference. The definition of "man" as "animal able to speak" is this kind of definition.

Like the definition by genus and specific difference in the strict sense, this type of definition is perfectly convertible with the thing defined. Just as every possible man is an animal able to speak (that is, has the basic powers requisite for speaking—although they may be undeveloped or impeded), so too every possible animal that is able to speak is a man.

[11] See pp. 248-252.

b—*Descriptive Definition by Logical Accidents.* Some descriptive definitions express the genus or quasi genus of the thing defined and state one or more logical accidents in place of the specific difference.

(1) A definition that states a single *physically necessary and characteristic property* (which, as we saw in the chapter on the predicables, is a logical accident) in place of the specific difference enables us to distinguish a thing from all other kinds of things. "Iron," for instance, is defined by this type of definition as a "metal whose atomic number is 26 and whose atomic weight is 55.85." So far as we know, all iron and only iron has this atomic number and atomic weight; still, we see no intrinsic necessity why iron must have this atomic number and atomic weight or why no other metal can have them.

(2) As a substitute for the specific difference, a definition may state a *combination of noncharacteristic properties* that are, as a matter of fact, found only in the thing defined. The definition of "man" as a "two-handed, featherless biped that holds its head erect" is this sort of definition. As a matter of fact, all men—at least almost all men—and only men are two-handed, featherless bipeds that hold their heads erect; still, there could be men in whom this definition is not verified, and there could be other beings in which it is verified.

(3) As a substitute for the specific difference, a definition can give logical accidents that are found either singly or collectively only in the thing defined. For instance, an "elephant" is "the largest extant land animal." As a matter of fact, an elephant is the largest extant land animal, but an elephant could cease being the largest extant land animal and still be an elephant.

Notice that all the definitions that define by stating logical accidents merely indicate subjects that have an essence; they do not unfold the essence itself. Hence, such definitions are often nominal definitions rather than real definitions.

2—Causal Definitions. A causal definition gives the genus or quasi genus of the thing defined and states a cause in place of the specific difference.

a—*Definition by Final Cause.* A definition by final cause, or a final definition, substitutes the final cause, or purpose, of a thing for its specific difference. Articles made by men are commonly defined by final definitions. A barometer, for instance, is an "instrument for determining atmospheric pressure and hence for judging probable changes of weather, for ascertaining the height of an ascent, and so on." The definition of logic as the "science and art of correct thinking" is a final definition, since it defines logic by stating its proximate end or purpose.

b–*Definition by Efficient Cause.* A definition by efficient cause substitutes the efficient cause of a thing for its specific difference. An efficient cause produces its effect by its activity. Diseases are often defined by stating the kind of bacterium, germ, or parasite that brings them on. Malaria, for instance, can be defined as a "febrile disease that is caused by animal parasites in the red blood corpuscles and is transferred to man by the bite of the anopheles mosquito."

c–*Definition by Material and Formal Cause.* A material cause is the stuff out of which a thing is made, and a formal cause is that in a thing that makes it the kind of thing it is. Marble, for instance, is the material cause of a marble statue, and the shape given the statue by the sculptor is its formal cause. The marble, before this particular shape had been given it, could indifferently have become a pedestal, a column, a tombstone, and so on; but once this particular shape has been given it, it is a statue. Now in definition the material cause of a thing may be used as a quasi genus and its formal cause as a substitute for its specific difference.

The definition of man as a being composed of an organized body and a rational soul is this type of definition. In this definition "organized body" is the quasi genus, as it expresses the nature of both man and the other animals; "rational soul" is the substitute for the specific difference, as it indicates the principle within man that differentiates him from the other animals.

Material and formal causes are treated at length in metaphysics and cosmology. We mention them only in passing, as a thorough explanation would take us out of the field of logic.

d–*Genetic Definition.* A genetic definition defines a thing by stating the process by which it is produced (or is imagined to be produced) and the elements that concur in its production. Geometric figures are often defined by genetic definitions. Thus, a circle is a "figure formed by revolving a line in a plane around one of its ends." An eclipse is an "obscuration of a heavenly body by the interposition of another." Bread is an "article of food made from flour or meal by moistening, kneading, and baking."

Exercise

Identify the following definitions. Note that some of them are of mixed type.

1. A body is a material substance.
2. A whale is the largest extant animal.
3. A clock is an instrument for measuring and indicating time by mechanical movement.
4. A mackerel is an Atlantic food fish, steel-blue above with blackish bars, and silvery beneath.
5. Carbon monoxide is a colorless, practically odorless gas, 0.967 times as heavy as air; it liquifies at $-192°$, and solidifies at $-207°$.
6. A watch is a pocket timepiece with a spring-driven movement.
7. The ear is the organ of hearing.
8. Man is a tool-using animal that cooks much of its food.
9. "Calamity" means "disaster."
10. "Geology" is a "science of the earth."
11. In the following pages we shall use "science" in the sense of "demonstrative habit."
12. Water is H_2O.
13. Prudence is the moral virtue that imparts readiness to act in accordance with right reason.
14. Prejudice is a judgment or opinion formed without due examination.
15. A misogynist is a "hater of women."
16. A sombrero is a broad-brimmed hat, usually of felt, much used in Mexico and southwestern United States.
17. Simple apprehension is the operation by which we grasp the essences of things.
18. A didelphys is a marsupial such as the opossum.
19. A square is a parallelogram having four equal sides and four right angles.
20. A real thing is an actually existing thing that exists in itself and not merely as an object of thought.

b. Rules Governing Definition

The following rules, which are traditional in treatises on logic, set forth the conditions that a good definition should fulfill. They will help us distinguish good definitions from defective definitions. Notice that all that logic can do to help us in the construction and evaluation of definitions is to supply us with general norms. In order to make and evaluate definitions we must also have a sufficient knowledge of the terms, or things, to be defined.

A good definition must be (1) *clear;* (2) *coextensive with the term or thing defined;* (3) *positive, when possible;* and (4) *brief.* We shall take each of these conditions in turn.

Rule 1. *A definition should be clear.*

The purpose of nominal definition is to indicate the thing signified by a term; the purpose of real definition is to declare the nature of the thing signified by a term. This purpose cannot be attained unless a definition is clearer than the term or thing defined.

In order to attain clarity in definition, we must avoid *metaphors, circular definition,* and *excessively difficult terminology.*

First, a definition should not be expressed in metaphorical or figurative language. The following definitions (perhaps they should not be called definitions at all) are defective on this count: "Sleep is the brother of death," "Bread is the staff of life," "Loyalty is the flame of the lamp of friendship," and "A myth is the voice of a dreamer and an idealist crying 'Why cannot these things be?' "

Secondly, a definition should not be circular; that is, it should not be so phrased that you cannot understand it unless you already understand the term that is being defined.

This rule is violated most openly in a *tautological definition,* which contains a part, or a cognate form, of the term to be defined —as in the definition of a "governor" as "one who performs gubernatorial functions" and of a "star" as a "stellar body."

This rule is violated more subtly by defining a term and then using the same term—generally a few pages later—to define words occurring in its definition. For instance, a writer might define "peace" as "the absence of war," and then define "war" as "the absence of peace."

Thirdly, in order to be clear, a definition should not contain excessively difficult terminology—as in Dr. Johnson's humorous definition of "net" as "a reticulated fabric, decussated at regular intervals, with interstices and intersections." This definition is also tautological, inasmuch as "reticulated" is simply another word for "netted."

This rule does not forbid difficult terminology if the matter defined is such as to require it. The definition, for instance, of the soul as "the first entelechy of an organized body having the potency of life" is an accurate technical definition, whose meaning is obvious to anyone familiar with Aristotelian philosophy.

In deciding whether or not a definition (especially a nominal definition) is clear, you must, to some extent, keep in mind the condition of the person for whom the definition is intended. A definition of table salt that will be perfectly satisfactory to a four-year-old will not suit a chemist, and vice versa.

Rule 2. *A definition should be coextensive with the term or thing defined.*

A definition should set off, or distinguish, the thing defined from all other things. In order to do this, it must be applicable to every example of the thing defined and only to examples of the thing defined. In other words, the term that is defined and the definition should have identical extension and should be perfectly convertible. Hence, supposing that "rational animal" is a correct definition of "man," then every possible man is a rational animal and every possible rational animal is a man.

Definitions by genus and specific difference and descriptive definitions that define by stating logical properties in the strict sense fulfill this rule most perfectly. Definitions by logical accidents fulfill it less perfectly, because there can be examples of the thing defined to which they do not apply and there can be other things to which they do apply. The definition, for instance, of "cod" as "an important food fish found especially in the Newfoundland Banks and along the New England and the Norwegian coast" might fit other fish besides cod; and cod would still be cod even if it ceased being used for food, as well as if it ceased to be found in these areas.

This rule is violated by the definition of a "wolf" as "a sheep-killing animal." This definition is at once too narrow and too broad. It is too narrow because it does not include all wolves, since there are wolves that do not kill sheep; it is too broad because it is applicable to animals other than wolves.

Rule 3. *A definition should be positive, when possible.*

A definition should state what a thing is rather than what it is not. Of course, negative terms can be defined only negatively. For instance, you cannot define "blindness" except as "the absence of sight in a subject that ought to have it," or "death" except as "the cessation of life."

Some things must be defined negatively on account of the limitations of human knowledge. We know so little about spirits, for instance, that we must define "spirit" negatively as "immaterial substance."

This rule is violated by the definitions of "virtue" as "the absence of vice" and of "wisdom" as "the avoidance of folly."

Rule 4. *A definition should be brief.*

A definition should contain no superfluous words. In the definition of "man" as "a rational, social, speaking, mortal animal," the words "social," "speaking," and "mortal" are superfluous, since they are implied in, and deducible from, "rational animal."

The ideally perfect definition is not supposed to give us the fullest possible knowledge of the thing defined but merely to state its essence.

We shall add one caution that might be called a fifth rule. In definition, a thing must be referred to its own proper genus. The definition of "to thresh" as "when you beat out grain" is defective on this count inasmuch as it refers threshing to the category of time although it belongs to the category of action.

Exercise

I. First, indicate the type of each of the following definitions. Then apply to them the rules governing definition.

1. A cat is a member of the feline species.
2. A square is a quadrilateral with four equal sides.
3. Deafness is deficiency in the sense of hearing.
4. Injustice is when one violates the rights of another.
5. Sin is the road to damnation.
6. Sin is a deliberate transgression of the law of God.

7. A lie is an intentional terminological inexactitude.
8. An archbishop is one who performs archiepiscopal functions.
9. A bachelor is a man who has not married.
10. A hat is a covering for the head.
11. A triangle is a plane figure bounded by three straight lines and enclosing three angles equal to two right angles.
12. "A cowboy is a raw-boned, tobacco-chewing, bronco-buster who walks as though he had been hit between the knees by a cannon ball."
13. A creature is anything made by God.
14. Poetry is a momentary glance through an open door.
15. Oats are a coarse grain used in England to feed horses and in Scotland to feed men.

II. Gather examples of definitions from dictionaries, textbooks, and so on. Indicate their type, and apply to them the rules governing definition.

6. LOGICAL DIVISION

Definition, as we saw in the last chapter, manifests the comprehension of a concept. A definition (at least, a definition that defines by stating a thing's genus and specific difference or its genus and a logical property) explicitly states various notes or intelligible elements that are contained implicitly in the concept it defines. Logical division, on the other hand, has to do with the extension of terms and concepts, and expresses the various kinds of inferiors in which a concept can be realized or of which a term can be predicated.

What we shall say about division is largely a development of what we said in Chapter 2 on the inverse ratio of comprehension and extension.

First, we shall treat of the notion of logical division; then, we shall treat of the rules governing logical division.

a. The Notion of Logical Division

Logical division is the resolution of a logical whole into its logical parts; that is, of a genus into its subgenera or species. Logical division is an answer to the question, In what kinds of subjects is a concept, essence, or quiddity, realized? The concept "triangle," for instance, is realized in equilateral, isosceles, and scalene triangles, which are the logical parts (or species) of the logical whole (or genus) "triangle." The concept "animal" is realized in man and in brute, which are the logical parts of the logical whole "animal."

Notice that the members into which a genus is divided are themselves universal. A species is not, properly speaking, divided into individuals.[12]

The notions of "logical whole" and "logical part" will be clarified if we contrast the relationship of a logical whole to its logical parts with the relationship of a physical whole to its physical parts. We are more familiar with the latter kind of whole and parts; so we shall begin with them.

A physical whole cannot be predicated of its physical parts. Body and soul, for instance, are the physical essential parts of a man; the two of them unite into one substantial whole and constitute one man. But neither of them, taken by itself, is a man: a man's body is not a man, and a man's soul is not a man. Or take integral heterogeneous parts of a man—parts, that is, like a man's head, trunk, arms, and legs. No single one of them is a man but only a part of a man. Or, again, take integral homogeneous parts of a thing—like the pieces into which a pie has been cut. No single piece of a pie is a whole pie.

A logical whole, on the contrary, can be predicated of each of its logical parts. "Man," as we have seen, is a logical part of the logical whole "animal." Still, every man is a *whole* animal and has the complete comprehension of "animal" realized in him in its entirety. Similarly, "equilateral triangle" is a logical part of "triangle." Nevertheless, an equilateral triangle is a whole triangle, and all that "triangle" signifies is verified in it. In other words, the entire comprehension of a genus is expressed by each of its species; a species adds something to the comprehension of a genus, but does not take anything away from it.

Logical division is effected by removing the indeterminacy of a logical whole, or genus, in either of two ways.

[12] The reason for this is that the individual being is more than the sum total of notes that can be abstracted from it and therefore predicated of it. The individual as such cannot be known by simple apprehension alone but only by judgment in conjunction with sense knowledge.

Besides, since there is no limit to the multiplicability of the members of a species, an exhaustive enumeration of all possible individuals is impossible.

First, the indeterminacy of a logical whole, or genus, can be removed by adding to its comprehension an attribute that is found in some, but not in all, of the inferiors of the genus. This method of division is illustrated by the division of "animal" into "man" and "brute" through the addition of "rational" and "irrational." "Rational" removes the indeterminacy of the genus "animal" by the addition of a note, or thought element, that is obviously something positive. Note, however, that "irrational" also adds something positive to "animal," even though it is expressed negatively. "Irrational" does not merely signify the absence of rationality; it also signifies the presence of some other attribute, whose exact nature we do not know or do not care to express, in place of rationality. Hence, "rational" and "irrational" are related to one another, not as contradictories, but as immediately opposed contraries within the genus "animal."

This method of division, which is known as dichotomy ("a cutting into two"), is valid and useful if the added attribute actually serves as a basis for division. For instance, having webbed feet or not having them is a legitimate basis for the division of birds, since all birds are actually divided into those that have webbed feet and those that do not have them; but having or not having webbed feet is not a legitimate basis for dividing men, since all men would be included in one of the intended divisions, namely, among those who do not have webbed feet. These examples show that divisions cannot be made without a consideration of the special character of the matter, or thought content, of the concepts to be divided. Division, in other words, is not a purely formal process.

Secondly, division can be effected by removing the indeterminacy of a logical whole, or genus, by adding to the comprehension of the genus the various ways in which some attribute found in every member of a genus is realized in each of them. This method of division is exemplified by the division of "triangle" into equilateral, isosceles, and scalene triangles on the basis of the comparative length of their sides. If all three sides are of equal length, the triangle is equilateral; if two and only two are equal, the triangle is isosceles; and if no sides are equal, the triangle is scalene. In every triangle the sides must stand in some relationship with one another on the basis of the comparative length of their sides; but it does not spring from the nature of a triangle that its sides have any one of these three possible relationships rather than the others.

A division is expressed by the predicate of a disjunctive proposition in the strict sense, whose subject is the genus, or logical whole, that is divided. Thus, the division of triangles on the basis of the comparative length of their sides is expressed, "Triangles are either equilateral, isosceles, or scalene." Sometimes, of course, the following formula is used, "Triangles are divided into equilateral, isosceles, and scalene."

The logical parts of a logical whole are sometimes called its *subjective* parts. The reason for this is that they are *subjects.* In the first place, they are subjects in which a genus is looked upon as inhering, somewhat as an accident inheres in a substance. In the second place—and this is the principal reason—they can be the subject of a proposition whose predicate is the logical whole.

Subdivision consists in submitting the parts of a logical whole to another process of division. "Term," for instance, can be divided into "univocal term," "equivocal term," and "analogous term." The last can be subdivided into terms that are analogous by analogy of proportionality and those that are analogous by analogy of attribution.

Co-division consists of more than one division of the some logical whole, each being made according to a different basis. Co-division is exemplified in the divisions of "triangle" on the basis of the relative length of the sides into equilateral, isosceles, and scalene triangles and on the basis of the size of the largest angle into obtuse-angled triangle (which has an angle of over ninety degrees), right-angled triangle (which has an angle of ninety degrees), and acute-angled triangle (all of whose angles are smaller than ninety degrees).

Notice that in connection with logical division, the terms "genus" and "species" are often used in a very broad sense. For instance, "barns" can be considered a quasi genus that is divided into "painted barns" and "unpainted barns" as quasi species.

Notice, too, that classification is the reverse of division. If you start with what is less general and work up to what is more general, you classify. If you begin with what is more general and work down to what is less general, you divide.

b. Rules Governing Logical Division

Four rules of division are traditionally given in treatises on logic. These rules aim at an ideal that, for practical reasons, cannot always be attained in actual divisions. We should observe them as perfectly as the matter allows.

Rule 1. *A division should be made on a single basis.*

The basis of a division is an attribute whose presence or absence, or whose modifications, in the various inferiors of a genus differentiate the inferiors from one another and thus divide the genus into species. Thus, on the basis of the presence of rationality or the absence of rationality (and the presence of something else in its place), the genus "animal" is divided into man and brute. On the basis of modifications in the comparative length of the sides, the genus "triangle" is divided into equilateral, isosceles, and scalene triangles. On the basis of modifications in the size of the largest angle, the genus "triangle" is divided into obtuse-angled, right-angled and acute-angled triangles.

Violation of this rule is known as *cross division.* You make a cross division if you divide triangles into equilateral, isosceles, and right-angled triangles, since you shift the basis of division from the comparative length of the sides to the size of the angles. You also make a cross division of Americans if you divide them into Republicans, Democrats, and Christians, since adherence to a political party is the basis for calling a man a Republican or Democrat, but religious belief is the basis for calling a man a Christian.

Rule 2. *A division should be exhaustive.*

A division is exhaustive if there is place for everything belonging to the genus in one or other of the members into which the genus has been divided. In other words, the members, when they are taken collectively, must be equal to the logical whole and coextensive with it. The division of Americans into Republicans and Democrats violates this rule. There are Americans who belong to neither of these parties.

Rule 3. *The members of a division should be mutually exclusive.*

This rule is violated when the members of a division overlap, so that something belonging to the genus can be referred to more than one of the members into which the genus has been divided.

Such overlapping takes place when a cross division is made, as in the division of Americans into Republicans, Democrats, and Christians. Some Americans are both Republicans and Christians; others are both Democrats and Christians; and so on. Such overlapping also takes place when a subordinate species is included in a series of coordinate species, as in the division of human beings into males, females and girls.

Rule 3 is a corollary of Rule 1 and of the rule that follows.

Rule 4. *A genus should be divided into its proximate species.*

Not only Rule 3 but also Rule 4 is violated in the division of human beings into males, females, and girls. "Human beings" should first be divided on the basis of sex into male and female, which are its proximate species or subclasses. Then "females" should be subdivided on the basis of age and maturity into women and girls.

Rule 4 is sometimes violated together with Rule 2, as in the division of rectilinear plane figures into equilateral triangles, squares, pentagons, hexagons, and so on. A complete list of the remote species of a genus is often difficult to make and there is great danger of omitting a species. This danger is eliminated if the genus is first divided into its proximate species and these are then subdivided. "Rectilinear plane figure," for example, should first be divided on the basis of thc number of sides into three-sided, four-sided, five-sided plane figures, and so on. Then these can be subdivided—"triangle," for instance, being subdivided into equilateral, isosceles, and scalene triangles.

Exercise

I. Which of the following are examples of logical division? Apply the rules governing division to all the examples of logical division. Correct the divisions that are made wrongly, adding extra members where necessary.

1. The division of a pie into four equal pieces.
2. The division of terms into univocal, analogous, and particular.
3. The division of terms into singular, particular, and universal.
4. The division of a man into head, trunk, arms, and legs.
5. The division of a city into its north and south sides.
6. The division of swords into curved, straight, long, and short.

7. The division of animals into carnivorous, herbivorous, and omnivorous.
8. The division of Americans into Protestants, Catholics, Jews, theists, and atheists.
9. The division of supposition into material, formal, and accidental.
10. The division of students into highly talented, moderately talented, and studious.
11. The division of definitions into nominal, real, essential, and accidental.
12. The division of musical instruments into percussion, wind, string, and brass.
13. The division of inference into material, formal, inductive, and deductive.
14. The division of the syllogism into the categorical syllogism and the enthymeme.
15. The division of sequence into valid and invalid.

II. Give original examples of logical division.

III. Examine various classifications of concepts, terms, supposition, and so on, and state whether or not the rules of division are observed.

PART V

THREE ADDITIONAL CHAPTERS

IN CHAPTERS 14, 15, AND 16 we shall treat of the kinds of propositions, of induction, and of the definition of logic by its formal object. These diverse topics are not grouped together because of any intrinsic relationship to one another but only because of convenience.

CHAPTER 14

Kinds of Propositions

We have already treated of several kinds of propositions. In Chapter 3 we gave a thorough explanation of the attributive proposition, of the division of propositions into affirmative and negative, and of the division into singular, particular, and universal (A, E, I, and O). We also mentioned the divisions into true and false and into existential and non-existential. In Chapter 8, as a prerequisite to the study of the hypothetical syllogism, we explained three kinds of hypothetical propositions—that is, the conditional proposition, the disjunctive proposition, and the conjunctive proposition. Finally, when we took up the enthymeme, we gave a partial explanation of causal propositions ("because . . . ," "since . . . ," "for . . ."). To avoid overburdening ourselves with terminology that was not a prerequisite to the study of inference, we postponed the treatment of the other kinds of propositions to the present chapter.

1. NECESSARY AND CONTINGENT PROPOSITIONS

That is necessary which is and cannot not be. That is contingent which is but can cease to be. Propositions are necessary or contingent, depending on whether the truth they express is a necessary truth or a contingent truth. This division of propositions is based on the special character of their thought content and not on their logical form.

a. Necessary Proposition

A necessary proposition expresses a necessary truth. It does not state a mere fact but expresses a truth that cannot be other than it is. The propositions "A triangle is a plane figure bounded by three straight lines" and "Man is a rational animal" are necessary propositions. A triangle that is not a plane figure bounded by three straight lines, as well as a man that is not a rational animal, is *conceptually repugnant* and therefore absolutely impossible. The proposition "A man is not a stone" is also a necessary proposition, since both a man that is a stone and a stone that is a man are impossible.

Every attributive proposition whose predicate is the genus, species, or property (in the strict sense) of the subject is a necessary proposition.

Notice that we cannot have philosophical demonstration unless we have necessary propositions as premises. As much as possible, science aims at attaining to necessary truths that are expressed in necessary propositions.

b. Contingent Proposition

A contingent proposition expresses a contingent truth. It states a mere fact—that is, it states something that is but could be, or could have been, other than it is. "Socrates sits" is a contingent proposition. Of course, on the supposition that Socrates is sitting, he cannot be simultaneously not sitting; but there is no conceptual repugnance in Socrates's not sitting.

Every attributive proposition whose predicate is a logical accident of the subject is a contingent proposition.

Exercise

Classify the following propositions as necessary or contingent, and give the reason for your answer.

1. Elephants exist.
2. Elephants are animals.
3. Squares are not circles.
4. God created the world.
5. Two and two are four.
6. If Socrates sits, he sits.
7. Not every criminal is caught.
8. Man is a creature.
9. Swans are white.
10. John ran quickly when the dog tried to bite him.

2. ABSOLUTE AND MODAL PROPOSITIONS

The proposition "A triangle is a figure" is a necessary proposition; not to be a figure is conceptually repugnant to a triangle. Still, in this proposition, no mention is made of the necessity—or the *necessary mode*—with which to be a figure belongs to a triangle. In the proposition "It is necessary that a triangle is a figure," however, not only is "figure" attributed to "triangle," but the necessity—or the *necessary mode*—with which a triangle is a figure is also expressed.

On the basis of whether or not the manner, or mode, with which the copula unites the subject and predicate (or with which the simple or qualified existence of a subject is posited, or relations among member propositions are asserted) is expressed, propositions are either absolute or modal. "A triangle is a figure" is an absolute proposition. "It is necessary that a triangle be a figure" is a modal proposition.

There are *four modes.* They are necessity, contingency, possibility, and impossibility. We shall define them in their concrete adjectival forms.

1. That is NECESSARY which is and cannot not be.
2. That is CONTINGENT which is but can cease to be.
3. That is POSSIBLE which is not but can be.
4. That is IMPOSSIBLE which is not and cannot be.

Sometimes "possible" is used in a broader sense so as to include what is as well as what is not but can be.

a. Absolute Proposition

An absolute proposition (as opposed to a modal proposition)[1] merely makes an assertion without stating whether what is asserted is necessary, contingent, possible, or impossible. An attributive proposition is absolute if it merely affirms or denies an attribute of a subject ("A dog is an animal" and "A dog is not a cat"). An existential proposition is absolute if it merely posits or sublates the existence of its subject ("God exists" and "Troy is not").

b. Modal Proposition

A modal proposition not only makes an assertion but also states whether what is asserted is necessary, contingent, possible, or impossible.

[1] In contrast to hypothetical propositions (that is, conditional, disjunctive, and conjunctive propositions), all other types are sometimes called absolute propositions.

The mode must state whether the objective relationship of the subject and predicate (or of the subject to existence) is necessary, contingent, possible, or impossible. The proposition "The ship sails *swiftly*" is not a modal proposition; "swiftly" belongs to the predicate itself, and does not express a relationship of the predicate to the subject. The proposition "It is *certainly* true" is also not a modal proposition, since "certainly" expresses the state of mind of the speaker rather than the objective relationship of "it" and "true."

The following are modal propositions. Notice the different ways in which the mode is expressed.

1. God exists necessarily.
2. That Socrates sits is contingent.
3. It is possible that men are living on Mars.
4. It is impossible that any square be a circle.

A modal proposition has two parts, the *dictum* and the *mode*. The *dictum* is the part that affirms or denies an attribute of a subject, or that posits or sublates the existence of a subject. The *dicta* of the examples given above are: "God exists," "Socrates sits," "Men are living on Mars," and "Any square is a circle." The *dictum* can be singular, particular, universal, or indeterminate, just as the corresponding absolute propositions.

The *mode* is the part that states whether the *dictum* is necessary, contingent, possible, or impossible. The mode can be expressed by an adverb ("necessarily," "contingently," "possibly," "impossibly"), by a clause ("It is necessary that . . . ," and so on), and sometimes by a verb ("I can . . .").

Necessity and impossibility are the *universal modes*, since what is necessary always takes place and what is impossible never takes place. For this reason, the modes expressing necessity and impossibility are construed as *A* and *E* respectively.

Possibility and contingency are the *particular modes*. Modal propositions expressing possibility are construed as *I* propositions, since they are the contradictories of those expressing impossibility, which are *E*. Those expressing contingency are construed as *O* propositions, since they are the contradictories of those expressing necessity, which are *A*.

c. *Opposition of Modal Propositions*

The nature of modal propositions will be made more clear if we consider the traditional square of opposition of modal propositions.

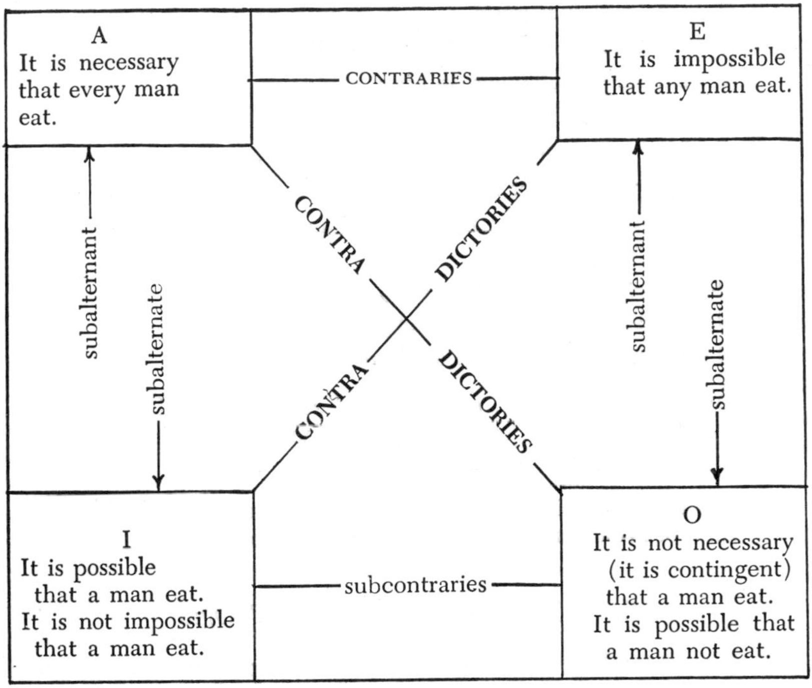

To refute the proposition "It is *necessary* that *every* man eat"(*A*), all you have to prove is that *some* man eats contingently—which is the same as proving that it is not necessary that every man eat or that it is possible for some man not to eat. The relationships of modal propositions towards one another are so obvious from a consideration of the square that it is not necessary to call attention to them in detail.

Exercise

I. Which of the following are modal propositions? Pick out the *dictum* and the *mode*. If the mode is expressed by an adverb, rephrase the proposition so as to express it by a clause, and vice versa.

1. God certainly exists.
2. That people live on Mars is doubtful.
3. People probably live on Mars.
4. God cannot lie.
5. That a creature be infinite is impossible.
6. A square cannot be a circle.
7. It is possible that men will some day encircle the earth in twenty-four hours.
8. The world exists contingently.
9. Houses can be painted purple.
10. Those who have done evil must be punished.

II. Give the contradictory, contrary, and subalternate of "It is impossible for all men to jump over the moon." Phrase them in several ways.

III. Give the contradictory, subcontrary, and subalternant of "It is possible for some man not to jump over the moon."

3. COMPOUND PROPOSITIONS

Before we explain the nature of compound propositions, we shall say a few words about simple propositions, because the former are best understood by contrasting them with the latter.

The propositions "God exists" and "A dog is an animal" are simple propositions. The first merely posits the existence of a subject; the second affirms an attribute of a subject. Notice that in both of these propositions our assent is expressed by the verb—by "exists" in the first, and by "is" in the second.

There are other propositions in which our assent is expressed by conjunctions, adverbs, and so on, as in the proposition "If the sun is shining, then it is day." In this proposition our assent is expressed by "*if . . . , then . . . ,*" and bears directly on the relationship of the first clause (the "if" clause) to the second clause (the "then" clause).

Propositions of this sort are compound propositions. Compound propositions, then, consist of at least two clauses; and in compound propositions our assent is expressed by conjunctions, adverbs, and so on, that indicate the relationship of the clauses towards one another.

Hypothetical propositions (that is, conditional, disjunctive, and conjunctive propositions) are compound. You will recall that we studied them before we took up the hypothetical syllogism. The causal propositions ("because . . ." propositions) mentioned in connection with the enthymeme are also compound propositions. In the present section we shall give a brief account—which will be little more than a catalog—of some other kinds of compound propositions.

The main division of compound propositions is into those that are openly compound and those that are occultly compound.

a. *Openly Compound Propositions*

A proposition is openly, or formally, compound if the plurality of clauses (exclusive of those that are merely parts of a complex term) is stated explicitly. There are several kinds. Some of these kinds have occultly compound variants.

1) **COPULATIVE PROPOSITIONS.** Copulative propositions are compound propositions that have two or more subjects, or predicates, or both, which are joined together by "and," "both . . . and," "neither . . . nor," and so on. The following is a copulative proposition that is openly, or formally, compound: "Peter was martyred in Rome, and Paul was martyred in Rome." The same truth can be expressed in an occultly compound proposition "Both Peter and Paul were martyred in Rome." "Neither wealth nor honors can make you happy" is likewise an occultly compound copulative proposition; it can be resolved into the openly compound proposition, "Wealth cannot make you happy, and honors cannot make you happy."

A copulative proposition is true if its every member is true; it is false if any member is false. The contradictory of a copulative proposition is a disjunctive in the broad sense. Thus, the contradictory of "Both Jimmy and Johnny are naughty boys" is "Either Jimmy is not a naughty boy, or Johnny is not a naughty boy (or neither is a naughty boy)." It can also be expressed: "Jimmy and Johnny are not both naughty boys." The contrary, however, of "Both Jimmy and Johnny are naughty boys" is "Neither Jimmy nor Johnny is a naughty boy."

2) ADVERSATIVE PROPOSITION. An adversative proposition is similar to a copulative proposition in that it has two or more subjects, or predicates, or both, which are joined together into a compound proposition. It differs from a copulative in that it also expresses a contrast of clauses by the use of conjunctions such as "but," "although," "nevertheless," "still," and so on. The clause introduced by the adversative conjunction is an assertion of something other than what you would expect to follow from, or to accompany, the other clause.

An adversative proposition is often a denial of the corresponding inferential, or illative, proposition. Let us examine the following example: "He is an American Indian but does not have black eyes." You would expect that he would have black eyes as a consequent of being an American Indian. The use of an adversative conjunction suggests what is included in the parentheses: "He is an American Indian (and therefore you would expect him to have black eyes), but he does not have black eyes."

For an adversative proposition to be true, each of the clauses must be true when it is taken by itself, and there must also be some kind of contrast between them. Thus, the example "He is an American Indian but does not have black eyes" is true if he is an American Indian and if he does not have black eyes, since you would expect an American Indian to have black eyes as a consequent of his being an American Indian. But the proposition "It is a razor but sharp" is not true even if the thing referred to is a razor and also is sharp. The reason for this is that there is no contrast between a thing's being a razor and its being sharp; sharpness is an attribute you would expect a razor to have.

3) CAUSAL PROPOSITION. A causal proposition is a compound proposition whose clauses are joined by the causal conjunctions "because," "since," "for," and so on. The clause introduced by the causal conjunction must state the cause, reason, occasion, or explanation, of what is asserted in the other clause. Sometimes it states the cause, occasion, or reason of the thing itself, as in the proposition

"He is wearing a cast because he broke his arm." Sometimes it states the reason for our knowledge of the thing, as in the proposition "He must have broken his arm because he is wearing a cast."

For a causal proposition to be true, each of its members must be true when it is taken by itself, and the clause introduced by the causal conjunction must actually state the cause, reason, occasion, or explanation, either of what is asserted in the other clause or of our knowledge of it. Thus, the proposition "Abraham Lincoln was elected president because he was a very tall man" is false although he was elected president and also was a very tall man; it is false because his being a very tall man was not the cause, occasion, and so on, either of his being elected president or of our knowledge of his election to the presidency.

Enthymemes, as we have seen, are frequently expressed by causal propositions.

4) **INFERENTIAL PROPOSITION.** An inferential (illative, or rational) proposition is a compound proposition whose clauses are joined by the conjunctions "therefore," "for this reason," "and so," and so on. As the name "inferential" suggests, an inferential proposition states an inference; the clause introduced by the inferential conjunction ("therefore," and so on) is the consequent, and the other clause is the antecedent.

For an inferential proposition to be true, each clause must be true when it is taken by itself, and the sequence expressed by the inferential conjunction must be valid.

Enthymemes, as we have seen, are frequently expressed in inferential propositions.

b. Occultly Compound Propositions

A proposition is occultly, or virtually, compound if it explicitly states only one clause (exclusive of clauses that are parts of terms) but implies one or more other clauses through the use of words such as "only," "except," "as such," and so on.

These propositions are called *exponibles* because they can be "exposed," or resolved, into two or more clauses by fully stating the clause that is implied by the word such as "only," and so on. There are several kinds.

1) EXCLUSIVE PROPOSITION. An exclusive proposition is an occultly compound proposition in which a word like "only," "alone," and so on, implies an entire clause. Sometimes the word "only" *excludes* the predicate from everything else than the subject, as in the proposition "Only citizens are voters." Here the word "only" restricts the applicability of "voter" to "citizens" and excludes "voter" from everything besides "citizens." Hence, this proposition can be exposed to "Non-citizens are not voters; (at least some) citizens are voters." The proposition "Only citizens are voters" is a sort of contrapositive of the *A* proposition "All voters are citizens" (notice the interchange of the subject and predicate) and, at least as far as its logical form is concerned, is perfectly equivalent to it. (Recall what was said about the equivalence of various logical forms when we studied conversion, obversion, and contraposition.)

Notice that the proposition "Only *some* houses are white" is different from the proposition given above. In this proposition the word "only" is affixed to the quantifier "some," not to "houses." Hence, this proposition does not mean that all white things are houses. This proposition is exposed to "Some houses are white, and some houses are not white."

2) EXCEPTIVE PROPOSITION. An exceptive proposition is an occultly compound proposition in which the subject term is restricted in its application by words such as "except," "save," "but," and so on. Notice that exceptive propositions are often equivalent to exclusive propositions. Thus, the exceptive proposition "None but (save, except) citizens are voters" is equivalent to the exclusive proposition "Only citizens are voters," and both of these propositions are exposed to "Non-citizens are not voters; (at least some) citizens are voters." The proposition "None but citizens are voters" is likewise equivalent to the *A* proposition "All voters are citizens."

3) INCEPTIVE AND DESITIVE PROPOSITIONS. Inceptive propositions express the beginning of a thing, action, or state. Desitive propositions express the ending of a thing, action, or state. Akin to these are propositions expressing continuance in being or action; but such propositions have no special name.

"He began to smoke last month" is an inceptive proposition. It is exposed as follows: "He did not smoke before last month; he did smoke and continued to do so last month."

"He gave up smoking" is a desitive proposition. It is exposed as follows: "He did smoke; then (for a while) he did not smoke."

The fallacy of many questions is frequently incurred by proposing a question in the form of an inceptive or desitive proposition; for instance, "Have you finally begun to behave yourself?," "Have you stopped beating your wife?," and "How long will you continue that nonsense?"

4) REDUPLICATIVE PROPOSITION. A reduplicative proposition is an occultly compound proposition that expresses the special aspect of the subject by reason of which the predicate belongs to it. It does this by words such as "as," "as such," "in so far as," "inasmuch as," and so on. "As logicians, we are concerned with the transition from data to conclusion; but, as rational beings, we are concerned with the attainment of truth" is a reduplicative proposition.

A reduplicative proposition is true if the proposition would be true without the reduplication and if, besides that, the reduplicated formality is the reason why the predicate belongs to the subject. The proposition "As a swimmer, he plays the trombone well" is false, even if he is a swimmer and does play the trombone well, because his being a swimmer is not the reason for his playing the trombone well.

5) COMPARATIVE PROPOSITION. A comparative proposition is an occultly compound proposition in which we compare the way an attribute is present in one subject with the way it is present in another; for instance, "John is bigger than James." This proposition can be exposed to "John has size; James has size; the size of John is greater than the size of James."

Exercise

I. Exercise on the implications of compound propositions.

1. If it is false that a superior is to be obeyed because he is prudent, which of the following must be true?

   (1). A superior is not to be obeyed.
   (2). A superior is not prudent.

(3). The prudence of a superior is not the reason why he is to be obeyed.

2. If it is false that Peter and Paul and James will go, which of the following must be true?
   (1). Peter will not go.
   (2). Neither Peter nor Paul nor James will go.
   (3). Either Peter or Paul or James will not go.
3. If it is true that he got sick because he ate green apples, which of the following must be true?
   (1). He got sick.
   (2). He ate green apples.
   (3). Everyone who ate green apples got sick.
   (4). His having eaten green apples was the reason for his getting sick.
4. If it is true that only George passed the Sanskrit test, which of the following must be true?
   (1). George passed the Sanskrit test.
   (2). All except George failed in the Sanskrit test.
   (3). None but George passed the Sanskrit test.
5. If it is true that you have not given up evil habits, which of the following must be true?
   (1). You still have evil habits.
   (2). You never had any evil habits.
   (3). You either never had, or still have, evil habits.
6. Expose the proposition "All but two of the crew were drowned."
7. State the contradictory of "All but two of the crew were drowned."
8. Is the following proposition true? "The figure is a triangle but has three sides." Explain.
9. State the contradictory of "He ate too many green apples and therefore got sick."
10. Expose "Only ten of the twenty passed the examination."

II. Criticize the following inferences. Indicate the formal flaws.

1. Anyone but an idiot would understand that;
   but Jack understands it;
   therefore Jack is an idiot.
2. None but the brave deserve the fair;
   but Jack is certainly brave;
   therefore Jack certainly deserves the fair.

3. Jack gave up stunt flying;
but people who do stunt flying run great risks;
therefore Jack ran great risks.

4. Jack did not give up stunt flying;
but people who do stunt flying run great risks;
therefore Jack runs great risks.

5. Only citizens are voters;
therefore all voters are citizens.

6. Only some women are voters;
therefore all voters are women.

CHAPTER 15

Induction

IT IS CUSTOMARY in logic courses to treat of deduction before induction. In the acquisition of knowledge, however, induction precedes deduction. Material beings known by sense experience are the starting points of all human knowledge. From a consideration of individual instances, our minds rise by induction to universal truths. These then serve as premises for deductive argumentation. Deduction, therefore, presupposes induction; and the universal principles arrived at by induction are applied to further concrete instances by deduction.

1. GENERAL NOTION OF INDUCTION

We have already defined induction as the process by which our minds proceed from a sufficient number of instances to a universal truth. This passage from the less universal, or particular, to the more universal is called the inductive ascent. Induction, then, proceeds from *I* to *A*. Now when we studied oppositional inference we were told that it was illicit to go from *I* to *A*. Notice, though, that we were then treating of *formal inference*, whereas induction is *material inference*. In induction we proceed from *I* to *A* by reason of the special character of the matter, or thought content, and not by reason of the form, or structure, of our argument.

The induction that we are chiefly concerned with begins with a knowledge of concrete individual material beings, which we know through sense experience. From these concrete individuals, we rise by this kind of induction to a universal truth. For instance, from the fact that this piece of copper conducts electricity and that pieces two, three, and four also conduct it, we might infer (rightly or wrongly) that all copper conducts electricity. But induction can also begin with universal truths and proceed to still more universal truths, as when we proceed from what is true of various species to a statement about the genus that these species belong to. For instance, from the fact that copper, iron, silver, and gold, which are species of the genus "metal," conduct electricity, we might infer (rightly or wrongly) that all metal conducts electricity.

We must distinguish (*a*) between incomplete induction, which some logicians misleadingly call imperfect induction, and complete, or perfect, induction and (*b*) between intellective and rational induction.[1] These two divisions overlap—that is, both incomplete and complete induction can be either intellective or rational.

First we shall briefly explain the distinction between incomplete and complete induction. Then, because of their very great importance, we shall treat of intellective and rational induction under separate headings. Finally we shall treat very briefly of the argument from analogy and make some further comments on induction.

Incomplete, or *imperfect, induction* proceeds from what is known of individual subjects having a nature to an assertion about a nature as such. It proceeds from *I* to *A*—from a limited number of instances to a universal statement—as when we infer that all copper conducts electricity because pieces one, two, three, and four conduct it.

We made extensive use of incomplete induction when we established the validity or invalidity of various logical forms. For instance, by insight into a single example ("Every dog is an animal; therefore some animal is a dog") we clearly understand the validity of the logical form "Every S is a P; therefore some P is an S." Likewise by insight into a single example ("Every dog is an animal; therefore every animal is a dog") we clearly understand the invalidity of the logical form "Every S is a P; therefore every P is an S."

When we speak of induction without qualification, we generally have in mind incomplete induction.

We shall now explain the nature of *complete induction.* According to certain logicians who misconstrue its nature, it consists in

[1] The terms "intellective" and "rational" induction are not in common use today. The explanations given here differ considerably from those given in many logic books, and it seemed desirable to emphasize this difference by coining new technical terms.

affirming something of all the individuals of a class, one by one, and then affirming it of the entire class. Suppose, for instance, that you want to find out whether all in this room are wearing shoes. You examine every individual and find out that he is wearing shoes. And then, from your assertions about each individual—from your assertions, that is, that Peter is wearing shoes, that John is wearing shoes, that Mary is wearing shoes, and so on—you proceed to an assertion about the whole class; namely, that all in this room are wearing shoes. Notice that the statement that all in this room are wearing shoes merely summarizes what has already been said and involves no advance in knowledge. It is a mere *enumerative universal*—a mere statement of fact—and does not even suggest that to wear shoes is a necessary attribute of everyone in this room or that being in this room is the reason why its occupants are wearing shoes. We mention this as an example of what induction is *not.*

Complete induction, rightly understood, consists in proceeding from what is true of each species of a genus to an assertion about the genus itself, as when we assert that copper, iron, silver, gold, and so on, and so on, conduct electricity and therefore all metal (not "all metals") conducts it. Notice that this is a true inference and that there is a true advance in knowledge (supposing, of course, that the inference is made correctly). To know that metal *as such* conducts electricity is more perfect knowledge than to know that various kinds of metal conduct it without also knowing that this is due to their generic nature as metals.

We also made extensive use of complete induction in establishing the validity or invalidity of various logical forms. Recall, for instance, how we showed that the mood I-E of a categorical syllogism is always invalid because it always involves an illicit process of the major term. First we showed by incomplete induction that I-E is invalid in each of the four figures. We clearly understood how these four figures include all possible arrangements of the syllogistic terms and that therefore I-E is always invalid. We proceeded from what is true of each of the four species of the genus "categorical syllogism in the mood I-E" to an assertion about the genus "categorical syllogism in the mood I-E" itself.

2. INTELLECTIVE INDUCTION

We shall lead up to a definition of intellective induction by analyzing a few examples and reflecting on how our minds proceed in regard to each of them.

a. Some Examples

First we shall examine two contingent propositions from which it is impossible for us to ascend to a universal truth. Then we shall examine a proposition from which we shall immediately see that we can ascend to a universal truth. While examining these propositions, we shall not pay attention to their form, but to the reality that they present to the mind.

1) "THIS HOUSE IS RED." Consider the following propositions, and suppose that what is asserted in them is true.

1. This house is red.
2. John is running down the street.

When you consider these propositions, you see no necessary connection between the subject and predicate. Of course, if the house is red, it cannot not be red in the respect in which it is red; and if John is running down the street, he cannot at the same time not be running down the street. But this is the only kind of necessity present; except on the supposition that the house is actually red or that John is actually running down the street, it is equally possible for the house not to be red or for John not to be running down the street. The actualities understood in these judgments are contingent; hence, it is impossible to ascend from them to universal statements about *house as such* or *man as such*. In the following example, however, from a consideration of a single instance, our minds spontaneously ascend to a universal truth.

2) "THIS WHOLE IS GREATER THAN THIS PART." [2] The entire rectangle represents a whole card; the dotted lines mark off a part of the whole card.

[2] Notice that the terms "whole" and "part" must be used univocally throughout an inductive process. What is true of the relationship of quantitative wholes to their parts need not be true of the relationship of essential wholes to their parts or of logical wholes to their parts, and so on.

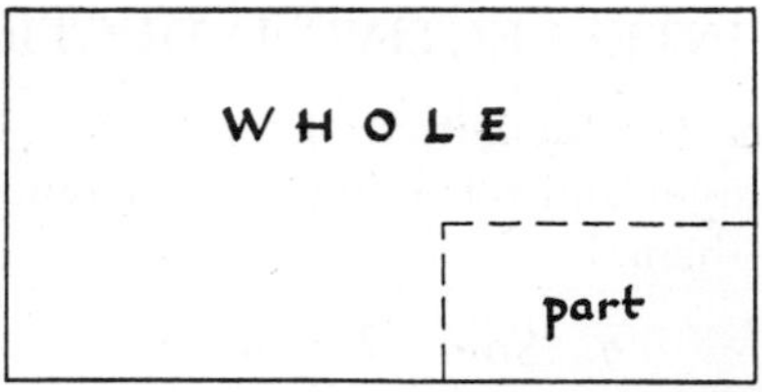

On seeing the whole card and the part, we know what is expressed in the proposition,

This whole card is greater than this part.

Insofar as it would be possible for this card and this part not to exist at all, this too is a contingent proposition. Yet there is an element of necessity in this proposition that is not found in the two previous examples. On looking at this card and its part, we clearly understand that the whole card is not greater than this part only as a matter of fact, but that it must be greater and cannot be otherwise. In other words, we grasp the *intelligibility of the fact* that this whole card is greater than this part and clearly perceive the intrinsic reason why it is impossible for the whole card not to be greater than its part. When we see a red house, we see nothing in the nature of the house requiring that it be red; and when we see a man running down the street, we see nothing in the nature of the man requiring that he run down the street. But on seeing this whole and this part, we clearly understand that the very nature of this whole and this part require that the whole be greater than the part. Moreover, we know and clearly understand that the reason why this whole is greater than this part is not that it is *this* whole and *this* part in these particular circumstances, but simply that it is *a* whole and *a* part. Once we have grasped this necessary relationship of a whole to its parts, our minds spontaneously pass from this concrete instance to the universal truth,

A whole is greater than any of its parts.

By insight into the particular example we know that this must be true. We cannot withhold our assent to the proposition "A whole is greater than any of its parts" because we clearly understand that it cannot be otherwise—we grasp the intelligible, necessary relationship between a whole and its parts so completely that we know with absolute certainty that, if a whole and a part exist at all, the whole must be greater than a part.

b. Definition of Intellective Induction

Our definition of intellective induction is nothing but a description of what we do when, on looking at the whole card and the part of the card, we pass from the proposition "This whole card is greater than this part" to the proposition "A whole as such is greater than any of its parts."

Intellective induction, then, is the process whereby our minds rise from a consideration of particular cases to a universal truth because we understand *through insight into the particular case* that the universal is necessarily true.

This definition will be understood better when, after illustrating, defining, and explaining rational induction, we make a detailed comparison of intellective and rational induction.

The rules of formal inference are established exclusively by intellective induction. In explaining these rules we always begin with examples whose validity or invalidity is obvious and then through insight into these examples we draw up our universal rules. For instance, to show the invalidity of the simple conversion of an *A* proposition we use an example like "Every dog is an animal; therefore every animal is a dog." The mere fact that the antecedent is true but the consequent (or pseudo consequent) is false shows that this logical form is invalid and then through insight into the quantitative relationship of the subject and predicate as illustrated in the terms "dog" and "animal" we clearly see the reason for the invalidity.

3. RATIONAL INDUCTION

First we shall re-examine the first two examples given in the last section and compare them with a third example. Then we shall give a definition of rational induction. Finally we shall compare intellective and rational induction in such a way as to throw further light on the nature of each of them.

a. Some Examples

Consider the following propositions, and suppose that what is asserted in them is true. Notice, again, that we are not now concerned with the form of these propositions, but with the reality that they present to the mind.

1. This house is red.
2. John is running down the street.
3. The apple, unsupported, falls toward the earth.

If we look at this third example in itself as a single concrete statement of fact and without reference to other knowledge or other instances, we see no necessities other than those seen in the first two propositions. But when we multiply instances in our experience—for example, the wind blows a tile loose and it falls, the man steps out of the window and he falls, the plate slips and it falls, ripe fruit breaks from the branch and it falls—when we multiply such instances, we perceive a similarity among the instances and, with or without accuracy, we generalize in some such fashion as follows:

Unsupported things fall toward the earth.[3]

In such a generalization we do not see the intelligibility of the fact any more clearly than in a single instance. Still, we are convinced that within the complexus of concrete realities there must be some factor, or combination of factors, that renders it necessary for unsupported things to fall toward the earth. In other words, we are sure that the only sufficient reason for the constancy with which unsupported things fall toward the earth is the presence of some necessity by reason of which they *must* fall toward the earth.

Such a generalization involves an *implicit deduction,* since the conclusion ("All unsupported things fall towards the earth") can be drawn only on the assumption that determined effects require a determined and intelligible ground.

b. Definition of Rational Induction

Our definition of rational induction is a description of what we do when, after experiencing, for instance, that countless things fall

[3] Perhaps we should add the qualification "provided they are heavier than air."

toward the earth when unsupported, we make a generalization such as "Unsupported things fall toward the earth."

Rational induction, then, is the process whereby our minds rise from a consideration of particular cases to a universal judgment because we know, or at least have reason to think, that the judgment is necessary, although we do not see the reason for this necessity.

c. *Comparison of Intellective and Rational Induction*

A comparison of intellective and rational induction will throw further light on the nature of each of them.

The most basic difference between intellective and rational induction is this: in intellective induction, *while considering the particular instance, we see and understand the intrinsic necessity*, and therefore the intelligibility, of the universal proposition, whereas in rational induction *we do not see this intrinsic necessity*, but are induced to admit the presence of some kind of necessity as the only sufficient reason for the constancy of the effects we have observed.

This difference implies two other differences. Intellective induction *depends on no previous judgments* and *gives absolute certainty*, because in it we see and clearly understand the full intelligibility of a truth. But rational induction *rests*, at least implicitly, on *previous judgments* (such as the principle of sufficient reason or intelligibility, the principle of causality, the principle of uniformity of nature, and so on) and *does not* by itself *give absolute certainty*.

There is a fourth difference between intellective and rational induction. In intellective induction a generalization can be made, in some cases at least, from a *single instance*. A multiplicity of instances may often be necessary, but only accidentally, for it serves only to direct our attention to the proper intelligibility of some complex situation and to stimulate our minds to proceed to generalization. But once our attention has been directed to the proper intelligibility of a concrete situation, there is no need whatsoever for further instances, since the generalization is implicit in the knowledge of each single instance. In rational induction, on the other hand, the *multiplicity of instances* is usually a formal part of the evidence—until a stage is reached (if it ever is reached) in which the intelligibility itself is displayed.

The aim of science is always full intelligibility; therefore the first type of induction (induction by insight, or intellective induction) remains the ideal. It sometimes happens in the course of scientific observation or experiment that a truth which was previously known only by rational induction suddenly becomes subject to immediate insight. At this point our assent no longer depends on previous observation and deduction except accidentally. In itself, the insight is immediate, and the previous process (observation, experiment, and so on) has merely displayed the factors involved so that the insight could be gained in immediate understanding.

We have examples of such development in astronomy. For instance, the first investigations of eclipses and other celestial phenomena interrelated certain factors with their occurrence; but when the structure and motion of the heavens was sufficiently understood, it became immediately evident why the occurrence of certain phenomena was necessarily related to the occurrence of an eclipse. The validity of the law formulating the functional relationship between these phenomena and the occurrence of eclipses no longer depended on the previous rational induction but was now self-evident.

4. THE ARGUMENT FROM ANALOGY

In this section we shall treat very briefly of the argument from analogy. First we shall define, or rather describe, it; then we shall call attention to its use and limitations; and finally we shall give two rules or cautions regarding the use of arguments from analogy.

a. Definition

The argument from analogy is a probable argument based on a resemblance. Suppose that *X* is known to resemble *Y* in the attributes *a, b, c, d,* and *e;* suppose, too, that *X* is also known to have the attribute *f*. If on the basis of *Y*'s similarity to *X* in the attributes *a, b, c, d,* and *e,* we argue that, since *X* has *f*, *Y* most likely also has *f*, we are using an argument from analogy. For instance, we might argue as follows: Deer are similar to cows, goats, and sheep in that they have horns and are cloven-footed and chew cud. Cows, goats, and sheep have stomachs with many chambers. Therefore, it seems, deer must have stomachs with many chambers.

The argument from analogy proceeds from one or more particular instances through an unexpressed universal to another particular instance that is similar to the former but not (logically) identical with them. The passage from the one or more particular instances to an unexpressed universal involves an implicit induction. The application of this universal to another instance involves an implicit deduction. If it is expressed completely, the argument given above will be stated as follows:

Cows, goats, and sheep have horns and are cloven-footed and chew cud.

But cows, goats, and sheep have stomachs with many chambers.

(Therefore, it seems, animals that have horns and are cloven-footed and chew cud have stomachs with many chambers.)

But deer have horns and are cloven-footed and chew cud.

Therefore, it seems, deer must have stomachs with many chambers.

From the particular instances of the cows, goats, and sheep we pass by induction to the implicit universal proposition stated in the parentheses; and then by an implicit deduction we apply this universal proposition to the particular case of the deer.

b. Use and Limitations

Arguments from analogy are of very great importance both in the practical concerns of every-day life and in scientific investigation. Think, for instance, of the advances that the science of medicine has made by experimenting on mice, guinea pigs, dogs, and so on, and then applying the lessons of these experiments to man on the basis of man's similarity to these animals. The historian's attempts to interpret present events in the light of the past are arguments from analogy. The housewife uses analogy when she argues that cooking herring in vinegar will improve its flavor because this method of cooking improves the flavor of smelt. In every-day life we continually solve our problems by reflecting on what we ourselves, or others, have done in situations similar to our present circumstances.

In itself, analogy does not lead to certainty but merely points the way to *probable* answers to our problems or suggests the direction that our investigations might take. What cured a guinea pig, for instance, *might* cure a man; but we will ordinarily not know for certain whether or not it will cure a man until we have tried it on a man—or maybe on many men. Unless arguments from analogy are used with extreme caution, they are as likely to lead to error as to truth.

c. *Rules or Cautions*

In the first place, if an argument from analogy is to be legitimate, *the resemblance on which it is based must be significant;* that is, there must be good reason to think that there is a necessary connection between the attributes in which two subjects are similar and the attribute we wish to predicate of the one subject because of its resemblances to the other. From the fact that John and James are of equal weight and height and of similar build, we can legitimately infer that they have about equal strength. All these factors have significance in relation to strength. But from the equality of their weight and height and the similarity of their builds we cannot legitimately infer that they are of equal intelligence, because these factors have no significance whatsoever in regard to intelligence.

Once we are certain that there is a causal connection between the attributes in which two subjects are similar and the attribute we wish to predicate of the second subject because of its similarity to the first, our argument ceases to be a mere probable argument from analogy and becomes a perfect syllogism that leads to a certain conclusion. This takes place whenever the implicit universal proposition is a necessary proposition.

Secondly, when we use arguments from analogy we must *take into account important differences.* As an example of how this caution is sometimes ignored we cite the tendency of certain evolutionists to concentrate solely on man's somatic resemblances to the other animals and to ignore the many ways in which he differs from them.

5. FURTHER COMMENTS ON INDUCTION

In this section we shall indicate the extent to which the study of induction belongs to logic and explain why there are no rules for induction as there are for deduction.

a. The Extent to Which Induction Belongs to Logic

To what extent does the study of induction belong to logic? To answer this question we must anticipate what we shall explain at length in Chapter 16, where we shall define logic in terms of its formal object. Logic, as we shall see in Chapter 16 (and as we have already indicated briefly in Chapter 1), is not a science of real beings but of second intentions. The scope of logic is therefore limited to what we can know by reflecting on our knowledge and on the attributes and relationships that things have as they exist in the mind and that they get as a result of being thought of. Now, when we reflect on our knowledge of various kinds of things, we advert to the fact that we know different things in different ways—and we discover the types of induction that we have just described. At the same time we clearly understand that their validity (unlike the validity of syllogisms) depends on the matter under consideration and not at all on the structure, or form, of our propositions and arguments.

Now, all that logic can do about the various kinds of induction is to acknowledge their existence, describe their nature, and confess its inability to make rules to regulate them.

b. No Rules for the Inductive Ascent

There are no rules governing induction as the rules of the syllogism, and so on, govern deduction. The reason for this is that inductive arguments are not reducible to logical forms that are valid regardless of their matter, but depend for their validity on the special character of the matter under consideration.

Directives on scientific investigation tell us how to conduct experiments, how to test hypotheses, and so on, but are not rules for making the inductive ascent itself. Besides, such directives lie outside the scope of logic inasmuch as they are instructions on the handling, not of second intentions, but of real beings.

CHAPTER 16

The Definition of Logic by Its Formal Object

In Chapter 1 we gave a preliminary definition of logic as the science and art of correct thinking. In the present chapter we shall consider logic from another point of view and define it in terms of its formal object.

First we shall treat of the differentiation of the sciences by their formal objects. Then we shall apply to logic what we have said about the sciences in general.

1. SCIENCES ARE SPECIFIED BY THEIR OBJECTS

One act of knowledge differs from another act of knowledge because it is knowledge either of a different thing or of a different aspect of the same thing. For instance, our knowledge of a walrus is different from our knowledge of a triangle because a walrus differs from a triangle; and the knowledge a stonecutter has of a stone differs from the knowledge a geologist has of the same stone because each considers a different aspect of the stone.

Sciences differ from one another in the same two ways: either they consider different kinds of things, or they consider different aspects of the same things. Thus, theology differs from anthropology in the first way, because the subject matter of theology is God, whereas the subject matter of anthropology is man. Anatomy differs from biochemistry in the second way: both consider living organisms, but under a different aspect.

The things a science considers—that is, the things as they are in themselves together with all their attributes—constitute its *material object.* Many sciences can have the same material object (or general subject matter); but each distinct science considers a distinct and special aspect of its material object. This special aspect is called the *formal object* of the science. Both anatomy and biochemistry, for instance, have the same material object, for both of them investigate living organisms; but they differ in their formal objects, for anatomy investigates the structural make-up of living organisms, whereas biochemistry investigates the chemical changes that take place within them. In their formal objects no two sciences are alike.

Differences in their objects, especially in their formal objects, are the most basic differences among the various sciences. The differences in method, in the nature of the laws they formulate, and in the kind of certainty they attain spring principally from the differences in their formal objects. For this reason the best way to define a particular science is to state its formal object. This, too, is the meaning of the statement that sciences are specified by their objects; for their formal objects place them in their species, making them the kind of science they are.

2. THE OBJECT OF LOGIC

We shall now state the material object of logic, then the formal object, and then give the actual definition of logic in terms of its formal object.

a. The Material Object

The *material object* of logic includes all things without exception. It includes all that the human mind can know, all that we can grasp by simple apprehension, judgment, and reasoning. Consequently, the material object of logic includes the material objects of all the other sciences. Logic is similar to metaphysics in this respect, for metaphysics is also a science of all things without exception.

b. The Formal Object

In its *formal object* logic differs from all the other sciences. Metaphysics, the philosophy of God, the philosophy of human nature, and all the purely speculative sciences study real beings—God, man, the world, and so on—as they exist (or can exist) independently of our thinking of them. They consider beings that human reason does not make but merely discovers and contemplates. Each science, it is true, considers only a particular aspect of things, and no single science investigates beings in all their aspects. Still, these aspects are really in things whether we think of them or not. For instance, Euclidean geometry considers abstract quantity, and quantity really is in things (although not in an abstract way). But logic is different. Logic does not consider things as they are in themselves independently of our thinking of them, but according to a new kind of being they get as a result of being known.

When we know a thing, we confer on it a new kind of being by giving it existence in thought. (For instance, when we know "triangle," "triangle" somehow exists in us by the mere fact of our knowing it.) In thought, things have many attributes and relationships that they do not have in the real order. They are universal. They can be predicated of one another; they stand towards one another as genus, specific difference, and so on; they can be minor, middle, and major terms in argumentation; and so on and so on. These attributes and relationships that things do not have in the real order but do have as they exist in the mind and that they get as a result of being known constitute the *formal object* of logic. They are called beings of reason (*entia rationis*) because they depend on reason for their very existence and cannot exist except in the mind. The logician examines these beings of reason and the various relationships they have towards one another, and draws up the laws of correct thinking in conformity with the requirements of this order of beings that his own mind has established.

In brief, the formal object of logic is not things as they are in themselves and independently of our knowledge of them, but things as reproduced in the mind together with all the attributes and relationships they get as a result of being mentally reproduced. These, together with the principle of contradiction, serve as guide posts to the logician when he formulates the laws of correct thinking.

c. The Definition Itself

In terms of its formal object, logic is defined as the science of the attributes and relationships that things have as they exist in the mind and get as a result of being known. In other words, it is the science of the mental representation of real beings, a science not directly of things but of certain aspects of our knowledge of things, a science of beings of reason.[1] Briefly, *logic is the science of second intentions.*[2]

Logic is the science of beings of reason, or second intentions, in several ways. In the first place, the kind of beings that logic considers is not—at least not directly—real beings but beings of reason. In the second place, the laws that logic formulates constitute an organized body of conclusions about beings of reason (such as subjects and predicates, genus and species, propositions, syllogisms, minor, middle, and major terms, and so on). In the third place, the purpose of logic is to guide the mind in the construction of more beings of reason (syllogisms, for instance). Still, when we apply the laws of logic we are thinking about things—about real things, that is, about things that exist (or can exist). And if our premises give us knowledge of real beings and we reason correctly, our conclusions will also give us knowledge of real beings.

3. COMPOSITE DEFINITION AND SYNOPSIS

Both of the definitions we have given are too broad if they are taken by themselves. The first definition ("logic is the science and art of correct thinking") is too broad for two reasons. In the first place, unless we arbitrarily restrict the meaning of "thinking" (as we did in Chapter 1), there are kinds of thinking that do not fall within the scope of logic; for instance, reverie, day-dreaming, and the chance association of ideas. In the second place, logic cannot lay down rules for the validity of material sequence or for the understanding of first principles, and so on. The second definition of logic ("logic is the science of the attributes and relationships that

[1] The *formal object* of logic does not include those beings of reason that have non-existence in their definitions, such as privations (blindness) and mere figments of the mind.

Note that the order of beings that logic considers does not include the entire order of thought or conceptual order. The conceptual order includes whatever exists in thought, whether it exists in the real order or not; but the "logical order" includes attributes and relationships that things have only in the conceptual order and that they cannot have in the real order.

[2] As we saw in Chapter 11, the beings of reason here referred to are called *second intentions.*

things have as they exist in the mind and get as a result of being known") is too broad because at least some aspects of these beings of reason fall outside the scope of logic; for instance, their relationship to real beings. But if we combine both of these definitions into one, we shall have a composite definition that accurately expresses the object and function of logic and clearly delineates its scope. Hence, we give the following definition:

Logic is the science of those beings of reason that the mind must consider in formulating the laws of correct thinking, and the art that applies these laws.

Logic considers beings of reason only insofar as they are the basis of the laws of correct thinking. Logic investigates and formulates the laws of correct thinking only insofar as they are determined by the nature of beings of reason.

Synopsis

Logic is the science which at least indirectly considers all beings (*material object*). It considers them according to the attributes and relationships they have as they exist in the mind and get as a result of being known (*formal object*). In accordance with the nature of these beings of reason, guided by the principle of contradiction (*first principle*), logic investigates and formulates the laws of correct thinking (*proximate end* or *purpose*) as a means of attaining truth (*ultimate end*). As an art, logic also applies these laws.

APPENDIX I

Some Remarks on Symbolic Logic

SYMBOLIC LOGIC GETS ITS NAME from its use of symbols that stand for various logical units and that are similar in many ways to the symbols of mathematics. Their purpose is to manifest the structure of propositions and arguments more clearly than can be done by ordinary language. They are to accomplish this by enabling us to avoid the obscurities, ambiguities, and cumbersomeness of ordinary language and to ignore the matter of our thought entirely and thus direct our attention solely to its form.

We shall now explain some very elementary symbolization of symbolic logic, restricting ourselves to a few types of propositions, and at the same time we shall call attention to interpretations at variance with those given in this book. We shall then conclude with a number of categorical assertions about the nature of symbolic logic and its relation to traditional Aristotelian and Thomistic logic.

The symbolism of symbolic logic has not been entirely standardized, but the following usages are rather common.

A single letter may signify either a complete proposition or a member of a compound proposition. Thus, the letter r may signify the proposition "If p, then q," and the letter a may signify a proposition like "John is a sailor."

Conjunction of propositions is signified by a dot (·). Thus, "Rover is a dog, and Felix is a cat" can be written "(Rover is a dog)·(Felix is a cat)," or, allowing p to stand for the first member and q for the second, we can symbolize it by $p \cdot q$ ("Both p and q"). The meaning of $p \cdot q$ is displayed in the following table:

p	q	$p \cdot q$
T	T	T
T	F	F
F	T	F
F	F	F

It is clear that $p \cdot q$ is true only in the first row where both p and q are true and that it is false in all other instances.

The contradictory of a proposition is indicated by prefixing a minus sign ($-$) to it or by placing an acute ($'$) after it, as well as in various other ways. The relationship of contradictories (p and $-p$) to one another as to truth and falsity is displayed in the following table:

p	$-p$
T	F
F	T

If one of two contradictories is true the other is false and vice versa.

A disjunctive proposition in the broad or inclusive sense is symbolized by a heavy "V," the first letter of the Latin word *vel,* which means "or." Thus, $p \vee q$ means "p or q—maybe both." This meaning is displayed in the following table:

p	q	$p \vee q$
T	T	T
T	F	T
F	T	T
F	F	F

You will notice that $p \vee q$ is false only in the last row where both p and q are false and that it is true in all other instances.

In a disjunctive proposition in the strict or exclusive sense one and only one member is true and the other members are false. Hence, a disjunctive in the strict or exclusive sense ("p or q—but not both") is symbolized as follows: $(p \vee q) \cdot (-p \vee -q)$. Its meaning is displayed in the following table:

p	q	$-p$	$-q$	$(p \vee q) \cdot (-p \vee -q)$
T	T	F	F	F
T	F	F	T	T
F	T	T	F	T
F	F	T	T	F

Thus, $(p \vee q) \cdot (-p \vee -q)$ is true when one of its members (either p or q) is true and the other is false, and is false when both members (that is, both p and q) are either true or false.

The "if-then" of a conditional proposition is symbolized by a horseshoe or reversed "C" ($\supset$). However, the interpretation of a conditional proposition as given by many symbolic logicians differs profoundly from the explanation we gave in Chapter 8.

According to the explanation given there, a conditional proposition is an assertion of a sequence and nothing else, and is true if the sequence is valid. The mere simultaneous truth of both the antecedent and consequent is not enough to make the conditional proposition true. There must also be some *connection* whereby the truth of the antecedent necessitates the truth of the consequent. Sometimes the connection arises only from the will of the speaker (as in the proposition "If you move, I'll shoot you") or maybe only from a subtle and unexpressed *a fortiori* argument regarding the consistent application of two metaphors (as in the proposition "If he's a lion, she's a wildcat")—but some connection there must always be.

Now, many symbolic logicians deny the necessity of any such connection and claim that all that is needed for a conditional proposition to be true is that *as a matter of fact* the consequent is not false when the antecedent is true. Hence, according to them, a conditional proposition is true (*a*) when both the antecedent and the consequent are true—as in the proposition "If you are human, then ocean water is salty," or (*b*) when the antecedent is false but the consequent true—as in "If you are a monkey, then you are human," or (*c*) when both the antecedent and consequent are false—as in "If you are a monkey, then you are a bird." In all these instances the antecedent is said to "imply" the consequent. A conditional proposition is false only when as a matter of fact the antecedent is true and the consequent false. Hence, the *minimum meaning* of "If *p*, then *q*" is merely $-(p \cdot -q)$, which means "It is false that *p* is true and *q* is false." This relationship of *p* and *q* is called *material implication*, and this is what is symbolized by the horseshoe or reversed "C" ($\supset$).

The meaning of $p \supset q$ is displayed in the following table:

p	q	$p \supset q$
T	T	T
T	F	F
F	T	T
F	F	T

Notice that $p \supset q$ is false only in the second row where *p* is true and *q* is false, and true in all other instances. Notice, too, that wherever $p \supset q$ is true, either *q* is true or *p* is false; hence, $p \supset q$ is equivalent to $-p \vee q$, which means "Either not *p*, or *q*."

The symbolic logician's symbolization and interpretation of the categorical, or attributive, proposition are very different from those of Aristotelian and Thomistic logic. Before we explain them it will be helpful to repeat and enlarge upon a few points already mentioned in Chapter 3, where we treated of the attributive proposition, and in Chapter 12, where we treated of the supposition of terms. In these chapters we explained how a subject term stands for a thing *as mentally conceived* and how the matter of a proposition and not merely its form, or structure, determines whether or not the actual real existence of a subject is asserted. The proposition "A chiliagon has a thousand sides" is a true proposition because a chiliagon as mentally conceived actually does have a thousand sides, and the proposition "A chiliagon has a million sides" is a false proposition because a chiliagon as mentally conceived does not have a million sides (but only a thousand). These propositions are true or false independently of the real existence of a chiliagon. However, *IF* a real chiliagon exists, it must exist as a figure having a thousand sides; still, the proposition "A chiliagon has a thousand sides" neither affirms nor denies the real existence of a chiliagon but prescinds from it. The same is true of the proposition "*Every* chiliagon has a thousand sides." Similarly, a particular proposition ("*Some* chiliagon has a thousand sides") does not necessarily assert the real existence of its subject but at least *can be* restricted to asserting something of the subject only as mentally conceived. Now the interpretation of *A, E, I,* and *O* propositions as given by symbolic logicians differs considerably from that given above, and this difference of interpretation is mirrored in their symbolization.

We shall begin with the singular proposition and in connection with it we shall explain and illustrate the meaning of *propositional function.* We shall use the capital of the first letter of the first word of the predicate term to symbolize the predicate, and the small letter of the first letter of the first word of the subject term to symbolize the subject. Thus, the proposition "John is a man" can be symbolized by the letters *Mj*—with *M* representing "man" and *j* representing "John"; and the proposition "Mary is a woman" can be symbolized by the letters *Wm*—with *W* standing for "*wo*man" and *m* for "Mary." Suppose, now, that we wish to indicate merely the predication of an attribute but without mentioning any subject at all—as though we wanted to say "______ is a man" or "______ is a woman," leaving a blank space for any subject we may wish to insert. Now, instead of using a blank space, we use the letter *x*, which is called a *variable* and which (like the blank space) stands for any *substitution instance* whatsoever. Thus, we get *Mx* and *Wx* —which are not called propositions but *propositional functions.* However, they become propositions when we retain the *constants* (*M* and *W*) and substitute actual subjects for *x*, as when in *Mx* we substitute *j* for *x* and get *Mj* ("John is a man") and in *Wx* we substitute *m* for *x* and get *Wm* ("Mary is a woman").

We shall now consider universal and particular propositions. According to symbolic logicians, the universal proposition does not signify that the subject as mentally conceived has (or does not have) the attribute signified by the predicate. All it signifies is the *factual coincidence* of the subject and predicate (or the factual absence of the predicate from the subject) *if* the subject exists—*IF* the subject exists in the real order, *THEN* it has (or does not have) the attribute signified by the predicate. The meaning, for instance, of the universal proposition "Every dog is an animal" is merely this: *if* there is a dog, *then* that dog is an animal. Now, using the variable

x, together with the sign of material implication ($\supset$)—and allowing an x in parentheses to signify "supposing that there is an x"—and having D signify "dog" and A signify "animal"—we get the following symbol:

$$(x)[Dx \supset Ax].$$

This symbol signifies: "Supposing that there is an x, then, if x is a dog, x is an animal." It does not assert the actual existence of x but merely the factual coincidence of "animal" with "dog" *if* a dog exists. Put negatively, it means simply that there exists no x such that if it is a dog it is not likewise an animal.

Notice the significance of this interpretation in relation to the truth or falsity of universal propositions about things that do not exist in the real order (that is, about so-called empty classes). Suppose, for instance, that no chiliagon actually exists in the real order. It would follow that every universal assertion whatsoever about a chiliagon would necessarily be true. Thus, all of the following propositions would be equally true:

1. Every chiliagon is a thousand-sided figure.
2. No chiliagon is a thousand-sided figure.
3. Every chiliagon is a million-sided figure.
4. No chiliagon is a million-sided figure.

The reason why all would be equally true is this: If there is (that is, if there exists) no chiliagon at all, obviously there is no chiliagon that either is or is not a thousand-sided figure; and, similarly, if there is no chiliagon at all, obviously there is no chiliagon that either is or is not a million-sided figure. This is why, according to symbolic logicians, it is possible for each of two contrary propositions to be true.

Particular propositions are always regarded as existential. The symbol of existence is a reversed "E" ($\exists$). Now, letting $\exists x$ signify that at least one x exists and, as above, letting D stand for "dog" and A for "animal," we can symbolize "Some dog is an animal" as follows:

$$(\exists x)[Dx \cdot Ax].$$

This signifies: "There exists at least one x such that this x is both a dog and an animal."

Notice that if particular propositions are always existential, then, unless the thing their subject stands for really exists, both *I* and *O* are always false. For instance, if no chiliagon exists, then the propositions "Some chiliagon is a thousand-sided figure" and "Some chiliagon is not a thousand-sided figure" are both false.

Symbolic logicians regard propositions expressing relations as a special type. Examine, for instance, the propositions "John is bigger than George" and "Mary is bigger than Ann." These propositions have a common element, or *constant* (the relation "is bigger than") and each has two proper names expressing the terms of the relation. Allowing *j*, *g*, *m*, and *a* to stand for "John," "George," "Mary," and "Ann," respectively, and using *B* to stand for the constant "is bigger than," we can symbolize the first of these propositions by *Bjg* and the second by *Bma*. Using the *variables* *x* and *y* in place of the proper names, we get the *propositional function Bxy*, which means "*x* has the relation *B* to *y*." Similarly, from *Tsp* ("Socrates is the teacher of Plato") we can get the propositional function *Txy*, and so on.

Notice that the words "is bigger than" and "is the teacher of" express *real* relations between a subject and a term that are *really* (and not just mentally) distinct from one another. There is not only a mental distinction but also a real distinction between John and George, between Mary and Ann, and between Socrates and Plato—John and George, Mary and Ann, Socrates and Plato, are different beings and not the same being grasped under different formalities. In contrast to this, the copula of Aristotelian and Thomistic logic—at least the affirmative copula—asserts the identity of terms that are not *really* distinct from one another but only *mentally* distinct. For instance, when we say "Rover is a dog," we are not speaking of two beings but of one being—and this one being is grasped first as Rover and then also as dog. There is not a real distinction but only a mental distinction between Rover and the dog that he is.

This indiscriminate use of propositional functions to express both *real* relations between really distinct terms and *logical* relations of identity of subject and predicate has profound implications regarding the symbolic logician's view of the nature of logic.

We shall conclude this appendix on symbolic logic by making a few categorical assertions about the nature of symbolic logic and its relation to Aristotelian and Thomistic logic.

First, symbolic logic is not a science of second intentions but either of real relations or of logical relations looked upon as though they were real relations. Hence, it is wrong to speak of Aristotelian and Thomistic logic as being a part of symbolic logic and vice versa. Neither is a part of the other, for they are distinct disciplines, although in some areas they overlap.

Secondly, in attempting to ignore matter entirely and restrict its attention to form, symbolic logic has cut itself off from the basis of necessary connections between antecedents and consequents and has limited itself to mere factual, or contingent, connections. Hence, it is unsuitable as a tool for attaining necessary truths.

Thirdly, however helpful symbolic logic may be as a tool of the so-called inductive sciences, it is useless as a tool of philosophy. Philosophy aims at insight into principles and into the relationship of conclusions to the principles from which they are derived. Symbolic logic, however, does not aim at giving such insight, but (at least according to many of its proponents) at a mechanical transition from a premise to a mere factual, or contingent, conclusion.

Fourthly, the omission by symbolic logicians of all treatment of the concept, as well as their claim that all universal propositions about non-existent objects are true, is based on metaphysical and epistemological suppositions at variance with Aristotelian and Thomistic metaphysics and epistemology. Many symbolic logicians are nominalists and logical positivists.

APPENDIX II

A Sample Multiple-Choice Test

THIS EXAMINATION covers much of the so-called mechanics of logic as well as a few other topics that lend themselves to treatment in this sort of test. A teacher will find it easy to construct similar tests by substituting other examples for those used here.

Instructions: Indicate the correct answer by writing the proper number, letter, or other symbol in the parentheses to the left of each question.

COMPREHENSION AND EXTENSION

( ) 1. Which of the following has the greatest comprehension?
- (1) Square.
- (2) Plane figure.
- (3) Parallelogram.
- (4) Rectangle.
- (5) Rectilinear plane figure.

( ) 2. Which member of Question 1 has the greatest extension?

( ) 3. Which of the following has the greatest comprehension?
- (1) Dog.
- (2) Animal.
- (3) Mammal.
- (4) Living organism.
- (5) Beagle hound.

( ) 4. Which member of Question 3 has the greatest extension?

QUANTITY AND QUALITY OF PROPOSITIONS

Indicate whether each of the following propositions is an *A, E, I,* or *O* proposition.

( ) 5. George Washington was the first president of the United States.

( ) 6. Many men are not bald.

( ) 7. A kangaroo is an animal.

( ) 8. A kangaroo is hopping across a field.

( ) 9. Kangaroos are not birds.

(E) 10. No kangaroo is native to America.

( ) 11. Some kangaroos are in zoos.

Indicate *A, E, I,* or *O* as in Questions 5-11.

( ) 12. Any building made of wood is combustible.

( ) 13. Not all modern buildings are fireproof.

( ) 14. Mothers love their children.

QUANTITY OF THE PREDICATE

Indicate whether each of the following predicates is singular, particular, or universal by writing *s, p,* or *u* in the parentheses.

( ) 15. Chicago is a very large city.

( ) 16. Chicago is the second-largest city in the United States.

( ) 17. Chicago is not the largest city in the United States.

( ) 18. Chicago is not a mere village.

( ) 19. Dogs are animals.

( ) 20. No dog is a cat.

( ) 21. John is a very good debater.

( ) 22. John is not a good athlete.

( ) 23. John is the best debater in the entire school.

( ) 24. Not all good students are good athletes.

( ) 25. Some good athletes are very good students.

EDUCTION, OPPOSITION, ETC.

Complete the following by writing *T, F,* or "?" (standing for "true," "false," or "doubtful") in the parentheses.

( ) 26. If the antecedent is false and the sequence valid, the consequent is . . .

( ) 27. If the consequent is false and the sequence valid, the antecedent is . . .

( ) 28. If the antecedent is true and the sequence invalid, the consequent is . . .

( ) 29. If *every A is a B* is true, that no A is a B is . . .

( ) 30. If *every A is a B* is false, that no A is a B is . . .

( ) 31. If *every A is a B* is true, that some A is a B is . . .

( ) 32. If *every A is a B* is true, that some A is not a B is . . .

( ) 33. If *every A is a B* is false, that some A is a B is . . .

( ) 34. If *every A is a B* is false, that some A is not a B is . . .

( ) 35. If *some A is a B* is true, that every A is a B is . . .

( ) 36. If *some A is not a B* is false, that every A is a B is . . .

( ) 37. If *some A is not a B* is false, that no A is a B is . . .

Write T, F, or ?, as above.

( ) 38. If *some A is not a B* is false, that some A is a B is . . .

( ) 39. If *every A is a B* is true, that no non-B is an A is . . .

( ) 40. If *every A is a B* is true, that no non-A is a B is . . .

( ) 41. If *every A is a B* is true, that some B is an A is . . .

( ) 42. If *every A is a B* is false, that no A is a non-B is . . .

( ) 43. If *no A is a B* is false, that no B is an A is . . .

( ) 44. If *no A is a B* is true, that every A is a non-B is . . .

( ) 45. If *no A is a B* is false, that every A is a non-B is . . .

( ) 46. If *no A is a B* is false, that every non-B is an A is . . .

( ) 47. If *some B is an A* is false, that no A is a B is . . .

( ) 48. If *some B is an A* is false, that no A is a non-B is . . .

( ) 49. If *some B is an A* is false, that some A is a B is . . .

( ) 50. If *some B is an A* is false, that some A is not a B is . . .

( ) 51. If it is true that all men have intellects, that all beings having intellects are men is . . .

( ) 52. If it is true that all men have intellects, that some being not having an intellect is a man is . . .

( ) 53. If it is false that both John and Mary will go, that John will not go is . . .

( ) 54. If it is false that either John or Mary will not go, that both John and Mary will go is . . .

( ) 55. If it is false that he eats ice cream because he likes it, that he likes ice cream is . . .

( ) 56. If it is true that he eats ice cream because he likes it, that he likes ice cream is . . .

( ) 57. If only citizens over twenty-one may vote, that all citizens over twenty-one may vote is . . .

( ) 58. If it were false that all women are human beings, then that some woman is not a human being would be . . .

( ) 59. If it is true that many labor unions are managed honestly, that some are not managed honestly is . . .

( ) 60. If it is true that no atheists are Christians, that only non-Christians are atheists is . . .

CATEGORICAL SYLLOGISM

Mark each syllogism 1, 2, 3, 4, or 5 as follows:

(1) Formally valid.
(2) Illicit process of the minor or major term.
(3) Undistributed middle.
(4) Invalid because of two negative premises.
(5) Not 1, 2, 3, or 4.

( ) 61. Most Americans are very generous; but all St. Louisans are Americans; therefore some St. Louisans are very generous.

( ) 62. Every good stenographer is a good copyist; but many good secretaries are good stenographers; therefore many good secretaries are good copyists.

( ) 63. Every good stenographer is a good copyist; but every good secretary is a good copyist; therefore some good secretary is a good stenographer.

( ) 64. Every dog is an animal; but every hound is a dog; therefore every dog is mortal.

( ) 65. No dog is feathered; but owls are feathered; therefore owls are not dogs.

( ) 66. All hawks are birds; but no dogs are hawks; therefore no dogs are birds.

( ) 67. No man is a pure spirit; but horses are not pure spirits; therefore horses are not men.

( ) 68. Since diamonds are stones and certain stones are very precious, it follows that diamonds are very precious.

( ) 69. Since diamonds, which are stones, are very precious, it follows that some stones are very precious.

( ) 70. No insects have eight legs; but human beings are not insects; therefore human beings do not have eight legs.

( ) 71. No insects have eight legs; now, spiders do have eight legs; therefore spiders are not insects.

( ) 72. Some Frenchmen are temperamental; but all Parisians are Frenchmen; therefore some Parisians are temperamental.

( ) 73. He who is not guilty need not be afraid; but John is not guilty; therefore John need not be afraid.

( ) 74. All metals are good conductors of electricity; but glass is not a metal; therefore glass is not a good conductor of electricity.

( ) 75. Since no triangles are circles and no circles are squares, it follows that no squares are triangles.

Mark each syllogism 1, 2, 3, 4, or 5 as follows:

( ) 76. Only good men and willing workers should be elected to the board of aldermen; but So-and-so is a good man and a willing worker; therefore So-and-so should be elected to the board of aldermen.

( ) 77. Only the brave deserve the fair; but So-and-so is not brave; therefore So-and-so does not deserve the fair.

( ) 78. All voters in our federal elections are citizens of the U. S. A.; but many people living within the territorial limits of the U. S. A. are not citizens of the U. S. A.; therefore many people living within the territorial limits of the U. S. A. are not voters in our federal elections.

( ) 79. Some A is a B; every B is a C; some C is a D; no D is an E; therefore some A is not an E.

( ) 80. Some A is not a B; every B is a C; every C is a D; every D is an E; therefore some A is not an E.

CONDITIONAL SYLLOGISM

Mark the syllogisms 1, 2, 3, 4, or 5 as follows:

(1) Valid; minor posits the antecedent.
(2) Valid; minor sublates the consequent.
(3) Invalid; minor posits the consequent.
(4) Invalid; minor sublates the antecedent.
(5) Invalid for some other reason.

( ) 81. If every A is a B, then every C is a D; but some A is a B; therefore some C is a D.

( ) 82. If every A is a B, then every C is a D; but some A is not a B; therefore some C is not a D.

( ) 83. If every A is a B, then every C is a D; but some C is a D; therefore some A is a B.

( ) 84. If every A is a B, then every C is a D; but some C is not a D; therefore some A is not a B.

( ) 85. If some A is a B, then no C is a D; but every A is a B; therefore no C is a D.

( ) 86. If some A is a B, then no C is a D; but some C is a D; therefore no A is a B.

( ) 87. Unless he has his appendix removed, he will surely die; now, he's going to have his appendix removed and therefore will not die.

( ) 88. These men should not be referred to as traitors. Unless the facts establish the existence of a conspiracy—and they certainly do not—these men should be spared the

Mark the syllogisms 1, 2, 3, 4, or 5 as follows:

shame and ignominy of that loathsome name.

( ) 89. If you have malaria, you have been bitten by an anopheles mosquito; but you have been bitten by an anopheles mosquito; therefore you have malaria.

( ) 90. If you have malaria, you have been bitten by an anopheles mosquito; therefore, since you do not have malaria, you have not been bitten by an anopheles mosquito.

( ) 91. If A, then B; and if C, then D; but either not A or not C; therefore either not B or not C.

( ) 92. If A, then B; and if C, then D; but either not B or not D; therefore either not A or not C.

( ) 93. If A, then B; if B, then C; if C, then D; if D, then not E. But E. Therefore not A.

( ) 94. If A, then B; if B, then C; if C, then D; if D, then E. But not A. Therefore not E.

UNIVOCAL, EQUIVOCAL, AND ANALOGOUS TERMS

Mark the italicized terms 1, 2, or 3 as follows:

(1) Univocal.
(2) Equivocal.
(3) Analogous.

( ) 95. Every plane figure bounded by three straight lines is a *triangle*.

( ) 96. The *pens* in which you keep pigs are very different from the *pens* with which you write.

( ) 97. *Sequence* is sometimes valid, sometimes invalid.

( ) 98. God and creatures, substance and accident, are *beings*.

( ) 99. Both squares and triangles are *figures*.

( ) 100. The *eye* of the intellect is keener than the *eye* of the body.

PREDICABLES

Mark the italicized terms 1, 2, 3, 4, 5, or 6 as follows:

(1) Species.
(2) Genus.
(3) Specific difference.
(4) Logical property.
(5) Logical accident.
(6) None of these.

( ) 101. Some men are *over six feet tall*.

( ) 102. A triangle is a *rectilinear figure*.

( ) 103. A triangle is a rectilinear figure *enclosed by three lines*.

( ) 104. God and creatures are *beings*.

( ) 105. Man is *mortal*.

SUPPOSITION OF TERMS

Indicate the supposition of the italicized terms by writing 1, 2, 3, 4, or 5 in the parentheses, as follows:

(1) Material.
(2) Logical.
(3) Absolute.
(4) At once personal and essential.
(5) At once personal and accidental.

( )106. *Man* is a creature.

( )107. *Man* is a word of three letters.

( )108. *Man* is the subject of a proposition.

( )109. *Man* is a universal concept.

( )110. Many *men* are over six feet tall.

( )111. Each and every *man* is mortal.

( )112. *Man* is a species, not a genus.

( )113. *Man* has existed for many thousands of years.

( )114. *Man* is a little less than the angels.

( )115. *Man* is a most interesting word.

Answers to the Test Questions

1-1	21-p	41-T	61-3	81-5	101-5
2-2	22-u	42-F	62-1	82-4	102-2
3-5	23-s	43-F	63-3	83-5	103-3
4-4	24-u	44-T	64-5	84-2	104-6
5-A	25-p	45-F	65-1	85-1	105-4
6-O	26-?	46-?	66-2	86-2	106-3
7-A	27-F	47-T	67-4	87-4	107-1
8-I	28-?	48-F	68-3	88-1	108-2
9-E	29-F	49-F	69-1	89-3	109-2
10-E	30-?	50-T	70-4	90-4	110-5
11-I	31-T	51-?	71-1	91-4	111-4
12-A	32-F	52-F	72-3	92-2	112-2
13-O	33-?	53-?	73-1	93-2	113-5
14-I	34-T	54-T	74-2	94-4	114-3
15-p	35-?	55-?	75-4	95-1	115-1
16-s	36-T	56-T	76-3	96-2	
17-s	37-F	57-?	77-1	97-3	
18-u	38-T	58-T	78-1	98-3	
19-p	39-T	59-?	79-3	99-1	
20-u	40-?	60-T	80-2	100-3	

INDEX